The British Aristocracy and
the Peerage Bill of 1719

PROBLEMS IN EUROPEAN HISTORY:
A DOCUMENTARY COLLECTION

The British Aristocracy and the Peerage Bill of 1719

EDITED BY

JOHN F. NAYLOR
State University of New York
at Buffalo

New York
OXFORD UNIVERSITY PRESS
London   Toronto   1968

FOREWORD

Problems in European History: A Documentary Collection has arisen from a collective teaching experience. The series seeks to take care of a shortcoming which the authors believe persists in college history instruction. Certainly the restricting confines of the traditional textbook have been expanded as numerous collections of "readings" have appeared. But the undergraduate still remains at a distance from the historian's workshop. A compilation of heavily edited "significant documents" does not make for the sense of contact with the past that the study of history ought to promote. And the predigested selections from contending historians, neatly arrayed on either side of "classic" controversies, do not get the student to probe the underlying evidence; in fact, these academic disputations often leave him bewildered.

The conviction that students learned little of the way in which historians actually worked prompted a group of young Harvard historians five years ago to develop a new approach. The course that resulted—Social Sciences 3: Problems in Modern European History—represented an attempt to focus intensively on a small number of problems. Each problem would involve careful analysis of a wide variety of original source material. The student could develop the skills and understanding of historical explanation. In learning to compare evidence, make and test hypotheses, and judge critically earlier accounts, he would encounter some of the problems of historical research as experienced by the working historian.

In Social Sciences 3 eight studies in historical analysis are presented in a year. Our intention here is to make these documentary collections available, not necessarily as a series except in their underlying aim, but as separate problems that can be studied individually in connection with courses in European history. Each book has been edited and introduced with that purpose in mind. Thus the student can wrestle with the problems inherent in historical writing and judgment while he studies intensively a segment of the history of the country or period being taught.

Social Sciences 3 has developed over the past four years through the efforts of our collaborators, who share in the creation of these books beyond what we can gratefully acknowledge. Individual problems were prepared or substantially recast by the respective authors, but each case study was discussed and scrutinized by the entire staff of Social Sciences 3. To all of them, to the Committee on General Education of Harvard College, which has generously given of its time and efforts, and to our students—whose criticisms and suggestions were a fundamental guideline—we extend our thanks.

Cambridge, Mass.
August 1967

RICHARD BIENVENU
JOHN F. NAYLOR

PREFACE

I have made no attempt to append a critical apparatus to the documents collected in this book; care has, however, been taken to edit these materials in a consistent fashion and to ensure that they are readily comprehensible to the student. For those interested in examining the sources of these documents, I have supplied full bibliographical information in the initial reference to each source. Particularly in the pamphlet material, words have sometimes been altered to clarify the sense of certain passages. With this intent, spelling and capitalization, along with matters of punctuation, have occasionally been modernized. I trust that this practice gives no offense and that I will be indulged whatever minor inconsistencies may come to the attention of the careful reader.

The purist may cavil with my use of the term British aristocracy in the title, but by this I mean only to indicate the peerage of the United Kingdom, as England, Wales, and Scotland were styled after 1707. That the Scottish peerage faced particular problems in the events of 1719 will emerge in the pages of this book.

Though the responsibility for any errors is mine alone, I am grateful to my colleagues for their suggestions concerning content; I am particularly indebted to A. Thomas Gleason, Edward Keenan, and Mack Walker, who participated actively and avidly in the initial compilation of the materials that this book draws upon. Without the editorial help of Mrs. Beverly Newton and Mrs. Marie Stanton of the Office of General Education at Harvard our ideas would not have been realized: I hope that our gratitude will help to discharge the debt to them.

Buffalo, New York
February 1968

J. F. N.

CONTENTS

The British Aristocracy and
the Peerage Bill of 1719

INTRODUCTION

When James II ascended the thrones of England and Scotland in 1685, few people in the kingdoms recalled that January day in 1649 when his father, Charles I, had paid the price on the block for the extravagant concepts by which he had governed. The three decades which followed had witnessed a bewildering succession of types of government—parliamentary, commonwealth, protectorate, monarchical. In 1660 the country decided that the least divisive form of government was that which they had overthrown two decades earlier, provided only that the excesses which had cost Charles I his life could be avoided. At that time the word "moderation" was restored to the English political vocabulary, spoken by the vast majority of its citizenry. James's elder brother, Charles II, respected that consensus: he accepted a role within the broad bounds of the constitutional settlement of 1660. That settlement might have long survived, had not James II chosen to challenge it. For that brazen challenge, he paid with the loss of his throne; his successors were confronted with a constitutional settlement far more restrictive of the powers of the king, in theory now as well as in practice. The pragmatic settlement of 1688 stemmed from his mistaken endeavors; by that time all but a few in the kingdom had abandoned his banner, on which "absolutism" rather than "moderation" was writ large.

James II was not particularly ill-fitted to reign in Great Britain: though aged fifty-four in 1685, weakened physically and perhaps mentally as well, his training, as soldier, sailor, and administrator, was wide. In the last years of his brother's reign James had stood at the center of affairs. He inherited capable ministers, men unburdened by excessive scruples and prepared to do his bidding if only he did not go too far. In addition to problems of temperament —vanity, impatience, bigotry—James was greatly handicapped in his capacity as Head of the English Church. He was a Roman Catholic, professing his faith openly, as if contemptuous of that religious course followed in his realm. His overt profession of faith was made in spite of (though given his personality, one might better say because of) his near exclusion from the succession to the throne in 1679–80. In that so-called Exclusion Crisis, a group of parliamentarians known as Whigs, led by the Earl of Shaftesbury, determined to limit the power of the king, failed in their attempt to secure James's removal from the succession. In the aftermath of that failure, the power of the crown again waxed; James, Duke of York, shared in the revival and returned from his exile in 1682. That group in Parliament, the Tories, which had stood by the Stuart monarch in the crisis, turned ruthlessly upon their opponents, developing a doctrine at the same time justifying and explaining Parliament's reversal. That theory of non-resistance held hereditary monarchy inviolable: to depose or exclude a ruler was regarded as an unnatural act, a grave sin against God, who had sanctioned that ruler. This extreme Tory dogma, widely associated with the revolution of 1688, was in fact grounded in the Exclusion Crisis of a decade earlier.

With the destruction of the parliamentary opposition—in several cases literally, for politics of the time promised glittering rewards and harsh penalties—the Whig faction was cowed and quiescent for the remaining years of Charles's reign. Nor had that monarch to worry greatly about Parliament at all, for he had chosen to turn for financial support not to the Commons, the traditional source, but rather to the French king, Louis XIV. In exchange for his Francophile foreign policy, Charles thus freed himself from parliamentary dependence. Tories and partisans of the Church of England supported him without question; the University of Oxford went on record that there could be no other choice, for resistance was proscribed. Such was the legacy of James II in 1685. His religion need not have posed a problem if confined to the royal chapel; he could have set up a working arrangement with a Tory-dominated House of Commons, and so freed himself from his brother's dependence upon the covert French subsidies. A promising legacy this, though nothing was left of it in three years' time: James II expended good will like a wastrel. When he fled the kingdom in 1688 he took with him the baggage of absolute kingship, the theory of non-resistance.

One need not chronicle the depressing course of James's alienation of the bulk of his subjects, for his actions were all of a piece, in the service of his religion and his absolutism. Those who stood in his way, whether individual ministers or Parliament itself, he consciously pushed aside; statute law he regularly violated, pressuring the judiciary to acquiesce. Seven bishops, however, refused to read his second Declaration of Indulgence in 1688; the nation rejoiced upon learning of their acquittal on charges lodged against them by the King. That demonstration was in marked counterpoint to the singular lack of enthusiasm which had greeted the announcement in June of the birth of a son to James II. That news was unexpected, unbelieved, and decidedly unwelcome, for the cannonade that heralded the birth might well have marked the preservation of the Catholic dynasty. Royal practices which might have been endured, given James's age and Protestant heirs, now gave promise of permanency. Setting aside the theoretical question of non-resistance, was there a practical course of opposition?

Neither of James's daughters approved of the direction of her father's catholicizing policies. The elder, Mary, born in 1662, had married the Protestant William of Orange; toward James they had behaved with complete propriety through 1687, but in that year they had opened communications with discontented politicians in London. The younger daughter, Anne, too had married into a Protestant dynasty, in this case Denmark; by 1687 Anne, as set in her Anglican ways as was James in his Catholic, was alienated from her father. Yet such family fallings-out might not have proved so significant in charting England's future course had not William of Orange grown concerned with the European implications of James's foreign policy. William, engaged in mortal combat with Louis XIV, reacted sharply to James's recall in January 1688 of six English and Scottish regiments serving under William's command in Holland; it was no coincidence that three months later William informed a Whig leader that he was prepared to lead an armed force to England if he were invited to do so by men of influence. He was not so concerned with the ancient rights of England as with the Protestant and Dutch cause in European affairs; shrewdly he saw no reason why the three ends could not be served simultaneously.

Thus the domestic situation in England played directly into William's hands. The birth of James's son—widely, though incorrectly, held supposititious—relegated Mary to a secondary place in the succession; William had her rights, as well as his own cause, to uphold. Late in 1688 a favorable breeze, long known to partisans of the revolution as a Protestant wind, enabled William to sail down the Channel past the frustrated Stuart supporters pinned in port, to the west of England. As the forces of Orange marched on London, James rode out to save his kingdom for himself and Rome. Increasingly uncertain of the morale of his troops, he wavered; ignoring the advice of John Churchill, one of his leading generals, to engage in combat, James turned round to disgrace and exile. Churchill rode out by cover of night to William's camp; shortly after, the Princess Anne defected. The highest councils of the nation had turned against their duly constituted king; the country did not hesitate to follow. James II lost his throne, though not his head; William and Mary ruled in his place.

That they assumed their responsibilities by the consent of the governed was quite clear: the parliamentary leaders, Whig and Tory alike, asked the new rulers to summon a Convention Parliament, which assembled in January 1689. The Commons and Lords attempted to justify in legal terms the act of revolution now a fact of political life. The two bodies espoused conflicting theories; two weeks of pedantic debates had accomplished little, when William asserted his desire to function as something more than his wife's gentleman usher. Mary, whose claim to the throne was clear, wished her husband to be king. Those parliamentarians who had sought logical consistency had to yield to practical reality, their attempt to stretch theory to cover the *fait accompli* a failure. They declared William and Mary king and queen, rendering the monarchy temporarily elective; only those few who adhered to the outmoded concept of divine right dissented and professed their allegiance to James II—henceforth they were known as Jacobites.

Parliament's offer of the crown was not unconditional, for William and Mary accepted with it a Declaration of Rights depriving the monarch of the power to suspend law and to maintain a standing army. To its stipulation that parliaments ought to be summoned frequently, the political leaders added an assurance of its implementation, by making the king's annual revenue contingent upon parliament's assembly. The succession they vested in any children of William and Mary, or lacking those, in Princess Anne and her heirs. Protestant rulers were assumed. Such an empirical political settlement, based upon reality rather than general constitutional principles, was designed not for the future but as a guard against the past: it looked not forward to democracy but backward, against absolutism. The men of 1689 considered themselves conservatives rather than revolutionaries; their settle-

ment did not end the dynamic tension between court and country—
or in other words, between the monarchical and parliamentary
forms of government—but simply ruled out certain weapons used
by Stuart monarchs. Both sides were left free to forge new means
of exerting influence in the future. That continuing conflict, de-
limited by law after 1689, is at the root of eighteenth-century
politics. One must not enter into that era with an eye fixed upon
contemporary practices; he must instead consciously plant his feet
in soil barren of democratic growth. Men were not without principles, to be sure, but often family connexions, binding together
factions of men, counted for more. An acknowledged system of
patronage existed, forging ministries acceptable to the court from
among these diverse and often inchoate groupings. With formal
political parties counting for little in the consensus atmosphere of
the last decade of the seventeenth century, private interests determined parliamentary acceptance of ministerial policies.

The practical settlement of 1689 left open the question of
theoretical justification, which the two Houses of Parliament had
not settled. In short order, however, the vacuum was filled by a
political theorist of unquestioned genius, John Locke; for nearly
three centuries men have looked to Locke's *Two Treatises of
Government*, first published anonymously in 1690, as a theory
based primarily upon the events of 1688, providing a form of
government for the ages. Locke's Oxford-based friendship with
the Earl of Shaftesbury, prominent Whig leader, had provided him
with a knowledge of the political, social, and intellectual climate
of Restoration England. After the Whig defeat in the Exclusion
Crisis, in which Locke worked closely with his political mentor,
and possibly in mortal peril, the philosopher fled to Holland in the
fall of 1683, there to remain until after the revolution. The British
political scientist Peter Laslett recently has asserted that Locke
feared discovery of a work which he had written in direct opposition to the Tory view of the basis of governmental power, in
terms too forceful for his personal safety: the work in question is

none other than the *Two Treatises*, which Laslett contends was written not as a consequence of the revolution, but as a tract in the Exclusionist controversy.[1] In effect he demanded revolutionary courses years before 1688! For a detailed reconstruction of the events which likely precipitated Locke's treatises—a concise and illustrative example in itself of historical methodology—I refer the student to Laslett's introduction. What is particularly relevant for our present purposes is that those selections from Locke's "Second Treatise" printed below probably date to 1679–80 and ought therefore to be studied with a mind to the events of those years.

In the "First Treatise," according to Laslett written after the Second, Locke sought to dispute the theories which the royal camp advanced against the possibility of exclusion. The foremost proponent of that position was Sir Robert Filmer, author of a lengthy work, *Patriarcha or A Defence of the Natural Power of Kings against the Unnatural Liberty of the People*, written in 1640 but not published till 1680, whose title does not belie its contents. Simply stated, Filmer had enlisted God in the Stuart cause; in terms of political philosophy, he maintained that government was based upon status and not consent. Locke challenged the thesis that because the kingly authority was an extension of the paternal order given to man by God, subjects had no right to rebel. The events of 1688 showed the practical limitation of the Filmer-Jacobite claim; Locke invested those events with the dignity of a universal principle. In a sense one can set aside the question of the dating of the *Two Treatises*; whenever written, they transcend the formative circumstances to stand for what Locke conceived of as the natural rights of man.

That Locke's thought was not without impact upon his own time is apparent in the pamphlet warfare centering on the Peerage Bill; the student can assess Locke's success in persuading his contemporaries that the events of 1688 ought to be viewed in a

---

[1]Peter Laslett, Introduction to John Locke's *Two Treatises of Government* (Cambridge, 1960), pp. 58–79.

conservative, rather than revolutionary, light. To convince all that revolution had been justified remained an impossible task, because emotion rather than logic characterized the Jacobite position. The possibility of their return to power meant danger for the author of the *Two Treatises*; not surprisingly, Locke refused to admit authorship until shortly before his death in 1704. Possibly the desire for deserved immortality moved him then; possibly a recognition that English politics had gradually become less intense in a decade and a half proved decisive.

Clearly, the passions of 1688 had abated even earlier, by the time of William's death in 1702; Mary had predeceased him by some eight years. William III had governed successfully, on the whole, though his austere personality cost him the gratitude which his successes would otherwise have engendered in his subjects. His attention had centered on matters of foreign policy, particularly the wars against France; domestic affairs did not greatly concern him, and politics he consequently disliked. Nor did he ever take English statesmen or generals into his confidence; Great Britain remained only a means in his grand design, though her control of the seas proved decisive in William's wars. He relied mainly upon Tories to staff his ministries; for the Whigs, who had done far more to secure his succession, he cared little—their persistent attempts to strengthen the House of Commons and reduce the crown prerogatives went unappreciated. Yet the Whigs commanded more votes in the Commons, where supplies for his campaigns were voted, and they obliged William in 1694 to accept a Triennial Bill, stipulating that a general election be held every three years. At about this time William developed some doubts about his Tory supporters, most of whom maintained contact with the court of James II, "the king across the waters." Nor were they, with roots deep in the countryside, completely in favor of William's continental wars, which then, as now, meant increased taxes. A number of Whigs entered his ministries, carrying through in the 1690's important financial reforms which supported the wars and spurred the growth of the English economy.

Though Louis XIV made significant concessions, including the recognition of William as king of England, in the Peace of Ryswick, signed in 1697, the electorate in the following year looked not backward to his successes but ahead to peace and financial retrenchment. Though one cannot readily impose a party framework on that election, the Commons which resulted followed generally a Tory course, reducing the size of William's army and paring expenditures. Distressed by such ingratitude, the King threatened to leave England: he did not, but English politics clearly had evaded his grasp. Given the complexity of the task, that ought not be surprising, even to the detached historian. The family connexions which played a major part in the workings of English politics, along with the court interest and the independent country gentry, produced a complicated pattern which does not readily lend itself to interpretation along orthodox Whig-Tory lines.[2] Though the composition of the family connexions continuously evolved, they remained a decisive element in English politics twenty years and two monarchs later.

When a new Parliament met in 1701, two formidable dynastic succession problems presented themselves. The English succession could be legislated: neither William nor Anne any longer had prospects of direct heirs—Anne having borne and lost sixteen children, a commentary on the state of medicine at the time—so the succession passed to the Electress Sophia of Hanover, an aged granddaughter of James I, and her heirs, whence stems the present line of British monarchs. Parliament's dissatisfaction with the actions of William are manifest in the very language of the Act of Settlement, "an act for the further limitation of the crown, and better securing the rights and liberties of the subject." Nearly all of the terms made binding upon the Hanoverian line were critical commentaries on William's reign; he and the nation had moved far apart.

The question of a second succession, to the throne of Spain

2Robert Walcott, Jr., *English Politics in the Early Eighteenth Century* (Cambridge, Mass., 1956), ch. 4.

and its vast empire, brought the two closer together in the last year of William's reign. Louis XIV could not resist that grand prize, offered to his grandson, and so broke the Partition Treaty so laboriously constructed by William to preserve his Dutch domains. Supplementing diplomatic injury with personal insult, Louis recognized James Edward, son of James II, as King of England in 1701, upon his father's death. This unnecessary and arrogant act served only to give the country element in Great Britain a stake in Louis's defeat: his triumph would mean the British monarchy would pass into the hands of a French client, and a papist at that. William's second alliance against Louis XIV was solidly supported in the English countryside and ably led by a son of that England, John Churchill, who had earned himself an earldom by his timely changing of sides in 1688. At William's death the conduct of the war fell to Marlborough's military genius.

Queen Anne was well pleased with that arrangement; for the most part slow-witted and unimaginative, she was possessed of several Stuart characteristics—obstinacy, passionate loyalty to her favorites, and a consuming faith, in her case fortunately the Anglican. For advice she relied on Marlborough's wife, Sarah, the military leader himself, and a skilled minister, Godolphin. Men mainly Tory in allegiance completed her first ministry, as the generation which had carried the revolution bestrode the stage for their final bows in the Queen's reign: the glories of that age are theirs; so too the follies which scarred its last years. Those errors were, however, hidden in the future as the Tory ministry evolved gradually toward one of no party; as Tory interest in the war waned under the pressure of increased land taxes, Godolphin turned to Whig-oriented factions for parliamentary support, though he made every effort to deny them all but a minimum role in the formulation of policy. Late in the decade the Whig pressure was ever present and the ministry Whig in all but name. Meanwhile the war went well, for in the words of his illustrious descendant, Winston Churchill, the Duke (as he was by now) of Marlborough never fought a battle which he did not win, nor lay a siege which he did not carry. The allies in the grand coalition forged by William III were not everywhere successful, however; in this flaw lay the seed of another near revolution for Great Britain.

Whig interest in the war continued unabated into 1709, so much so that the major purpose of England's entry—keeping the French out of the Low Countries—now secure through Marlborough's victories, slipped from view. The Godolphin ministry, pledged with England's allies to secure a Habsburg succession to the Spanish crown, persisted in that end despite the Bourbon successes in Spain. Had the will to peace existed, terms could likely have been arranged with Louis XIV, for France, like England, was war-weary. Godolphin had yet another pressing reason to settle terms quickly, for the chief prop of any ministry was working its way loose: he was losing the support of the monarch. Queen Anne resented the Whig composition of that ministry, forced upon her by her principal advisers; indeed she had fallen out with the Duchess of Marlborough, who hitherto had exercised great influence. Anne's High Church and Tory sympathies were further provoked by the reopening of the religious question, in abeyance since the revolution. The Sacheverell affair of 1709 revived talk of non-resistance and brought a portion of the Tories full circle to espousal of doctrines which verged on Jacobitism; at the same time it provided them with a rallying cry against the Godolphin ministry. His fall in 1710 thus indicated the widespread measure of support for the Church and the desire for peace.

That ministry had accomplished one major legislative change which we must take into account. The age-old enmity of England and Scotland, settled on numerous occasions in centuries past by force of arms, eased as a result of a daring pacific initiative. Despite the personal union of the two crowns under the Stuarts, relations between the two countries had not much improved since 1603: the two realms remained divided religiously, politically, economically, even in legal institutions. Englishmen viewed their backward northern neighbors with contempt, and the Scots reciprocated the feeling. They made no move to secure the Hanoverian succession following upon the Act of Settlement in 1701; the possibility of a rupture between the two countries loomed more menacingly, when in 1704 the Scottish Parliament provided that the dynastic union of England and Scotland would terminate upon the death of Queen Anne, unless in the meanwhile Scotland decided otherwise. This worsening of relations thus provided the impetus for discussion of legislative and dynastic union, initiated in 1706. In a way the poor relations made negotiation easier, because concessions were clearly required on both sides. Godolphin blended proposed economic concessions to Scotland with thinly veiled threats of reprisals if union were rejected. Although there were those in the northern kingdom bitterly opposed to union, influential Scots saw that Scottish independence was not really at issue: they were already economically dependent upon England; to opt for union was but to maximize the commercial opportunities open to them.

The spirit of compromise is well illustrated by the degree of representation given Scotland in the House of Commons. Entitled by its wealth and share of taxation to thirteen seats at Westminster, though to eighty-five by population, the Scots accepted a representation of forty-five. Sixteen Scottish peers were to sit in the House of Lords; they were to be chosen by the whole body of the Scottish peerage, yearly assembled in Edinburgh. Scots were, however, eligible for English peerages, sitting by that right. Legislative union and the Hanoverian succession in Scotland as well as England were of course secured; the expected economic boon for Scotland proved slow in arriving, and confidence in a continuance of the Union was carefully controlled. The Pretender was not forgotten in Scotland.[3]

Godolphin's Tory successor, Robert Harley, confirmed in office by a decisive electoral triumph, implemented the deeply held

[3]George Macaulay Trevelyan, *Ramillies and the Union with Scotland* (London, 1932), chs. 10–14.

feeling for the Church and for peace which had brought him to power. Pressured by his clever colleague, Henry St. John, covetous of more power even at Harley's expense, Harley resorted to unscrupulous and dishonest practices to force a peace upon Britain's reluctant allies. Great Britain and France came to terms in 1711, and two years later the Peace of Utrecht, negotiated by St. John, brought an end to British participation in the war. For Great Britain the gains were considerable, for Utrecht opened Britain's path to empire. To St. John, now Viscount Bolingbroke, must go a major portion of the credit for the far-sighted terms; to him also the responsibility for the methods which led to Utrecht, methods which left a residual bad taste after the exclamations of joy uttered by most of his countrymen. Bolingbroke was now in a position to challenge Harley, by this time Earl of Oxford, for supremacy within the ministry. For the moment they united to defeat a Whig challenge to the Utrecht treaty in the House of Lords. Queen Anne showed her complete domination by the Tories in yielding to her ministers' entreaty to create a dozen Tory peers, required to secure the House of Lords' assent to the treaty. Her exercise of royal prerogative greatly disturbed the Whigs, who did not soon forget the crown's direct intervention in politics.

In matters of religion as well the Tories acted in a way consistent with their intention to strengthen the Church. Protestant dissenters were sharply handicapped by the passage of a bill designed to prevent the assumption of public office by those who only occasionally conformed to Church of England rites. To this they added in 1714 the Schism Act, intended to take education from the hands of dissenting ministers, thus drying up Protestant non-conformity at its source. The ministry pushed the Whigs into a desperate corner, where they could hold no hopes of recovery under the Tory and High Church Queen.

Time, however, was running out for Anne, and her Tory ministers as well. The latter had to choose whether to remain loyal to the Act of Settlement, which would bring an eighty-four-year-old German princess to the throne, or to attempt to raise up the Pretender in her place, as James III. Given their retrograde movement, the decision to approach the Pretender is not surprising: early in 1714 Oxford informed him that the government would attempt to secure parliamentary reversal of the Act of Settlement if he would agree to give up Roman Catholicism. The Tory leadership became conditional Jacobites. Unlike the French monarch who had decided that Paris was well worth a Mass and embraced Catholicism, the Pretender held to his faith, evidently reasoning that London was not worth a Book of Common Prayer. Stuart obstinacy finally had caught up with the Tories. Meanwhile their overtures had cost them room for maneuver between the two claimants; the Whigs had showered their attentions upon Hanover, for the succession to them was a matter of political life or death. Sophia and her son George Lewis were now in the Whig camp.

At this critical juncture the struggle between Bolingbroke and Oxford was resolved in the former's favor, but he could do little with the power he had sought, because Anne proved no Jacobite: she refused to intervene to win the nation for her half-brother. Moderate elements within the ministry regained control, and Bolingbroke failed to rally his forces in the few days remaining to him to stage a *coup d'état*. England was spared another revolution, for a Catholic king was simply unacceptable to the majority of its men of influence. So calm was the situation that the Hanoverian Elector, George—for Sophia had after all died several months before Anne—could in 1714 repair to his new kingdom in leisurely fashion. Unfortunately he understood neither its language nor its politics. He did, however, recognize which faction had favored his cause.

George I was no paragon of regal virtue. Nor did he care greatly for his new domain; he imported a good portion of his Hanoverian court, ministers and mistresses alike, to Britain, there to put the resources of that great nation at the disposal of a middling-size German electorate. The ministry he put under the charge of the Whigs, with but two exceptions. The man generally regarded as the leading member of that administration was Viscount Townshend, an experienced diplomat and the brother-in-law of Sir Robert Walpole, a Whig parliamentarian of recognized ability who was content with a lesser governmental office, albeit a lucrative one, for office could be put to private purposes. Cowper, a sound Whig but a trying colleague, became Lord Chancellor and strove mightily to ingratiate himself with the King, as the reader will perceive in the documents. Sunderland, son-in-law to Marlborough, now restored to favor, expressed disappointment with his appointment as Lord Lieutenant of Ireland, a post which removed him from the center of affairs, and he did not long remain there. The new ministry presented a surprise in the person of General Stanhope, appointed to a secretaryship of state for southern affairs; a distinguished soldier with military ambitions, Stanhope's political career stemmed from his early and continuing association with the Hanoverian court.

Upon the assembly of Parliament, the Whig leaders took steps to secure their victory by depriving their rivals of the possibility of a return to power. Impeachment proceedings were instituted against Bolingbroke and Oxford for the allegedly treasonous betrayal of the allies before Utrecht. Bolingbroke fled to France, taking up service under the Pretender, which served the Whig purposes well; Oxford was imprisoned in the Tower for two years but his conviction was never secured, at least in part because of a falling-out among the Whig ministers, which can be followed in the documents. In 1714, however, the Tories were as crushed as the Whigs had been just a short time before. Perhaps the shock of that quick reversal of fate spurred the Jacobite exiles in France to expectation of a successful restoration of James Edward to the throne of his fathers; Bolingbroke, having learned the hard way, warned the Pretender against exaggerating Jacobite support in Great Britain, but James Edward refused to curb his adherents in Scotland, where rebellion broke out in 1715. Townshend and

Stanhope had anticipated a challenge from the north and quickly restored order. The 1715 rebellion posed no serious threat to the Hanoverian dynasty; the ministry utilized the rebellion to purge its ranks of the last non-Whig members. In Parliament, Tory opposition was moribund, sharply reduced in size, stripped of its former leadership, and twice discredited—once by its treasonous acts when in power, and a second time by association with rebellion. As a result of these events, the Tory party possessed little national political significance, for forty years hence. Yet the Whigs had taken no chances: in 1717 the ministry secured the passage of a Septennial Act, which prolonged by four years the sitting of the Whig-dominated House of Commons. So complete was the Whig triumph, so inarticulate the voice of parliamentary opposition, that British parliamentary government might well have faltered in the period of Whig supremacy had not the Whig ministry itself split, promoting a revival of opposition criticism.

That internal struggle reflected a contest for control of the government, clearly enough, but also at issue was the course of British foreign policy. Stanhope, who had been engaged in the unsuccessful efforts in Spain in the late war, remained unhappy about its results; anxious for an aggressive role in European affairs, he strove to break the isolation of British policy since its pre-Utrecht desertion of its allies. By 1717 he had secured good relations both with the Dutch and the French; he conducted a daring diplomacy in northern Europe, repeatedly running the risk of war, subsidizing new allies, and hiring mercenaries at a high cost. In the process George's Hanoverian domains were well served, and the monarch approved; yet the ministry exposed itself to the same cries which had assailed William's continental ventures. Supporting Stanhope was the ever-intriguing Sunderland, eager for power.

Increasingly distrustful of his machinations and disturbed by Stanhope's policies was the Walpole-Townshend faction. At Stanhope's behest, Walpole had undertaken the monumental task of dealing with the national debt, and his efforts were just making their impact apparent; his policy was based upon a strict limitation of that debt. An aggressive foreign policy likely would entail expensive alliances, possibly even a ruinous war. Fiscal responsibility Walpole stressed, but Stanhope had the ear of George, accompanying him to Hanover when he left Britain to visit his beloved electorate in 1716; Sunderland typically exerted his influence through George's mistresses. Walpole and Townshend, on the contrary, had no such means of access to the King. How to articulate their dissent from Stanhope's policy? In years past, the Whigs had looked to the Hanoverians as a focus for their opposition; in similar fashion the Tories, after their fall, had looked to the Pretender. If Walpole and Townshend were forced from the ministry by their colleagues, might they find a focus for their opposition? Where could they turn? Who might stand with them?

The answer to these questions lies in the matrix of personalities and policies which converged in the Peerage Bill of 1719.

. . .

To answer those questions there exists a wealth of contemporary materials which are drawn upon in the collection following. First, however, it is well to be acquainted with the period itself, the context in which the Peerage Bill must be studied. To meet that requirement this introduction has been drawn up: with this knowledge one then can approach Locke as did the men of the eighteenth century and subsequently measure the impact of his political thought upon the men drawn into the vortex of the Peerage Bill. The Hanoverian dynasty, particularly George and his Hanoverian advisers, are colorfully described in a selection from Thackeray, who had no trouble extracting humor from their collective foibles. One can then read the document presented to George shortly after his arrival in England by a leading Whig politician, who assessed the course of events in the realm since the time of the Exclusion Crisis. Cowper's detailed letter presents an insight into the Whig point of view: one ought to remember that history is more than historians subsequently make it out to be; it is also what men at the time thought they were doing.

With the scene thus set, the falling-out among the Whig ministry can be reconstructed from the wide variety of letters presented below. The principal problem confronting the historian in any such collection is separating fact from fiction, the accurate description from that account written to serve its author's interest. This self-serving need not even be deliberate: a man can deceive himself as readily as he can his correspondent. The historian's task is to prevent him from deceiving history. To accomplish this purpose, the historian must weigh and evaluate evidence, a process which the student must adopt to utilize this collection. He can himself measure diverse, even contradictory, points of view against one another in order to produce an ordered account of what really happened.

In a similar fashion, the student may assess other contemporary materials, bearing directly upon the Peerage Bill. Polemical pamphlet warfare was waged by men whose names have justly survived in English literature; these readings add dimension and force to the controversy and provide it with a flavor all too often missing from the. pages of history. And they are of distinct relevance in indicating the intentions and motivations of the rival politicians. In this connection it is interesting to recall Locke's formulations and to ask whether they were utilized—or simply assumed—by the protagonists. Or were they of less significance to the men of 1719 than we might assume, with our longer perspective on Locke's impact?

The same questions can also be posed with regard to the course of men's actions in Parliament when the Peerage Bill was debated, as an early nineteenth-century reconstruction of those debates, drawing upon sources closer to the actual debate, is printed below. In those pages one finds the resolution of the struggle which we have surveyed. What finally persuaded more members of Parliament to vote against a restricted peerage than to vote for it? How effective had the pamphlets been in persuading them one way or the other? Were their arguments reiterated, or had the House of Commons other considerations in mind? Interest, or principle? Which seemed more at stake in the Commons debate?

Letters exist also which enable us to consider the reaction of several of the participants to the defeat of the Peerage Bill. Were Stanhope and Townshend brought up short in their ways? Had Walpole's role demonstrated to one and all the political predominance which he was to exercise for the next two decades? What is there to be said about the quality of his mind and the force of his arguments? The historian must ask himself these questions, and others; the documents collected here enable the student to arrive at answers to these questions and to sense the tortuous path into the past which the historian must follow to illume that past for his readers.

I

THE HISTORICAL SETTING

The materials grouped in this section should be read and evaluated in connection with the introduction and the student's own knowledge of the period. Two rather different types of evaluation are involved, however. With the first selection, the student can set aside the involved question of the dating of Locke's "Second Treatise" and concentrate his attention upon the impact of Locke's thought. A political philosopher associated with the concepts underlying the American revolution of the eighteenth century as well as the English revolution of his own time, Locke sets forth in relatively few pages views upon the state of nature and the concept of property which reflect an optimistic interpretation of human nature—in marked contrast to those espoused by Thomas Hobbes. Given such a point of view, Locke's ordering of the common-wealth, by which men choose freely to govern themselves, is not surprising. In the selection, one may perceive that structuring and the political consequences which follow from it—such as the role of prerogative. Such conclusions are not difficult to draw, though a critical evaluation of Locke's concept of individual rights and government must hinge upon a consideration of the "Second Treatise" in its entirety. Evaluation of Locke's impact upon his own time is, however, here possible, though one must not assume it is definitive; the scope of the materials printed later in this book is not sufficiently great, but they provide indications useful to the historian. By having Locke's precepts fixed in mind, a critical approach to the pamphlet controversy surrounding the Peerage Bill is made possible; thus, a document can enable the historian to evaluate other materials.

And, of course, documents can be measured against a knowledge of the period. Lord Chancellor Cowper, in the final selection in this section, purports to offer an "impartial" history of the period of what was to him the immediate past. How impartial was that assessment? If it is less than complete, then the student will see how motivation can sometimes twist the facts into strange, even unrecognizable, patterns. Or perhaps Cowper was deceiving himself; in any event, the historian must be on guard against all claims to impartiality, including his own.

The Victorian novelist William Makepeace Thackeray (1811–63) was sufficiently clever with his pen so that he had not to lay claim to impartiality when dealing with some of his least favorite monarchs, the Hanoverian dynasty; he developed his critical views of the "Four Georges" in the course of a lecture tour in America in 1855. Yet curiously his comments are not without some redeeming historical value, for Thackeray's acerbic comments upon the realm which the Hanoverians inherited remind us that the early eighteenth century was a grasping, acquisitive age: governmental codes of ethics, if at present a charade, were then not even contemplated. And finally, Thackeray reminds us that history may entertain as well as enlighten. Given the foibles of the eighteenth century, humor is hardly out of the question.

Locke's Two Treatises

Chapter I

1. It having been shown in the foregoing discourse:

(*1*) That Adam had not, either by natural right of fatherhood or by positive donation from God, any such authority over his children or dominion over the world as is pretended.

(*2*) That if he had, his heirs yet had no right to it.

(*3*) That if his heirs had, there being no law of nature nor positive law of God that determines which is the right heir in all cases that may arise, the right of succession, and consequently of bearing rule, could not have been certainly determined.

(*4*) That if even that had been determined, yet the knowledge of which is the eldest line of Adam's posterity being so long since utterly lost that in the races of mankind and families of the world there remains not to one above another the least pretense to be the eldest house, and to have the right of inheritance.

All these premises having, as I think, been clearly made out, it is impossible that the rulers now on earth should make any benefit or derive any the least shadow of authority from that which is held to be the fountain of all power: Adam's private dominion and paternal jurisdiction; so that he that will not give just occasion to think that all government in the world is the product only of force and violence, and that men live together by no other rules but that of beasts, where the strongest carries it, and so lay a foundation for perpetual disorder and mischief, tumult, sedition, and rebellion—things that the followers of that hypothesis so loudly cry out against—must of necessity find out another rise of government, another original of political power, and another way of designing and knowing the persons that have it than what Sir Robert Filmer has taught us.

2. To this purpose, I think it may not be amiss to set down what I take to be political power; that the power of a magistrate over a subject may be distinguished from that of a father over his children, a master over his servants, a husband over his wife, and a lord over his slave. All which distinct powers happening sometimes together in the same man, if he be considered under these different relations, it may help us to distinguish these powers one from another, and show

John Locke, "Of Civil Government," the second of *Two Treatises of Government,* first published anonymously in 1690 (6th edition, London, 1764).

the difference betwixt a ruler of a commonwealth, a father of a family, and a captain of a galley.

3. Political power, then, I take to be a right of making laws with penalties of death and, consequently, all less penalties for the regulating and preserving of property, and of employing the force of the community in the execution of such laws and in the defense of the commonwealth from foreign injury; and all this only for the public good.

Chapter II
Of the State of Nature

4. To understand political power right and derive it from its original, we must consider what state all men are naturally in, and that is a state of perfect freedom to order their actions and dispose of their possessions and persons as they think fit, within the bounds of the law of nature, without asking leave or depending upon the will of any other man.

A state also of equality, wherein all the power and jurisdiction is reciprocal, no one having more than another; there being nothing more evident than that creatures of the same species and rank, promiscuously born to all the same advantages of nature and the use of the same faculties, should also be equal one amongst another without subordination or subjection; unless the lord and master of them all should, by any manifest declaration of his will, set one above another, and confer on him by an evident and clear appointment an undoubted right to dominion and sovereignty.

5. This equality of men by nature the judicious Hooker* looks upon as so evident in itself and beyond all question that he makes it the foundation of that obligation to mutual love amongst men on which he builds the duties we owe one another, and from whence he derives the great maxims of justice and charity. His words are:

> The like natural inducement hath brought men to know that it is no less their duty to love others than themselves; for seeing those things which are equal must needs all have one measure; if I cannot but wish to receive good, even as much at every man's hands as any man can wish unto his own soul, how should I look to have any part of my desire herein satisfied unless myself be careful to satisfy the like desire, which is

[*Richard Hooker (1554–1600), Anglican theologian and author of *The Laws of Ecclesiastical Polity*, an influential work in the development of political theory—Ed.]

undoubtedly in other men, being of one and the same nature? To have anything offered them repugnant to this desire must needs in all respects grieve them as much as me; so that, if I do harm, I must look to suffer, there being no reason that others should show greater measure of love to me than they have by me showed unto them; my desire therefore to be loved of my equals in nature, as much as possibly may be, imposeth upon me a natural duty of bearing to them-ward fully the like affection; from which relation of equality between ourselves and them that are as ourselves, what several rules and canons natural reason hath drawn, for direction of life, no man is ignorant. (*Eccl. Pol.* lib. i.).

6. But though this be a state of liberty, yet it is not a state of license; though man in that state have an uncontrollable liberty to dispose of his person or possessions, yet he has not liberty to destroy himself, or so much as any creature in his possession, but where some nobler use than its bare preservation calls for it. The state of nature has a law of nature to govern it, which obliges every one; and reason, which is that law, teaches all mankind who will but consult it that, being all equal and independent, no one ought to harm another in his life, health, liberty, or possessions; for men being all the workmanship of one omnipotent and infinitely wise Maker—all the servants of one sovereign master, sent into the world by his order, and about his business—they are his property whose workmanship they are, made to last during his, not one another's, pleasure; and being furnished with like faculties, sharing all in one community of nature, there cannot be supposed any such subordination among us that may authorize us to destroy another, as if we were made for one another's uses as the inferior ranks of creatures are for ours. Every one, as he is bound to preserve himself and not to quit his station wilfully, so by the like reason, when his own preservation comes not in competition, ought he, as much as he can, to preserve the rest of mankind, and may not, unless it be to do justice to an offender, take away or impair the life, or what tends to the preservation of the life, the liberty, health, limb, or goods of another.

7. And that all men may be restrained from invading others' rights and from doing hurt to one another, and the law of nature be observed, which wills the peace and preservation of all mankind, the execution of the law of nature is, in that state, put into every man's hands, whereby everyone has a right to punish the transgressors of that law to such a degree as may hinder its violation; for the law of nature would, as

all other laws that concern men in this world, be in vain if there were nobody that in that state of nature had a power to execute that law and thereby preserve the innocent and restrain offenders. And if anyone in the state of nature may punish another for any evil he has done, everyone may do so; for in that state of perfect equality, where naturally there is no superiority or jurisdiction of one over another, what any may do in prosecution of that law, everyone must needs have a right to do.

8. And thus in the state of nature one man comes by a power over another; but yet no absolute or arbitrary power to use a criminal, when he has got him in his hands, according to the passionate heats or boundless extravagance of his own will; but only to retribute to him, so far as calm reason and conscience dictate, what is proportionate to his transgression, which is so much as may serve for reparation and restraint; for these two are the only reasons why one man may lawfully do harm to another, which is that we call punishment. In transgressing the law of nature, the offender declares himself to live by another rule than that of reason and common equity, which is that measure God has set to the actions of men for their mutual security; and so he becomes dangerous to mankind, the tie which is to secure them from injury and violence being slighted and broken by him. Which being a trespass against the whole species and the peace and safety of it provided for by the law of nature, every man upon this score, by the right he has to preserve mankind in general, may restrain; or, where it is necessary, destroy things noxious to them, and so may bring such evil on any one who has transgressed that law, as may make him repent the doing of it and thereby deter him, and by his example others, from doing the like mischief. And in this case, and upon this ground, *every man has a right to punish the offender and be executioner of the law of nature.*

9. I doubt not but this will seem a very strange doctrine to some men; but before they condemn it, I desire them to resolve me by what right any prince or state can put to death or punish any alien for any crime he commits in their country. It is certain their laws, by virtue of any sanction they receive from the promulgated will of the legislative, reach not a stranger; they speak not to him, nor, if they did, is he bound to hearken to them. The legislative authority, by which they are in force over the subjects of that commonwealth, has no power over him. Those who have the supreme power of making laws in England, France, or Holland, are to an Indian but like the

rest of the world—men without authority; and therefore, if by the law of nature every man has not a power to punish offenses against it as he soberly judges the case to require, I see not how the magistrates of any community can punish an alien of another country, since, in reference to him, they can have no more power than what every man naturally may have over another.

10. Besides the crime which consists in violating the law and varying from the right rule of reason, whereby a man so far becomes degenerate and declares himself to quit the principles of human nature and to be a noxious creature, there is commonly injury done to some person or other, and some other man receives damage by his transgression; in which case he who has received any damage has, besides the right of punishment common to him with other men, a particular right to seek reparation from him that has done it; and any other person, who finds it just, may also join with him that is injured and assist him in recovering from the offender so much as may make satisfaction for the harm he has suffered.

11. From these two distinct rights—the one of punishing the crime for restraint and preventing the like offense, which right of punishing is in everybody; the other of taking reparation, which belongs only to the injured party—comes it to pass that the magistrate, who by being magistrate has the common right of punishing put into his hands, can often, where the public good demands not the execution of the law, remit the punishment of criminal offenses by his own authority, but yet cannot remit the satisfaction due to any private man for the damage he has received. That he who has suffered the damage has a right to demand in his own name, and he alone can remit; the damnified person has this power of appropriating to himself the goods or service of the offender by right of self-preservation, as every man has a power to punish the crime to prevent its being committed again, by the right he has of preserving all mankind and doing all reasonable things he can in order to that end; and thus it is that every man, in the state of nature, has a power to kill a murderer, both to deter others from doing the like injury, which no reparation can compensate, by the example of the punishment that attends it from everybody, and also to secure men from the attempts of a criminal who, having renounced reason—the common rule and measure God has given to mankind—has, by the unjust violence and slaughter he has committed upon one, declared war against all mankind, and therefore may be destroyed as a lion or a tiger, one of those

wild savage beasts with whom men can have no society nor security. And upon this is grounded that great law of nature, "Whoso sheddeth man's blood, by man shall his blood be shed." And Cain was so fully convinced that every one had a right to destroy such a criminal that, after the murder of his brother, he cries out, "Every one that findeth me, shall slay me"; so plain was it written in the hearts of mankind.

12. By the same reason may a man in the state of nature punish the lesser breaches of that law. It will perhaps be demanded: with death? I answer: Each transgression may be punished to that degree and with so much severity as will suffice to make it an ill bargain to the offender, give him cause to repent, and terrify others from doing the like. Every offense that can be committed in the state of nature may in the state of nature be also punished equally, and as far forth as it may in a commonwealth; for though it would be beside my present purpose to enter here into the particulars of the law of nature, or its measures of punishment, yet it is certain there is such a law, and that, too, as intelligible and plain to a rational creature and a studier of that law as the positive laws of commonwealths, nay, possibly plainer, as much as reason is easier to be understood than the fancies and intricate contrivances of men, following contrary and hidden interests put into words; for so truly are a great part of the municipal laws of countries, which are only so far right as they are founded on the law of nature, by which they are to be regulated and interpreted.

13. To this strange doctrine—viz., that in the state of nature every one has the executive power of the law of nature—I doubt not but it will be objected that it is unreasonable for men to be judges in their own cases, that self-love will make men partial to themselves and their friends, and, on the other side, that ill-nature, passion, and revenge will carry them too far in punishing others, and hence nothing but confusion and disorder will follow; and that therefore God has certainly appointed government to restrain the partiality and violence of men. I easily grant that civil government is the proper remedy for the inconveniences of the state of nature, which must certainly be great where men may be judges in their own case; since it is easy to be imagined that he who was so unjust as to do his brother an injury will scarce be so just as to condemn himself for it; but I shall desire those who make this objection to remember that absolute monarchs are but men, and if government is to be the remedy of those evils which necessarily follow from men's being judges in their own cases, and the state of nature is therefore not to be endured, I desire to know

what kind of government that is, and how much better it is than the state of nature, where one man commanding a multitude has the liberty to be judge in his own case, and may do to all his subjects whatever he pleases, without the least liberty to any one to question or control those who execute his pleasure, and in whatsoever he does, whether led by reason, mistake, or passion, must be submitted to? Much better it is in the state of nature, wherein men are not bound to submit to the unjust will of another; and if he that judges, judges amiss in his own or any other case, he is answerable for it to the rest of mankind.

14. It is often asked as a mighty objection, "Where are or ever were there any men in such a state of nature?" To which it may suffice as an answer at present that since all princes and rulers of independent governments all through the world are in a state of nature, it is plain the world never was, nor ever will be, without numbers of men in that state. I have named all governors of independent communities, whether they are, or are not, in league with others; for it is not every compact that puts an end to the state of nature between men, but only this one of agreeing together mutually to enter into one community and make one body politic; other promises and compacts men may make one with another and yet still be in the state of nature. The promises and bargains for truck, etc., between the two men in the desert island, mentioned by Garcilasso de la Vega, in his history of Peru, or between a Swiss and an Indian in the woods of America, are binding to them, though they are perfectly in a state of nature in reference to one another; for truth and keeping of faith belongs to men as men, and not as members of society.

15. To those that say there were never any men in the state of nature, I will not only oppose the authority of the judicious Hooker, *Eccl. Pol.*, lib. i., sect. 10, where he says,

> The laws which have been hitherto mentioned (i.e., the laws of nature) do bind men absolutely, even as they are men, although they have never any settled fellowship, never any solemn agreement amongst themselves what to do, or not to do; but forasmuch as we are not by ourselves sufficient to furnish ourselves with competent store of things needful for such a life as our nature doth desire, a life fit for the dignity of man; therefore to supply those defects and imperfections which are in us, as living singly and solely by ourselves, we are naturally induced to seek communion and fellowship with others. This was the cause of men's uniting themselves at first in politic societies.

But I, moreover, affirm that all men are naturally in that state and remain so till by their own consents they make themselves members of some politic society; and I doubt not in the sequel of this discourse to make it very clear.

Chapter V
Of Property

25. Whether we consider natural reason, which tells us that men, being once born, have a right to their preservation, and consequently to meat and drink and such other things as nature affords for their subsistence; or revelation, which gives us an account of those grants God made of the world to Adam, and to Noah and his sons; it is very clear that God, as King David says (Psalm cxv. 16), "has given the earth to the children of men," given it to mankind in common. But this being supposed, it seems to some a very great difficulty how any one should ever come to have a property in anything. I will not content myself to answer that if it be difficult to make out property upon a supposition that God gave the world to Adam and his posterity in common, it is impossible that any man but one universal monarch should have any property upon a supposition that God gave the world to Adam and his heirs in succession, exclusive of all the rest of his posterity. But I shall endeavor to show how men might come to have a property in several parts of that which God gave to mankind in common, and that without any express compact of all the commoners.

26. God, who has given the world to men in common, has also given them reason to make use of it to the best advantage of life and convenience. The earth and all that is therein is given to men for the support and comfort of their being. And though all the fruits it naturally produces and beasts it feeds belong to mankind in common, as they are produced by the spontaneous hand of nature; and nobody has originally a private dominion exclusive of the rest of mankind in any of them, as they are thus in their natural state; yet, being given for the use of men, there must of necessity be a means to appropriate them some way or other before they can be of any use or at all beneficial to any particular man. The fruit or vension which nourishes the wild Indian, who knows no enclosure and is still a tenant in common, must be his, and so his, i. e., a part of him, that another can no longer have any right to it before it can do him any good for the support of his life.

27. Though the earth and all inferior creatures be common to all men, yet every man has a property in his own person; this nobody

has any right to but himself. The labor of his body and the work of his hands, we may say, are properly his. Whatsoever then he removes out of the state that nature has provided and left it in, he has mixed his labor with, and joined to it something that is his own, and thereby makes it his property. It being by him removed from the common state nature has placed it in, it has by this labor something annexed to it that excludes the common right of other men. For this labor being the unquestionable property of the laborer, no man but he can have a right to what that is once joined to, at least where there is enough and as good left in common for others.

28. He that is nourished by the acorns he picked up under an oak, or the apples he gathered from the trees in the wood, has certainly appropriated them to himself. Nobody can deny but the nourishment is his. I ask, then when did they begin to be his? When he digested or when he ate or when he boiled or when he brought them home? Or when he picked them up? And it is plain, if the first gathering made them not his, nothing else could. That labor put a distinction between them and common; that added something to them more than nature, the common mother of all, had done; and so they became his private right. And will anyone say he had no right to those acorns or apples he thus appropriated because he had not the consent of all mankind to make them his? Was it a robbery thus to assume to himself what belonged to all in common? If such a consent as that was necessary, man had starved, notwithstanding the plenty God had given him. We see in commons, which remain so by compact, that it is the taking any part of what is common and removing it out of the state nature leaves it in which begins the property, without which the common is of no use. And the taking of this or that part does not depend on the express consent of all the commoners. Thus the grass my horse has bit, the turfs my servant has cut, and the ore I have digged in any place where I have a right to them in common with others, become my property without the assignation or consent of anybody. The labor that was mine, removing them out of that common state they were in, has fixed my property in them.

. . .

31. It will perhaps be objected to this that "if gathering the acorns, or other fruits of the earth, etc., makes a right to them, then any one may engross as much as he will." To which I answer: not so. The same law of nature that does by this means give us property does also bound that property, too. "God has given us all things richly" (1 Tim. vi. 17), is the voice of reason confirmed by inspiration. But how far

has he given it us? To enjoy. As much as any one can make use of to any advantage of life before it spoils, so much he may by his labor fix a property in; whatever is beyond this is more than his share and belongs to others. Nothing was made by God for man to spoil or destroy. And thus considering the plenty of natural provisions there was a long time in the world, and the few spenders, and to how small a part of that provision the industry of one man could extend itself and engross it to the prejudice of others, especially keeping within the bounds set by reason of what might serve for his use, there could be then little room for quarrels or contentions about property so established.

32. But the chief matter of property being now not the fruits of the earth and the beasts that subsist on it, but the earth itself, as that which takes in and carries with it all the rest, I think it is plain that property in that, too, is acquired as the former. As much land as a man tills, plants, improves, cultivates, and can use the product of, so much is his property. He by his labor does, as it were, enclose it from the common. Nor will it invalidate his right to say everybody else has an equal title to it, and therefore he cannot appropriate, he cannot enclose, without the consent of all his fellow commoners—all mankind. God, when he gave the world in common to all mankind, commanded man also to labor, and the penury of his condition required it of him. God and his reason commanded him to subdue the earth, i. e., improve it for the benefit of life, and therein lay out something upon it that was his own, his labor. He that in obedience to this command of God subdued, tilled, and sowed any part of it, thereby annexed to it something that was his property, which another had no title to, nor could without injury take from him.

33. Nor was this appropriation of any parcel of land by improving it any prejudice to any other man, since there was still enough and as good left, and more than the yet unprovided could use. So that, in effect, there was never the less left for others because of his enclosure for himself; for he that leaves as much as another can make use of does as good as take nothing at all. Nobody could think himself injured by the drinking of another man, though he took a good draught, who had a whole river of the same water left him to quench his thirst; and the case of land and water, where there is enough for both, is perfectly the same.

34. God gave the world to men in common; but since he gave it them for their benefit and the greatest conveniences of life they were capable to draw from it, it cannot be supposed he meant it should

always remain common and uncultivated. He gave it to the use of the industrious and rational—and labor was to be his title to it—not to the fancy or covetousness of the quarrelsome and contentious. He that had as good left for his improvement as was already taken up needed not complain, ought not to meddle with what was already improved by another's labor; if he did, it is plain he desired the benefit of another's pains which he had no right to, and not the ground which God had given him in common with others to labor on, and whereof there was as good left as that already possessed, and more than he knew what to do with, or his industry could reach to.

35. It is true, in land that is common in England or any other country where there are plenty of people under government who have money and commerce, no one can enclose or appropriate any part without the consent of all his fellow commoners; because this is left common by compact, i. e., by the law of the land, which is not to be violated. And though it be common in respect of some men, it is not so to all mankind, but is the joint property of this country or this parish. Besides, the remainder after such enclosure would not be as good to the rest of the commoners as the whole was when they could all make use of the whole; whereas in the beginning and first peopling of the great common of the world it was quite otherwise. The law man was under was rather for appropriating. God commanded, and his wants forced, him to labor. That was his property which could not be taken from him wherever he had fixed it. And hence subduing or cultivating the earth and having dominion, we see, are joined together. The one gave title to the other. So that God, by commanding to subdue, gave authority so far to appropriate; and the condition of human life which requires labor and material to work on necessarily introduces private possessions.

36. The measure of property nature has well set by the extent of men's labor and the conveniences of life. No man's labor could subdue or appropriate all, nor could his enjoyment consume more than a small part, so that it was impossible for any man, this way, to entrench upon the right of another, or acquire to himself a property to the prejudice of his neighbor, who would still have room for as good and as large a possession—after the other had taken out his—as before it was appropriated. This measure did confine every man's possession to a very moderate proportion, and such as he might appropriate to himself without injury to anybody, in the first ages of the world, when men were more in danger to be lost by wandering from their company in the then vast wilderness of the earth than to be straitened for want

of room to plant in. And the same measure may be allowed still without prejudice to anybody, as full as the world seems; for supposing a man or family in the state they were at first peopling of the world by the children of Adam or Noah, let him plant in some inland, vacant places of America; we shall find that the possessions he could make himself, upon the measures we have given, would not be very large, nor, even to this day, prejudice the rest of mankind, or give them reason to complain or think themselves injured by this man's encroachment, though the race of men have now spread themselves to all the corners of the world and do infinitely exceed the small number which was at the beginning. Nay, the extent of ground is of so little value without labor that I have heard it affirmed that in Spain itself a man may be permitted to plough, sow, and reap, without being disturbed, upon land he has no other title to but only his making use of it. But, on the contrary, the inhabitants think themselves beholden to him who by his industry on neglected and consequently waste land has increased the stock of corn which they wanted. But be this as it will, which I lay no stress on, this I dare boldly affirm—that the same rule of property, viz., that every man should have as much as he could make use of, would hold still in the world without straitening anybody, since there is land enough in the world to suffice double the inhabitants, had not the invention of money and the tacit agreement of men to put a value on it introduced—by consent—larger possessions and a right to them; which, how it has done, I shall by-and-by show more at large.

.   .   .

39. And thus, without supposing any private dominion and property in Adam over all the world exclusive of all other men, which can in no way be proven, nor any one's property be made out from it; but supposing the world given, as it was, to the children of men in common, we see how labor could make men distinct titles to several parcels of it for their private uses, wherein there could be no doubt of right, no room for quarrel.

40. Nor is it so strange, as perhaps before consideration it may appear, that the property of labor should be able to overbalance the community of land; for it is labor indeed that put the difference of value on everything; and let anyone consider what the difference is between an acre of land planted with tobacco or sugar, sown with wheat or barley, and an acre of the same land lying in common without any husbandry upon it, and he will find that the improvement of labor makes the far greater part of the value. I think it will be but

a very modest computation to say that, of the products of the earth useful to the life of man, nine-tenths are the effects of labor; nay, if we will rightly estimate things as they come to our use and cast up the several expenses about them, what in them is purely owing to nature, and what to labor, we shall find that in most of them ninety-nine hundredths are wholly to be put on the account of labor.

. . .

44. From all which it is evident that, though the things of nature are given in common, yet man, by being master of himself and proprietor of his own person and the actions or labor of it, had still in himself the great foundation of property; and that which made up the greater part of what he applied to the support or comfort of his being, when invention and arts had improved the conveniences of life, was perfectly his own and did not belong in common to others.

45. Thus labor, in the beginning, gave a right of property wherever anyone was pleased to employ it upon what was common, which remained a long while the far greater part and is yet more than mankind makes use of. Men, at first, for the most part contented themselves with what unassisted nature offered to their necessities; and though afterwards, in some parts of the world—where the increase of people and stock, with the use of money, had made land scarce and so of some value—the several communities settled the bounds of their distinct territories and, by laws within themselves, regulated the properties of the private men of their society, and so, by compact and agreement, settled the property which labor and industry began. And the leagues that have been made between several states and kingdoms either expressly or tacitly disowning all claim and right to the land in the others' possession have, by common consent, given up their pretenses to their natural common right which originally they had to those countries, and so have, by positive agreement, settled a property amongst themselves in distinct parts and parcels of the earth; yet there are still great tracts of ground to be found which—the inhabitants thereof not having joined with the rest of mankind in the consent of the use of their common money—lie waste, and are more than the people who dwell on it do or can make use of, and so still lie in common; though this can scarce happen amongst that part of mankind that have consented to the use of money.

46. The greatest part of things really useful to the life of man, and such as the necessity of subsisting made the first commoners of the world look after, as it does the Americans now, are generally

things of short duration, such as, if they are not consumed by use, will decay and perish of themselves; gold, silver, and diamonds are things that fancy or agreement has put the value on, more than real use and the necessary support of life. Now of those good things which nature has provided in common, every one had a right, as has been said, to as much as he could use, and property in all that he could effect with his labor; all that his industry could extend to, to alter from the state nature had put it in, was his. He that gathered a hundred bushels of acorns or apples had thereby a property in them; they were his goods as soon as gathered. He was only to look that he used them before they spoiled, else he took more than his share and robbed others. And indeed it was a foolish thing, as well as dishonest, to hoard up more than he could make use of. If he gave away a part to anybody else so that it perished not uselessly in his possession, these he also made use of. And if he also bartered away plums that would have rotted in a week for nuts that would last good for his eating a whole year, he did no injury; he wasted not the common stock, destroyed no part of the portion of the goods that belonged to others, so long as nothing perished uselessly in his hands. Again, if he would give his nuts for a piece of metal, pleased with its color, or exchange his sheep for shells, or wool for a sparkling pebble or a diamond, and keep those by him all his life, he invaded not the right of others; he might heap as much of these durable things as he pleased; the exceeding of the bounds of his just property not lying in the largeness of his possession, but the perishing of anything uselessly in it.

47. And thus came in the use of money—some lasting thing that men might keep without spoiling, and that by mutual consent men would take in exchange for the truly useful but perishable supports of life.

48. And as different degrees of industry were apt to give men possessions in different proportions, so this invention of money gave them the opportunity to continue and enlarge them; for supposing an island, separate from all possible commerce with the rest of the world, wherein there were but a hundred families, but there were sheep, horses, and cows, with other useful animals, wholesome fruits, and land enough for corn for a hundred thousand times as many, but nothing in the island, either because of its commonness or perishableness, fit to supply the place of money; what reason could anyone have there to enlarge his possessions beyond the use of his family and a plentiful supply to its consumption, either in what their own industry

produced or they could barter for like perishable, useful commodities with others? Where there is not something both lasting and scarce, and so valuable to be hoarded up, there men will not be apt to enlarge their possessions of land were it ever so rich, ever so free for them to take. For, I ask, what would a man value ten thousand or a hundred thousand acres of excellent land, ready cultivated and well stocked, too, with cattle, in the middle of the inland parts of America where he had no hopes of commerce with other parts of the world to draw money to him by the sale of the product? It would not be worth the enclosing, and we should see him give up again to the wild common of nature whatever was more than would supply the conveniences of life to be had there for him and his family.

49. Thus in the beginning all the world was America, and more so than that is now; for no such thing as money was anywhere known. Find out something that has the use and value of money amongst his neighbors, you shall see the same man will begin presently to enlarge his possessions.

50. But since gold and silver, being little useful to the life of man in proportion of food, raiment, and carriage, has its value only from the consent of men, whereof labor yet makes, in great part, the measure, it is plain that men have agreed to a disproportionate and unequal possession of the earth, they having, by a tacit and voluntary consent, found out a way how a man may fairly possess more land than he himself can use the product of, by receiving in exchange for the overplus gold and silver which may be hoarded up without injury to any one, these metals not spoiling or decaying in the hands of the possessor. This partage of things in an inequality of private possessions men have made practicable out of the bounds of society and without compact, only by putting a value on gold and silver, and tacitly agreeing in the use of money; for, in governments, the laws regulate the right of property, and the possession of land is determined by positive constitutions.

51. And thus, I think, it is very easy to conceive how labor could at first begin a title of property in the common things of nature, and how the spending it upon our uses bounded it. So that there could then be no reason of quarreling about title, nor any doubt about the largeness of possession it gave. Right and convenience went together; for as a man had a right to all he could employ his labor upon, so he had no temptation to labor for more than he could make use of. This left no room for controversy about the title, nor for encroachment on

the right of others; what portion a man carved to himself was easily seen, and it was useless, as well as dishonest, to carve himself too much or take more than he needed.

Chapter XI
Of the Extent of the Legislative Power

134. The great end of men's entering into society being the enjoyment of their properties in peace and safety, and the great instrument and means of that being the laws established in that society, the first and fundamental positive law of all commonwealths is the establishing of the legislative power; as the first and fundamental natural law which is to govern even the legislative itself is the preservation of the society and, as far as will consist with the public good, of every person in it. This legislative is not only the supreme power of the commonwealth, but sacred and unalterable in the hands where the community have once placed it; nor can any edict of anybody else, in what form soever conceived or by what power soever backed, have the force and obligation of a law which has not its sanction from that legislative which the public has chosen and appointed; for without this the law could not have that which is absolutely necessary to its being a law: the consent of the society over whom nobody can have a power to make laws, but by their own consent and by authority received from them. And therefore all the obedience, which by the most solemn ties any one can be obliged to pay, ultimately terminates in this supreme power and is directed by those laws which it enacts; nor can any oaths to any foreign power whatsoever, or any domestic subordinate power, discharge any member of the society from his obedience to the legislative acting pursuant to their trust, nor oblige him to any obedience contrary to the laws so enacted, or farther than they do allow; it being ridiculous to imagine one can be tied ultimately to obey any power in the society which is not supreme.

135. Though the legislative, whether placed in one or more, whether it be always in being, or only by intervals, though it be the supreme power in every commonwealth; yet:

First, it is not, nor can possibly be, absolutely arbitrary over the lives and fortunes of the people; for it being but the joint power of every member of the society given up to that person or assembly which is legislator, it can be no more than those persons had in a state of nature before they entered into society and gave up to the community; for nobody can transfer to another more power than he has in himself, and nobody has an absolute arbitrary power over himself or over any other, to destroy his own life or take away the life or property of another. A man, as has been proved, cannot subject himself to the arbitrary power of another; and having in the state of nature no arbitrary power over the life, liberty, or possession of another, but only so much as the law of nature gave him for the preservation of himself and the rest of mankind, this is all he does or can give up to the commonwealth, and by it to the legislative power, so that the legislative can have no more than this. Their power, in the utmost bounds of it, is limited to the public good of the society. It is a power that has no other end but preservation, and therefore can never have a right to destroy, enslave, or designedly to impoverish the subjects. The obligations of the law of nature cease not in society but only in many cases are drawn closer and have by human laws known penalties annexed to them to enforce their observation. Thus the law of nature stands as an eternal rule to all men, legislators as well as others. The rules that they make for other men's actions must, as well as their own and other men's actions, be conformable to the law of nature—i. e., to the will of God, of which that is a declaration—and the fundamental law of nature being the preservation of mankind, no human sanction can be good or valid against it.

136. Secondly, the legislative or supreme authority cannot assume to itself a power to rule by extemporary, arbitrary decrees, but is bound to dispense justice and to decide the rights of the subject by promulgated, standing laws, and known authorized judges. For the law of nature being unwritten, and so nowhere to be found but in the minds of men, they who through passion or interest shall miscite or misapply it, cannot so easily be convinced of their mistake where there is no established judge; and so it serves not, as it ought, to determine the rights and fence the properties of those that live under it, especially where every one is judge, interpreter, and executioner of it, too, and that in his own case; and he that has right on his side, having ordinarily but his own single strength, has not force enough to defend himself from injuries or to punish delinquents. To avoid these inconveniences which disorder men's properties in the state of nature, men unite into societies that they may have the united strength of the whole society to secure and defend their properties, and may have standing rules to bound it by which every one may know what is his. To this end it is that men give up all their natural power to the society which they enter into, and the community put the legislative power into such hands

as they think fit with this trust, that they shall be governed by declared laws, or else their peace, quiet, and property will still be at the same uncertainty as it was in the state of nature.

137. Absolute arbitrary power or governing without settled standing laws can neither of them consist with the ends of society and government which men would not quit the freedom of the state of nature for, and tie themselves up under, were it not to preserve their lives, liberties, and fortunes, and by stated rules of right and property to secure their peace and quiet. It cannot be supposed that they should intend, had they a power so to do, to give to any one or more an absolute arbitrary power over their persons and estates and put a force into the magistrate's hand to execute his unlimited will arbitrarily upon them. This were to put themselves into a worse condition than the state of nature wherein they had a liberty to defend their right against the injuries of others and were upon equal terms of force to maintain it, whether invaded by a single man or many in combination. Whereas, by supposing they have given up themselves to the absolute arbitrary power and will of a legislator, they have disarmed themselves and armed him to make a prey of them when he pleases, he being in a much worse condition who is exposed to the arbitrary power of one man who has the command of 100,000, than he that is exposed to the arbitrary power of 100,000 single men, nobody being secure that his will, who has such a command, is better than that of other men, though his force be 100,000 times stronger. And, therefore, whatever form the commonwealth is under, the ruling power ought to govern by declared and received laws and not by extemporary dictates and undetermined resolutions; for then mankind will be in a far worse condition than in the state of nature if they shall have armed one or a few men with the joint power of a multitude, to force them to obey at pleasure the exorbitant and unlimited decrees of their sudden thoughts or unrestrained and, till that moment, unknown wills, without having any measures set down which may guide and justify their actions. For all the power the government has, being only for the good of the society, as it ought not to be arbitrary and at pleasure, so it ought to be exercised by established and promulgated laws; that both the people may know their duty and be safe and secure within the limits of the law; and the rulers, too, kept within their bounds, and not be tempted by the power they have in their hands to employ it to such purposes and by such measures as they would not have known, and own not willingly.

138. Thirdly, the supreme power cannot take from any man part of his property without his own consent; for the preservation of property being the end of government and that for which men enter into society, it necessarily supposes and requires that the people should have property; without which they must be supposed to lose that, by entering into society, which was the end for which they entered into it—too gross an absurdity for any man to own. Men, therefore, in society having property, they have such right to the goods which by the law of the community are theirs, that nobody has a right to take their substance or any part of it from them without their own consent; without this, they have no property at all, for I have truly no property in that which another can by right take from me when he pleases, against my consent. Hence it is a mistake to think that the supreme or legislative power of any commonwealth can do what it will and dispose of the estates of the subject arbitrarily, or take any part of them at pleasure. This is not much to be feared in governments where the legislative consists, wholly or in part, in assemblies which are variable, whose members, upon the dissolution of the assembly, are subjects under the common laws of their country, equally with the rest. But in governments where the legislative is in one lasting assembly, always in being, or in one man, as in absolute monarchies, there is danger still that they will think themselves to have a distinct interest from the rest of the community, and so will be apt to increase their own riches and power by taking what they think fit from the people; for a man's property is not at all secure, though there be good and equitable laws to set the bounds of it between him and his fellow subjects, if he who commands those subjects have power to take from any private man what part he pleases of his property and use and dispose of it as he thinks good.

139. But government, into whatsoever hands it is put, being, as I have before shown, entrusted with this condition, and for this end, that men might have and secure their properties, the prince, or senate, however it may have power to make laws for the regulating of property between the subjects one amongst another, yet can never have a power to take to themselves the whole or any part of the subject's property without their own consent; for this would be in effect to leave them no property at all. And to let us see that even absolute power, where it is necessary, is not arbitrary by being absolute, but is still limited by that reason and confined to those ends which required it in some cases to be absolute, we need look no farther than the common

practice of martial discipline; for the preservation of the army, and in it of the whole commonwealth, requires an absolute obedience to the command of every superior officer, and it is justly death to disobey or dispute the most dangerous or unreasonable of them; but yet we see that neither the sergeant, that could command a soldier to march up to the mouth of a cannon or stand in a breach where he is almost sure to perish, can command that soldier to give him one penny of his money; nor the general, that can condemn him to death for deserting his post or for not obeying the most desperate orders, can yet, with all his absolute power of life and death, dispose of one farthing of that soldier's estate or seize one jot of his goods, whom yet he can command anything, and hang for the least disobedience. Because such a blind obedience is necessary to that end for which the commander has his power, viz., the preservation of the rest; but the disposing of his goods has nothing to do with it.

140. It is true, governments cannot be supported without great charge, and it is fit every one who enjoys his share of the protection should pay out of his estate his proportion for the maintenance of it. But still it must be with his own consent—i.e., the consent of the majority, giving it either by themselves or their representatives chosen by them. For if any one shall claim a power to lay and levy taxes on the people, by his own authority and without such consent of the people, he thereby invades the fundamental law of property and subverts the end of government; for what property have I in that which another may by right take, when he pleases, to himself?

141. Fourthly, the legislative cannot transfer the power of making laws to any other hands; for it being but a delegated power from the people, they who have it cannot pass it over to others. The people alone can appoint the form of the commonwealth, which is by constituting the legislative and appointing in whose hands that shall be. And when the people have said, we will submit to rules and be governed by laws made by such men, and in such forms, nobody else can say other men shall make laws for them; nor can the people be bound by any laws but such as are enacted by those whom they have chosen and authorized to make laws for them. The power of the legislative, being derived from the people by a positive voluntary grant and institution, can be no other than what that positive grant conveyed, which being only to make laws, and not to make legislators, the legislative can have no power to transfer their authority of making laws and place it in other hands.

142. These are the bounds which the trust that is put in them by

the society and the law of God and nature have set to the legislative power of every commonwealth, in all forms of government:

First, they are to govern by promulgated established laws, not to be varied in particular cases, but to have one rule for rich and poor, for the favorite at court and the countryman at plough.

Secondly, these laws also ought to be designed for no other end ultimately but the good of the people.

Thirdly, they must not raise taxes on the property of the people without the consent of the people, given by themselves or their deputies. And this property concerns only such governments where the legislative is always in being, or at least where the people have not reserved any part of the legislative to deputies to be from time to time chosen by themselves.

Fourthly, the legislative neither must nor can transfer the power of making laws to anybody else, or place it anywhere but where the people have.

Chapter XII
Of the Legislative, Executive, and
Federative Power of the Commonwealth

143. The legislative power is that which has a right to direct how the force of the commonwealth shall be employed for preserving the community and the members of it. But because those laws which are constantly to be executed, and whose force is always to continue, may be made in a little time, therefore there is no need that the legislative should be always in being, not having always business to do. And because it may be too great a temptation to human frailty, apt to grasp at power, for the same persons who have the power of making laws to have also in their hands the power to execute them, whereby they may exempt themselves from obedience to the laws they make, and suit the law, both in its making and execution, to their own private advantage, and thereby come to have a distinct interest from the rest of the community contrary to the end of society and government; therefore, in well ordered commonwealths, where the good of the whole is so considered as it ought, the legislative power is put into the hands of diverse persons who, duly assembled, have by themselves, or jointly with others, a power to make laws; which when they have done, being separated again, they are themselves subject to the laws they have made, which is a new and near tie upon them to take care that they make them for the public good.

144. But because the laws that are at once and in a short time made have a constant and lasting force and need a perpetual execution or an attendance thereunto; therefore, it is necessary there should be a power always in being which should see to the execution of the laws that are made and remain in force. And thus the legislative and executive power come often to be separated.

145. There is another power in every commonwealth which one may call natural, because it is that which answers to the power every man naturally had before he entered into society; for though in a commonwealth the members of it are distinct persons still in reference to one another, and as such are governed by the laws of the society, yet, in reference to the rest of mankind, they make one body which is, as every member of it before was, still in the state of nature with the rest of mankind. Hence it is that the controversies that happen between any man of the society with those that are out of it are managed by the public, and an injury done to a member of their body engages the whole in the reparation of it. So that, under this consideration, the whole community is one body in the state of nature in respect of all other states or persons out of its community.

146. This, therefore, contains the power of war and peace, leagues and alliances, and all the transactions with all persons and communities without the commonwealth, and may be called 'federative,' if anyone pleases. So the thing be understood, I am indifferent as to the name.

147. These two powers, executive and federative, though they be really distinct in themselves, yet one comprehending the execution of the municipal laws of the society within itself upon all that are parts of it, the other the management of the security and interest of the public without, with all those that it may receive benefit or damage from, yet they are always almost united. And though this federative power in the well or ill management of it be of great moment to the commonwealth, yet it is much less capable to be directed by antecedent, standing, positive laws than the executive, and so must necessarily be left to the prudence and wisdom of those whose hands it is in to be managed for the public good; for the laws that concern subjects one amongst another, being to direct their actions, may well enough precede them. But what is to be done in reference to foreigners, depending much upon their actions and the variation of designs and interests, must be left in great part to the prudence of those who have this power committed to them, to be managed by the best of their skill for the advantage of the commonwealth.

148. Though, as I said, the executive and federative power of every

community be really distinct in themselves, yet they are hardly to be separated and placed at the same time in the hands of distinct persons; for both of them requiring the force of the society for their exercise, it is almost impracticable to place the force of the commonwealth in distinct and not subordinate hands, or that the executive and federative power should be placed in persons that might act separately, whereby the force of the public would be under different commands, which would be apt some time or other to cause disorder and ruin.

Chapter XIII
Of the Subordination of the Powers
of the Commonwealth

149. Though in a constituted commonwealth, standing upon its own basis and acting according to its own nature, that is, acting for the preservation of the community, there can be but one supreme power which is the legislative, to which all the rest are and must be subordinate, yet, the legislative being only a fiduciary power to act for certain ends, there remains still in the people a supreme power to remove or alter the legislative when they find the legislative act contrary to the trust reposed in them; for all power given with trust for the attaining an end being limited by that end; whenever that end is manifestly neglected or opposed, the trust must necessarily be forfeited and the power devolve into the hands of those that gave it, who may place it anew where they shall think best for their safety and security. And thus the community perpetually retains a supreme power of saving themselves from the attempts and designs of anybody, even of their legislators whenever they shall be so foolish or so wicked as to lay and carry on designs against the liberties and properties of the subject; for no man or society of men having a power to deliver up their preservation, or consequently the means of it, to the absolute will and arbitrary dominion of another, whenever any one shall go about to bring them into such a slavish condition, they will always have a right to preserve what they have not a power to part with, and to rid themselves of those who invade this fundamental, sacred, and unalterable law of self-preservation for which they entered into society. And thus the community may be said in this respect to be always the supreme power, but not as considered under any form of government, because this power of the people can never take place till the government be dissolved.

150. In all cases, while the government subsists, the legislative is the supreme power; for what can give laws to another must needs be

superior to him; and since the legislative is not otherwise legislative of the society but by the right it has to make laws for all the parts and for every member of the society, prescribing rules to their actions, and giving power of execution where they are transgressed, the legislative must needs be the supreme, and all other powers in any members or parts of the society derived from and subordinate to it.

151. In some commonwealths where the legislative is not always in being, and the executive is vested in a single person who has also a share in the legislative, there that single person in a very tolerable sense may also be called supreme; not that he has in himself all the supreme power, which is that of lawmaking, but because he has in him the supreme execution from whom all inferior magistrates derive all their several subordinate powers, or at least the greatest part of them. Having also no legislative superior to him, there being no law to be made without his consent which cannot be expected should ever subject him to the other part of the legislative, he is properly enough, in this sense, supreme. But yet it is to be observed that though oaths of allegiance and fealty are taken to him, it is not to him as supreme legislator, but as supreme executor of the law made by a joint power of him with others; allegiance being nothing but an obedience according to law, which, when he violates, he has no right to obedience nor can claim it otherwise than as the public person invested with the power of the law, and so is to be considered as the image, phantom, or representative of the commonwealth, acted by the will of the society, declared in its laws; and thus he has no will, no power, but that of the law. But when he quits this representation, this public will, and acts by his own private will, he degrades himself and is but a single private person without power and without will that has no right to obedience—the members owing no obedience but to the public will of the society.

152. The executive power, placed anywhere but in a person that has also a share in the legislative, is visibly subordinate and accountable to it and may be at pleasure changed and displaced, so that it is not the supreme executive power that is exempt from subordination, but the supreme executive power vested in one who, having a share in the legislative, has no distinct superior legislative to be subordinate and accountable to, farther than he himself shall join and consent; so that he is no more subordinate than he himself shall think fit, which one may certainly conclude will be but very little. Of other ministerial and subordinate powers in a commonwealth we need not speak, they being so multiplied with infinite variety in the different customs and

constitutions of distinct commonwealths that it is impossible to give a particular account of them all. Only thus much, which is necessary to our present purpose, we may take notice of concerning them, that they have no manner of authority, any of them, beyond what is by positive grant and commission delegated to them, and are all of them accountable to some other power in the commonwealth.

153. It is not necessary, no, nor so much as convenient, that the legislative should be always in being; but absolutely necessary that the executive power should, because there is not always need of new laws to be made but always need of execution of the laws that are made. When the legislative has put the execution of the laws they make into other hands, they have a power still to resume it out of those hands, when they find cause, and to punish for any maladministration against the laws. The same holds also in regard of the federative power, that and the executive being both ministerial and subordinate to the legislative which, as has been shown, in a constituted commonwealth is the supreme. The legislative also in this case being supposed to consist of several persons—for if it be a single person, it cannot but be always in being, and so will, as supreme, naturally have the supreme executive power, together with the legislative—may assemble and exercise their legislature at the times that either their original constitution or their own adjournment appoints, or when they please, if neither of these has appointed any time, or there be no other way prescribed to convoke them. For the supreme power being placed in them by the people, it is always in them, and they may exercise it when they please, unless by their original constitution they are limited to certain seasons, or by an act of their supreme power they have adjourned to a certain time; and when that time comes, they have a right to assemble and act again.

154. If the legislative, or any part of it, be made up of representatives chosen for that time by the people, which afterwards return into the ordinary state of subjects and have no share in the legislature but upon a new choice, this power of choosing must also be exercised by the people, either at certain appointed seasons, or else when they are summoned to it; and in this latter case the power of convoking the legislative is ordinarily placed in the executive, and has one of these two limitations in respect of time: that either the original constitution requires their assembling and acting at certain intervals, and then the executive power does nothing but ministerially issue directions for their electing and assembling according to due forms; or else it is left to his prudence to call them by new elections, when the occasions or

exigencies of the public require the amendment of old or making of new laws, or the redress or prevention of any inconveniences that lie on or threaten the people.

155. It may be demanded here, what if the executive power, being possessed of the force of the commonwealth, shall make use of that force to hinder the meeting and acting of the legislative, when the original constitution or the public exigencies require it? I say using force upon the people without authority, and contrary to the trust put in him that does so, is a state of war with the people who have a right to reinstate their legislative in the exercise of their power; for having erected a legislative with an intent they should exercise the power of making laws, either at certain set times or when there is need of it, when they are hindered by any force from what is so necessary to the society, and wherein the safety and preservation of the people consists, the people have a right to remove it by force. In all states and conditions, the true remedy of force without authority is to oppose force to it. The use of force without authority always puts him that uses it into a state of war, as the aggressor, and renders him liable to be treated accordingly.

156. The power of assembling and dismissing the legislative, placed in the executive, gives not the executive a superiority over it, but is a fiduciary trust placed in him for the safety of the people, in a case where the uncertainty and variableness of human affairs could not bear a steady fixed rule; for it not being possible that the first framers of the government should, by any foresight, be so much masters of future events as to be able to prefix so just periods of return and duration to the assemblies of the legislative, in all times to come, that might exactly answer all the exigencies of the commonwealth, the best remedy could be found for this defect was to trust this to the prudence of one who was always to be present and whose business it was to watch over the public good. Constant, frequent meetings of the legislative, and long continuations of their assemblies without necessary occasion, could not but be burdensome to the people and must necessarily in time produce more dangerous inconveniences, and yet the quick turn of affairs might be sometimes such as to need their present help. Any delay of their convening might endanger the public; and sometimes, too, their business might be so great that the limited time of their sitting might be too short for their work, and rob the public of that benefit which could be had only from their mature deliberation. What then could be done in this case to prevent the community from being exposed, some time or other, to eminent hazard, on one side or the other, by fixed intervals and periods set to the meeting and acting

of the legislative, but to entrust it to the prudence of some who, being present and acquainted with the state of public affairs, might make use of this prerogative for the public good? And where else could this be so well placed as in his hands who was entrusted with the execution of the laws for the same end? Thus supposing the regulation of times for the assembling and sitting of the legislative not settled by the original constitution, it naturally fell into the hands of the executive, not as an arbitrary power depending on his good pleasure but with this trust always to have it exercised only for the public weal, as the occurrences of times and change of affairs might require. Whether settled periods of their convening, or a liberty left to the prince for convoking the legislative, or perhaps a mixture of both, has the least inconvenience attending it, it is not my business here to inquire; but only to show that though the executive power may have the prerogative of convoking and dissolving such conventions of the legislative, yet it is not thereby superior to it.

157. Things of this world are in so constant a flux that nothing remains long in the same state. Thus people, riches, trade, power change their stations, flourishing mighty cities come to ruin and prove in time neglected, desolate corners, while other unfrequented places grow into populous countries, filled with wealth and inhabitants. But things not always changing equally, and private interest often keeping up customs and privileges when the reasons of them are ceased, it often comes to pass that in governments where part of the legislative consists of representatives chosen by the people, that in tract of time this representation becomes very unequal and disproportionate to the reasons it was at first established upon. To what gross absurdities the following of custom when reason has left it may lead, we may be satisfied when we see the bare name of a town of which there remains not so much as the ruins, where scarce so much housing as a sheepcote or more inhabitants than a shepherd is to be found, sends as many representatives to the grand assembly of lawmakers as a whole county numerous in people and powerful in riches. This strangers stand amazed at, and everyone must confess needs a remedy; though most think it hard to find one, because the constitution of the legislative being the original and supreme act of the society, antecedent to all positive laws in it and depending wholly on the people, no inferior power can alter it. And, therefore, the people, when the legislative is once constituted, having in such a government as we have been speaking of no power to act as long as the government stands, this inconvenience is thought incapable of a remedy.

158. *Salus populi suprema lex* [The public good is the supreme law]

is certainly so just and fundamental a rule that he who sincerely follows it cannot dangerously err. If, therefore, the executive who has the power of convoking the legislative, observing rather the true proportion than fashion of representation, regulates, not by old custom but true reason, the number of members in all places that have a right to be distinctly represented—which no part of the people, however incorporated, can pretend to but in proportion to the assistance which it affords to the public—it cannot be judged to have set up a new legislative but to have restored the old and true one, and to have rectified the disorders which succession of time had insensibly as well as inevitably introduced. For it being the interest as well as intention of the people to have a fair and equal representative, whoever brings it nearest to that is an undoubted friend to and establisher of the government and cannot miss the consent and approbation of the community. Prerogative being nothing but a power in the hands of the prince to provide for the public good in such cases which, depending upon unforeseen and uncertain occurrences, certain and unalterable laws could not safely direct, whatsoever shall be done manifestly for the good of the people and the establishing the government upon its true foundations is, and always will be, just prerogative. The power of erecting new corporations, and therewith new representatives, carries with it a supposition that in time the measures of representation might vary, and those places have a just right to be represented which before had none; and by the same reason those cease to have a right and be too inconsiderable for such a privilege, which before had it. It is not a change from the present state, which perhaps corruption or decay has introduced, that makes an inroad upon the government, but the tendency of it to injure or oppress the people, and to set up one part or party with a distinction from, and an unequal subjection of, the rest. Whatsoever cannot but be acknowledged to be of advantage to the society and people in general, upon just and lasting measures, will always, when done, justify itself; and whenever the people shall choose their representatives upon just and undeniably equal measures, suitable to the original frame of the government, it cannot be doubted to be the will and act of the society, whoever permitted or caused them so to do.

Chapter XIV
Of Prerogative

159. Where the legislative and executive power are in distinct hands —as they are in all moderated monarchies and well-framed govern-

ments—there the good of the society requires that several things should be left to the discretion of him that has the executive power; for the legislators not being able to foresee and provide by laws for all that may be useful to the community, the executor of the laws, having the power in his hands, has by the common law of nature a right to make use of it for the good of the society, in many cases where the municipal law has given no direction, till the legislative can conveniently be assembled to provide for it. Many things there are which the law can by no means provide for; and those must necessarily be left to the discretion of him that has the executive power in his hands, to be ordered by him as the public good and advantage shall require; nay, it is fit that the laws themselves should in some cases give way to the executive power, or rather to this fundamental law of nature and government, viz., that, as much as may be, all the members of the society are to be preserved; for since many accidents may happen wherein a strict and rigid observation of the laws may do harm—as not to pull down an innocent man's house to stop the fire when the next to it is burning—and a man may come sometimes within the reach of the law, which makes no distinction of persons, by an action that may deserve reward and pardon, it is fit the ruler should have a power in many cases to mitigate the severity of the law and pardon some offenders; for the end of government being the preservation of all as much as may be, even the guilty are to be spared where it can prove no prejudice to the innocent.

160. This power to act according to discretion for the public good, without the prescription of the law and sometimes even against it, is that which is called 'prerogative'; for since in some governments the lawmaking power is not always in being, and is usually too numerous and so too slow for the dispatch requisite to execution, and because also it is impossible to foresee, and so by laws to provide for, all accidents and necessities that may concern the public, or to make such laws as will do no harm if they are executed with an inflexible rigor on all occasions and upon all persons that may come in their way, therefore there is a latitude left to the executive power to do many things of choice which the laws do not prescribe.

161. This power, while employed for the benefit of the community and suitably to the trust and ends of the government, is undoubted prerogative, and never is questioned; for the people are very seldom or never scrupulous or nice in the point; they are far from examining prerogative while it is in any tolerable degree employed for the use it was meant, that is, for the good of the people, and not manifestly

against it. But if there comes to be a question between the executive power and the people about a thing claimed as a prerogative, the tendency of the exercise of such prerogative to the good or hurt of the people will easily decide that question.

162. It is easy to conceive that in the infancy of governments, when commonwealths differed little from families in number of people, they differed from them too but little in number of laws; and the governors, being as the fathers of them, watching over them for their good, the government was almost all prerogative. A few established laws served the turn, and the discretion and care of the ruler supplied the rest. But when mistake or flattery prevailed with weak princes to make use of this power for private ends of their own and not for the public good, the people were fain by express laws to get prerogative determined in those points wherein they found disadvantage from it; and thus declared limitations of prerogative were by the people found necessary in cases which they and their ancestors had left in the utmost latitude to the wisdom of those princes who made no other but a right use of it, that is, for the good of their people.

163. And therefore they have a very wrong notion of government who say that the people have encroached upon the prerogative when they have got any part of it to be defined by positive laws; for in so doing they have not pulled from the prince anything that of right belonged to him, but only declare that that power which they indefinitely left in his or his ancestors hands to be exercised for their good was not a thing which they intended him when he used it otherwise. For the end of government being the good of the community, whatsoever alterations are made in it tending to that end cannot be an encroachment upon anybody, since nobody in government can have a right tending to any other end; and those only are encroachments which prejudice or hinder the public good. Those who say otherwise speak as if the prince had a distinct and separate interest from the good of the community and was not made for it—the root and source from which spring almost all those evils and disorders which happen in kingly governments. And, indeed, if that be so, the people under his government are not a society of rational creatures entered into a community for their mutual good, they are not such as have set rulers over themselves to guard and promote that good; but are to be looked on as a herd of inferior creatures under the dominion of a master who keeps them and works them for his own pleasure or profit. If men were so void of reason and brutish as to enter into society upon such terms, prerogative might indeed be what some men would have it: an arbitrary power to do things hurtful to the people.

164. But since a rational creature cannot be supposed, when free, to put himself into subjection to another for his own harm—though, where he finds a good and wise ruler, he may not perhaps think it either necessary or useful to set precise bounds to his power in all things—prerogative can be nothing but the people's permitting their rulers to do several things of their own free choice where the law was silent, and sometimes, too, against the direct letter of the law, for the public good, and their acquiescing in it when so done. For as a good prince who is mindful of the trust put into his hands and careful of the good of his people cannot have too much prerogative, that is, power to do good, so a weak and ill prince, who would claim that power which his predecessors exercised without the direction of the law as a prerogative belonging to him by right of his office, which he may exercise at his pleasure to make or promote an interest distinct from that of the public, gives the people an occasion to claim their right, and limit that power which, while it was exercised for their good, they were content should be tacitly allowed.

165. And, therefore, he that will look into the history of England will find that prerogative was always largest in the hands of our wisest and best princes, because the people, observing the whole tendency of their actions to be the public good, contested not what was done without law to that end, or, if any human frailty or mistake—for princes are but men, made as others—appeared in some small declinations from that end, yet it was visible the main of their conduct tended to nothing but the care of the public. The people, therefore, finding reason to be satisfied with these princes whenever they acted without or contrary to the letter of the law, acquiesced in what they did, and without the least complaint let them enlarge their prerogative as they pleased, judging rightly that they did nothing herein to the prejudice of their laws since they acted conformably to the foundation and end of all laws—the public good.

166. Such godlike princes, indeed, had some title to arbitrary power by that argument that would prove absolute monarchy the best government, as that which God himself governs the universe by, because such kings partook of his wisdom and goodness. Upon this is founded that saying that the reigns of good princes have been always most dangerous to the liberties of their people; for when their successors, managing the government with different thoughts, would draw the actions of those good rulers into precedent and make them the standard of their prerogative, as if what had been done only for the good of the people was a right in them to do for the harm of the people if they so pleased, it has often occasioned contest, and sometimes public disorders, before

the people could recover their original right and get that to be declared not to be prerogative which truly was never so, since it is impossible that anybody in the society should ever have a right to do the people harm, though it be very possible and reasonable that the people should not go about to set any bounds to the prerogative of those kings or rulers who themselves transgressed not the bounds of the public good; for *prerogative is nothing but the power of doing public good without a rule.*

167. The power of calling parliaments in England, as to precise time, place, and duration, is certainly a prerogative of the king, but still with this trust that it shall be made use of for the good of the nation, as the exigencies of the times and variety of occasions shall require; for it being impossible to foresee which should always be the fittest place for them to assemble in, and what the best season, the choice of these was left with the executive power, as might be most subservient to the public good, and best suit the ends of parliaments.

168. The old question will be asked in this matter of prerogative: But who shall be judge when this power is made a right use of? I answer: Between an executive power in being with such a prerogative, and a legislative that depends upon his will for their convening, there can be no judge on earth; as there can be none between the legislative and the people, should either the executive or the legislative, when they have got the power in their hands, design or go about to enslave or destroy them. The people have no other remedy in this, as in all other cases where they have no judge on earth, but to appeal to heaven; for the rulers, in such attempts, exercising a power the people never put into their hands—who can never be supposed to consent that anybody should rule over them for their harm—do that which they have not a right to do. And where the body of the people, or any single man, is deprived of their right, or is under the exercise of a power without right and have no appeal on earth, then they have a liberty to appeal to heaven whenever they judge the cause of sufficient moment. And, therefore, though the people cannot be judge so as to have by the constitution of that society any superior power to determine and give effective sentence in the case, yet they have, by a law antecedent and paramount to all positive laws of men, reserved that ultimate determination to themselves which belongs to all mankind, where there lies no appeal on earth—viz., to judge whether they have just cause to make their appeal to heaven. And this judgment they cannot part with, it being out of a man's power so to submit himself to another as to give him a liberty to destroy him, God and nature never allowing a

man so to abandon himself as to neglect his own preservation; and since he cannot take away his own life, neither can he give another power to take it. Nor let anyone think this lays a perpetual foundation for disorder; for this operates not till the inconvenience is so great that the majority feel it and are weary of it and find a necessity to have it amended. But this the executive power, or wise princes, never need come in the danger of; and it is the thing, of all others, they have most need to avoid, as of all others the most perilous.

The Four Georges

Very few years since, I knew familiarly a lady who had been asked in marriage by Horace Walpole, who had been patted on the head by George I. This lady had knocked at Doctor Johnson's door; had been intimate with Fox, the beautiful Georgina of Devonshire, and that brilliant Whig society of the reign of George III; had known the Duchess of Queensberry, the patroness of Gay and Prior, the admired young beauty of the Court of Queen Anne. I often thought as I took my kind old friend's hand, how with it I held on to the old society of wits and men of the world. I could travel back for seven score years of time—have glimpses of Brummel, Selwyn, Chesterfield, and the men of pleasure; of Walpole and Conway; of Johnson, Reynolds, Goldsmith; of North, Chatham, Newcastle; of the fair maids of honour of George II's Court; of the German retainers of George I's where Addison was Secretary of State; where Dick Steele held a place; whither the great Marlborough came with his fiery spouse; when Pope, and Swift, and Bolingbroke yet lived and wrote. Of a society so vast, busy, brilliant, it is impossible in four brief chapters to give a complete notion; but we may peep here and there into that bygone world of the Georges, see what they and their Courts were like; glance at the people round about them; look at past manners, fashions, pleasures, and contrast them with our own. I have to say thus much by way of preface, because the subject of these lectures has been misunderstood, and I have been taken to task for not having given grave historical treatises, which it never was my intention to attempt. Not about battles, about politics, about statesmen and measures of State, did I ever think to lecture you: but to sketch the manners and life of the old world; to amuse for a few hours with talk about the old society; and, with the

W. M. Thackeray, *The Four Georges*, first published in 1861 (*The Works of W. M. Thackeray*, vol. XI (London, 1911)).

result of many a day's and night's pleasant reading, to try and while away a few winter evenings for my hearers.

. . .

It was the first Elector of Hanover who made the fortunate match which bestowed the race of Hanoverian Sovereigns upon us Britons. Nine years after Charles Stuart lost his head, his niece Sophia, one of many children of another luckless dethroned sovereign, the Elector Palatine, married Ernest Augustus of Brunswick, and brought the reversion to the crown of the three kingdoms in her scanty trousseau.

One of the handsomest, the most cheerful, sensible, shrewd, accomplished of women was Sophia, daughter of poor Frederick, the winter King of Bohemia. The other daughters of lovely unhappy Elizabeth Stuart went off into the Catholic Church; this one, luckily for her family, remained, I cannot say faithful to the Reformed Religion, but at least she adopted no other. An agent of the French King's, Gourville, a convert himself, strove to bring her and her husband to a sense of the truth; and tells us that he one day asked Madame the Duchess of Hanover of what religion her daughter was, then a pretty girl of thirteen years old. The Duchess replied that the princess *was of no religion as yet*. They were waiting to know of what religion her husband would be, Protestant or Catholic, before instructing her! And the Duke of Hanover having heard all Gourville's proposal, said that a change would be advantageous to his house, but that he himself was too old to change.

This shrewd woman had such keen eyes that she knew how to shut them upon occasion, and was blind to many faults which it appeared that her husband the Bishop of Osnaburg and Duke of Hanover committed. He loved to take his pleasure like other sovereigns—was a merry prince, fond of dinner and the bottle; liked to go to Italy, as his brothers had done before him; and we read how he jovially sold 6,700 of his Hanoverians to the Seigniory of Venice. They went bravely off to the Morea, under command of Ernest's son, Prince Max, and only 1,400 of them ever came home again. The German princes sold a good deal of this kind of stock. You may remember how George III's Government purchased Hessians, and the use we made of them during the War of Independence.

The ducats Duke Ernest got for his soldiers he spent in a series of the most brilliant entertainments. Nevertheless, the jovial Prince was economical, and kept a steady eye upon his own interests. He achieved the electoral dignity for himself: he married his eldest son George to his beautiful cousin of Zell; and sending his sons out in command of armies to fight—now on this side, now on that—he lived on, taking his pleasure, and scheming his schemes, a merry wise prince enough—not, I fear, a moral prince, of which kind we shall nave but very few specimens in the course of these lectures.

Ernest Augustus had seven children in all, some of whom were scapegraces, and rebelled against the parental system of primogeniture and non-division of property which the Elector ordained. "Gustchen," the Electress writes about her second son: "Poor Gus is thrust out, and his father will give him no more keep. I laugh in the day, and cry all night about it; for I am a fool with my children." Three of the six died fighting against Turks, Tartars, Frenchmen. One of them conspired, revolted, fled to Rome, leaving an agent behind him, whose head was taken off. The daughter, of whose early education we have made mention, was married to the Elector of Brandenburg, and so her religion settled finally on the Protestant side.

A niece of the Electress Sophia—who had been made to change her religion, and marry the Duke of Orleans, brother of the French King; a woman whose honest heart was always with her friends and dear old Deutschland, though her fat little body was confined at Paris, or Marly, or Versailles—has left us, in her enormous correspondence (part of which has been printed in German and French), recollections of the Electress, and of George her son. Elizabeth Charlotte was at Osnaburg when George was born (1660). She narrowly escaped a whipping for being in the way on that auspicious day. She seems not to have liked little George, nor George grown up; and represents him as odiously hard, cold, and silent. Silent he may have been: not a jolly prince like his father before him, but a prudent, quiet, selfish potentate, going his own way, managing his own affairs, and understanding his own interests remarkably well.

In his father's lifetime, and at the head of the Hanover forces of 8,000 or 10,000 men, George served the Emperor, on the Danube against Turks, at the siege of Vienna, in Italy, and on the Rhine. When he succeeded to the Electorate, he handled its affairs with great prudence and dexterity. He was very much liked by his people of Hanover. He did not show his feelings much, but he cried heartily on leaving them; as they used for joy when he came back. He showed an uncommon prudence and coolness of behaviour when he came into his kingdom; exhibiting no elation; reasonably doubtful whether he should not be turned out some day; looking upon himself only as a lodger, and making the most of his brief tenure of St. James's and Hampton

Court; plundering, it is true, somewhat, and dividing amongst his German followers; but what could be expected of a sovereign who at home could sell his subjects at so many ducats per head, and make no scruple in so disposing of them? I fancy a considerable shrewdness, prudence, and even moderation in his ways. The German Protestant was a cheaper, and better, and kinder king than the Catholic Stuart in whose chair he sat, and so far loyal to England that he let England govern herself.

.   .   .

In the year 1700 the little Duke of Gloucester, the last of poor Queen Anne's children, died, and the folks of Hanover straightway became of prodigious importance in England. The Electress Sophia was declared the next in succession to the English throne. George Louis was created Duke of Cambridge; grand deputations were sent over from our country to Deutschland; but Queen Anne, whose weak heart hankered after her relatives at Saint Germains, never could be got to allow her cousin, the Elector Duke of Cambridge, to come and pay his respects to Her Majesty, and take his seat in her House of Peers. Had the Queen lasted a month longer; had the English Tories been as bold and resolute as they were clever and crafty; had the Prince whom the nation loved and pitied been equal to his fortune, George Louis had never talked German in Saint James's Chapel Royal.

When the crown did come to George Louis he was in no hurry about putting it on. He waited at home for awhile; took an affecting farewell of his dear Hanover and Herrenhausen; and set out in the most leisurely manner to ascend "the throne of his ancestors," as he called it in his first speech to Parliament. He brought with him a compact body of Germans, whose society he loved, and whom he kept round the Royal person. He had his faithful German chamberlains; his German secretaries; his negroes, captives of his bow and spear in Turkish wars; his two ugly elderly German favourites, Mesdames of Kielmansegge and Schulenberg, whom he created respectively Countess of Darlington and Duchess of Kendal. The Duchess was tall, and lean of stature and hence was irreverently nicknamed the Maypole. The Countess was a large-sized noblewoman, and this elevated personage was denominated the Elephant. Both of these ladies loved Hanover and its delights; clung round the linden trees of the great Herrenhausen avenue, and at first would not quit the place. Schulenberg, in fact, could not come on account of her debts; but finding the Maypole would not come, the Elephant packed up her trunk and slipped out of Hanover, unwieldy as she was. On this the Maypole straightway put herself in motion, and followed her beloved George Louis. One seems to be speaking of Captain Macheath, and Polly, and Lucy. The King we had selected; the courtiers who came in his train; the English nobles who came to welcome him, and on many of whom the shrewd old cynic turned his back—I protest it is a wonderful satirical picture. I am a citizen waiting at Greenwich pier, say, and crying hurrah for King George; and yet I can scarcely keep my countenance, and help laughing at the enormous absurdity of this advent!

Here we are, all on our knees. Here is the Archbishop of Canterbury prostrating himself to the Head of his Church, with Kielmansegge and Schulenberg with their ruddled cheeks grinning behind the Defender of the Faith. Here is my Lord Duke of Marlborough kneeling too, the greatest warrior of all times; he who betrayed King William—betrayed King James II—betrayed Queen Anne—betrayed England to the French, the Elector to the Pretender, the Pretender to the Elector; and here are my Lords Oxford and Bolingbroke, the latter of whom has just tripped up the heels of the former; and if a month's more time had been allowed him, would have had King James at Westminster. The great Whig gentlemen made their bows and congées with proper decorum and ceremony; but yonder keen old schemer knows the value of their loyalty. "Loyalty," he must think, "as applied to me—it is absurd! There are fifty nearer heirs to the throne than I am. I am but an accident, and you fine Whig gentlemen take me for your own sake, not for mine. You Tories hate me; you archbishop, smirking on your knees, and prating about Heaven, you know I don't care a fig for your Thirty-nine Articles, and can't understand a word of your stupid sermons. You, my Lords Bolingbroke and Oxford—you know you were conspiring against me a month ago; and you, my Lord Duke of Marlborough—you would sell me or any man else, if you found your advantage in it. Come, my good Melusina, come, my honest Sophia, let us go into my private room, and have some oysters and some Rhine wine, and some pipes afterwards: let us make the best of our situation; let us take what we can get, and leave these bawling, brawling, lying English to shout, and fight, and cheat, in their own way!"

If Swift had not been committed to the statesmen of the losing side, what a fine satirical picture we might have had of that general *sauve qui peut* amongst the Tory party! How mum the Tories became; how the House of Lords and House of Commons chopped round; and how decorously the majorities welcomed King George!

.　.　.

Delightful as London city was, King George I liked to be out of it as much as ever he could; and when there, passed all his time with his Germans. It was with them as with Blucher, a hundred years afterwards, when the bold old Reiter looked down from Saint Paul's, and sighed out, "Was für Plunder!" The German women plundered; the German secretaries plundered; the German cooks and intendants plundered; even Mustapha and Mahomet, the German negroes, had a share of the booty. Take what you can get, was the old monarch's maxim. He was not a lofty monarch, certainly: he was not a patron of the fine arts: but he was not a hypocrite, he was not revengeful, he was not extravagant. Though a despot in Hanover, he was a moderate ruler in England. His aim was to leave it to itself as much as possible, and to live out of it as much as he could. His heart was in Hanover. When taken ill on his last journey, as he was passing through Holland, he thrust his livid head out of the coach-window, and gasped out, "Osnaburg, Osnaburg!" He was more than fifty years of age when he came amongst us: we took him because we wanted him, because he served our turn; we laughed at his uncouth German ways, and sneered at him. He took our loyalty for what it was worth; laid hands on what money he could; kept us assuredly from Popery and wooden shoes. I, for one, would have been on his side in those days. Cynical and selfish as he was, he was better than a king out of Saint Germains with the French King's orders in his pocket, and a swarm of Jesuits in his train.

.　.　.

The days are over in England of that strange religion of king-worship, when priests flattered princes in the Temple of God; when servility was held to be ennobling duty; when beauty and youth tried eagerly for Royal favour; and woman's shame was held to be no dishonour. Mended morals and mended manners in Courts and people are among the priceless consequences of the freedom which George I came to rescue and secure. He kept his compact with his English subjects; and if he escaped no more than other men and monarchs from the vices of his age, at least we may thank him for preserving and transmitting the liberties of ours. In our free air, Royal and humble homes have alike been purified; and Truth, the birthright of high and low among us, which quite fearlessly judges our greatest personages, can only speak of them now in words of respect and regard. There are stains in the portrait of the first George, and traits in it which none of us need admire; but among the nobler features are justice, courage, moderation—and these we may recognise ere we turn the picture to the wall.

An Impartial History of Parties. [1714]

Note: Lord Chancellor Cowper (d. 1723) drew up the following memoir for the perusal of George I upon the latter's accession to the throne. In its original language, here reproduced, this document would have proved a closed book to George I; Lady Cowper, however, prepared a French translation which she presented to Bernstorff, the Hanoverian Minister, to be submitted to the King at an auspicious moment. Campbell asserts that the memoir was not without effect upon George, who continued Cowper in office until 1718.

"May it please your Majesty,
It being probable that many of those who have had the honour of serving you as Lords Justices during your Majesty's absence, will think themselves obliged, on your Majesty's arrival in your kingdom, severally to offer their thoughts, concerning the first settlement of your government, as that upon which not only the security, but also the tranquillity and comfort of your Majesty's whole reign, will entirely depend, I humbly beg leave (not being sufficiently master of the French tongue to explain myself fully, by speaking on a matter of so great consequence) to offer to your Majesty's judgment, in this manner, the best information I can, together with a few thoughts on that important subject; which is done with an entire resignation to your wisdom, and a most cordial disinterested zeal for your Majesty's service.

Nothing can sooner conduce to your Majesty's entering on right measures, at this juncture, than the giving a true idea of the parties into which, to our great misfortune, your people are divided. When that is once done, none is so well able from thence to make proper inferences, and form the most useful rules of government, as your Majesty; whose wisdom, experience, application, and success in that particular, are known and admired by all Europe.

That part of your people which consists of Papists and nonjurors, who manifest their disaffection to your Majesty's government by denying to give those assurances which the laws require, are, in England, but few in proportion to the rest of your Majesty's subjects; but I choose to mention these first, because all that need be suggested con-

John Lord Campbell, *The Lives of the Lord Chancellors*, vol. IV (London, 1846).

cerning them is in a very narrow compass. There are several penal laws in force contrived to curb and restrain them as there is occasion; and accordingly, those laws have been used to be put in execution with more or less rigour, as they who are obnoxious to them have behaved themselves with more or less duty and submission to the government, and sometimes with respect to the usage the Protestants meet with in the countries of Roman Catholic princes or states; and there is no question but your Majesty will be advised to deal with them in the same manner.

The residue of your Majesty's subjects, who take the oaths, and give all the assurances the laws require, are, notwithstanding, divided into two parties with respect to the government.

These parties began to form themselves and give names to each other about the time the Bill of Exclusion was set on foot, in the reign of King Charles II., though some affect to carry their beginning so far back as the civil wars, which is part of the scandal one of them is pleased to fling upon the other, without the least ground of truth, since, to do them right, both are sincerely for the Monarchy of Great Britain and the Church of England (excepting as to the Church the Protestant Dissenters, who range themselves with those called Whigs, as the Papists do with those called Tories, almost in all state controversies whatsoever).

The Tories accuse the others of being inclined to set up a commonwealth, and the Whigs them of a design to introduce Popery, or at least to bring the Church of England nearer to that of Rome. Whereas, on one side, there are hardly ten in the whole kingdom that may be justly suspected of being for a commonwealth; and, on the other side, whenever the danger has been near and imminent, have shown themselves firm against Popery; and they among them who are projecting a union with the Gallican Church, are either Non-jurors or as few in number and as inconsiderable as the commonwealth men have been said to be on the other side. So that, laying by the reproaches which the parties unjustly make use of one against the other, their real differences of any consequence are but two, which began in this manner:

King Charles II., as was believed, by the influence of his brother, the Duke of York, had set on foot a violent prosecution against the Protestant Dissenters, to divide the Protestant interest, so that the Papists might the easier take advantage of those divisions. This was mightily exclaimed against and opposed to the utmost of their power by those who were afterwards called Whigs, and was much encouraged and promoted by the other party. And hence it was that this Act of Toleration, or at least an exception of Protestant Dissenters from the penal laws was one great point the parties at first divided upon. The other was this:

About the year 1678, the Popish plot being discovered, turned the thoughts of such as were zealous for the security of the Protestant religion to consider the danger it would incur if a Popish successor should come to the throne, and the Duke of York being known to be a Roman Catholic, Bills of Exclusion were voted by the House of Commons in three successive parliaments to set aside the Duke of York, and limit the Crown to the next Protestant heir.* One of the most forward and zealous of the members of the House of Commons in this business was Sir William Cowper (father of the Chancellor and M.P. for Hertford), whose grandfather, Sir William Cowper, had been a zealous royalist.

This Bill was promoted by members of the Church of England (there being but two or three Dissenters or thereabouts in any of those parliaments), and by such, generally speaking, who themselves or their ancestors had been royalists and taken part with King Charles I.

The court strenuously opposed it, and kept it from passing, either by getting a majority of votes against it in the House of Lords, or dissolving the parliament as soon as it was seen that it would pass the House of Commons.

This contest was also managed by a paper war; wherein they who were for excluding the Duke of York were by their adversaries in division called Whigs; and the others, who struggled to secure the crown to him, were called Tories.

The opinions the Whigs stood upon in general were, that although the monarchy was undoubtedly hereditary, and not elective, yet that for the preservation of the whole constitution, and particularly to prevent a Popish successor from succeeding to the Crown, whom they held to be incompatible with a Protestant kingdom, it was lawful for the King by Act of Parliament so to limit and bind the descent of the Crown as to incapacitate the next Popish successor or successors, and declare that it should descend and come to the next protestant heir. And this they contended very clearly would make such Protestant heir, when in possession of the Crown, in all respects, a lawful and a rightful King.

[*Cowper fails to note that the Whig faction led by Shaftesbury attempted to vest this succession in Charles II's bastard son, the irresponsible but ambitious Duke of Monmouth, rather than in James's daughter Mary.—Ed.]

On the other side the Tories contended, that though they could not but grant that the religion of the kingdom, and consequently the constitution, would run a great hazard under a Popish successor, yet that, by the laws of the land and the law of God, Providence only was to be trusted to in such a case, and the worst that could be expected was to be borne rather than so great and national a guilt should be incurred, as the setting aside, though by Act of Parliament, the person who was next to the Crown, in the course of descent, according to the common law, which, in this particular, they said was unalterable, and that therefore such a statute would be void, and consequently an allegiance still due to the person so excluded.

The arguments and authorities brought to support these opinions, it would be impertinent and tedious to trouble your Majesty with. It sufficeth to show what was the opinion of each of the parties at that time touching that important point, which was then agitated, and has been very lately revived on account of your Majesty's succession between the same parties in pamphlets, addresses, sermons, and laboured treatises, though not expressly in the debates or proceedings of either houses of parliament.

It is well known the Tories of that time prevailed, and the Duke of York succeeded to the Crown; but in less than four years' time, the foresight of the Whigs was so far justified by his government that most of the great men and leaders of the Tory party joined with them, if not led the way, to desire assistance from the then Prince of Orange for the preservation of the religion, laws, and liberties of the kingdom.

The success of his glorious enterprise will ever be remembered with gratitude, and the merciful hand of God is now more visible in it than ever, when by a plain connection of causes and effects, it has made way for your Majesty's accession to the throne, and the securing it to your Royal Family, wherein we have an unusual but most delightful prospect of safety, in so many Protestant Princes in being at the same time.

But the Prince of Orange had no sooner overcome all difficulties, and rescued them from the danger they apprehended, than the parties began again to divide. The Tories relapsed into their former notions, and it was argued in both Houses of Parliament, that the course of succession was not to be interrupted for any reason whatsoever; therefore, that King James and his Family with him abroad were to be invited to return, that the Government should be continued in his name, and because they would not trust a Prince, who had in so many instances declared his design to subvert their religion and civil rights, and who had been so lately exasperated by them, they fell into an absurdity, or rather inconsistency, with their own pretences of being zealous for the prerogative, by proposing a Regency over him in power though not in style, or so to restrain his authority that there should be no fear of his invading the Religion and Laws of the Kingdom any more; choosing in that manner to alter the very nature of the monarchy, and reduce it almost to a commonwealth, rather than exclude a Papist from the throne, and entail, after King William's decease, on the next Protestant Heirs.

But the majority of the Convention Parliament then sitting being of the Whig party, and not being willing to trust to such measures, the Prince of Orange was crowned King with his Queen, and the Crown, by an Act of the 1st year of King William and Queen Mary, became entailed on the heirs of the body of that Queen, and after, on the Princess Ann of Denmark, and the heirs of her body, and after, on the heirs of the body of King William.

And not only so, but the other disputed point of a toleration for Protestant Dissenters was settled by Act of Parliament, as the Whigs always desired it should be; and an exemption of Protestant Dissenters from the penalties of all the laws which affected them, was carefully and clearly enacted: the subsequent experience of which law, in bringing so much quiet and riches to the kingdom as it has done, has convinced many of the Tories of their error in that particular.

It may now reasonably be wondered at, since the two points in dispute were thus silenced by the two mentioned laws, how the parties could keep any longer divided, and what was remaining for them to continue about? This is answered by observing, that the Tory party became very uneasy at seeing the opinions they had been so long contending for borne down by two Acts of Parliament. They could then, indeed, no longer dispute the passing those laws, but they could and did sufficiently, on all safe occasions, manifest their dislike of them and resolution to get rid of them the first fair opportunity.

So that the only change produced among the parties was this, that as the struggle before was either to procure or hinder those two important acts for the security of the Protestant interest, so now it became a contest between them, (covertly, at least,) whether what was so obtained should be preserved and continued?

'Tis true, indeed, that by much greater part of the Tory party, seeing a necessity, either of owning the Government or quitting all hopes of employments in Church and State, besides being liable to double taxes, (as the Papists and Non-jurors were,) soon addressed themselves to find out such distinction as might leave them at liberty to own the then present Government, and to take such preferments under it as they could get. The topic they generally went upon was, that in opposing or not helping the Revolution Settlement, (though some of them had appeared in arms with the Prince to enable him to settle things to their mind,) they had acquitted themselves, in their opinions, of all guilt which they thought was contracted by those who had been busy in that work. And now that the law required them, under penalties, in case of disobedience to take certain oaths, they might as good Christians submit to the present powers and take them accordingly, intending still to own the King only as a King *de facto*, and not *de jure*; and that they might likewise for the support of order and government, till the rightful owner should find an opportunity of being restored, conscientiously take and execute any places of profit and trust in Church or State, the rather because their so doing might, in time, be a help to the setting things again, upon what they called, the right foot.

Books were wrote and sermons preached, using arguments of different sorts to support, or at least colour, these and the like notions.

On these grounds, all of that party, (except a very few,) took the oaths of allegiance, &c., to King William and Queen Mary, and many of them were admitted into places and some into those of the greatest dignity and trust. Several also into the Church, and even of those that had made difficulties of owning the Revolution Settlement, and stood out till near the last minute allowed them for it, were notwithstanding countenanced and preferred.

From this false step proceeded all the difficulties and troubles which that King met with in his whole reign.

And when he found himself beset with a war against France, commotions in Scotland, and an almost total defection of Ireland, he then perceived his mistake, and that he had occasion for another kind of service than that which flowed from a principle of submission and acquiescence only to his Government.

Accordingly, he made some alterations and put his principal affairs into the hands of them who had been zealous for bringing him to the Throne and making a Protestant Settlement, so far as was then established; and these carried him through that expensive war to the peace of Ryswick, with a zeal and application equal to their affections to his cause, at the same time effecting with success, what was thought impossible though almost necessary to be done during the war, the recoinage of the whole silver species of money, without debasing the standard, either in weight or fineness.

'Tis true the Tories were by the credit many of them obtained, in the beginning of his reign (as before observed), so raised that though they fell very short of a majority in Parliament, while the Court favoured the other party, yet they were able by raising objections to, and clogging the easier methods proposed for raising money, not only to make the supplies come later sometimes than was convenient, but also to necessitate raising them by way of funds, or anticipation of several excises for perpetuity, or long terms of years, rightly judging that such a course would, at one time or other, load and distress the Government. Whereas, if near as many duties as are now mortgaged had been given at once, those with the Land tax would have maintained the current service of the war, and civil government in each year by the product of the same year, and consequently the nation, not weary of the war till a good peace could be had, and out of debt or near it, when the war was finished.

I was then in the House of Commons, and one of those that proposed this method of raising the supplies within the year; but it was effectually opposed by the Tory party, they drawing into their opinion, as to that particular, several well meaning gentlemen, by suggesting that so easy and commodious a way of raising money might prove dangerous to liberty.

'Tis true that on many occasions the party last named has had the dexterity to object this mistake of running the nation into so great a debt to their adversaries then in the ministry, but I can aver it with the greater certainty, they were far from electing that method, otherwise than that they had rather supply the King that way than not at all, or unseasonably late, one of which would have fallen out; if they had endeavored to have broke through the opposition made to the raising the money any other way.

The peace of Ryswick being made, his then Majesty was prevailed on to experience once more, if he could render his affairs easy, by trying to win the Tories with the principal places of trust, which they might probably execute well enough to support the Government in time of peace.

This trial was made but did not answer expectation, for the King became more uneasy with them in power than before, which, together with his foreseeing the necessity of a new war, made it evident, that as he had begun to advise with his old servants in private, so they would quickly have been restored to their former power, had his Majesty lived but a little longer than he did.

It must be confessed, that the Act for the further Limitation of the

Succession to the Crown passed in the 12th year of this King, while the Tories were in such credit, and had a majority in the House of Commons; it is therefore to be observed, that the true reason why such a Bill passed in such a Parliament was: That the King having, by his own inclination, and probably the advice of some of his old ministry whom he continued to hear, earnestly recommended that Bill to Parliament in his speech from the throne, the Tories, for fear of losing the King's favour, did not endeavour to reject it, but set themselves to clog it, and indeed render it absurd by some of the restrictions your Majesty is undoubtedly apprised of, and to show their contempt and aversion whenever it came on, except when it was necessary to be present in order to load it, and by calling Sir J. B. to the chair of the Committee for that Bill, who was then thought to be distracted, and was soon after confined for being so.

Thus, that Bill went through the House of Commons, and many there who had let it pass, hoped that the House of Lords, where the Whigs had yet a majority, would, by disputing at least some of those restrictions which were most absurd and impracticable, lose the Bill. But the friends to your Majesty's family were better advised; they took and passed the Bill with all its faults, and without any amendment, wisely depending, that if they secured the main, the succession, whatsoever was absurdly and unreasonably annexed to it, would, at some fitting opportunity or other, be easily laid aside. Which, their opinion, has already in a great measure proved true. One of those restrictions, which enacted that all public business should be transacted only in the Privy Council, and that every Privy Councillor should set his name to the resolutions drawn up in form, being repealed in the reign of the late Queen, and by the same act another of those restrictions, that no officer should sit in either House of Parliament after the Queen's decease, was reduced so as to extend to some few officers only, and that, as well in the Queen's time, as after the Protestant succession, should take place.

King William, having passed this Bill for the further limitation of the Crown, soon after died, leaving that invaluable legacy to his people.

Her late Majesty, upon her accession to the Crown, did not only continue to employ those of the Tory party she found in power, but added many others of the same, and set herself plainly and avowedly to govern by it; and as a natural consequence of so doing, was advised in her first speech from the Throne to reflect on the memory of her glorious predecessor (without whose hazardous and successful expedition the sceptre had certainly been in another hand), by saying very

emphatically, that *her heart was entirely English*; which, however, her
Majesty intended, they who persuaded her to use that expression, and
every one who heard of it, understood to be an insinuation that King
William's being born abroad had occasioned his not having the interest
of this kingdom so entirely at his heart as he should have had, which
was very far from having any foundation in truth, considering that he
had ventured his life and fortunes more than once for our preservation,
and had shown no greater favours to the States General than were
necessary to cultivate a good understanding between the two nations
for their common security.

Yet, notwithstanding this manifest resolution to uphold the Tory
party and discountenance the other, the war had not been renewed
and continued any long time before the Duke of Marlborough and
Lord Treasurer Godolphin, then in principal credit with the Queen,
discovered that they could not carry on the war with any hope of
success by a set of men who, though they were willing to profit and
govern under the Queen's authority, yet, had not so cordial an affection
to a Government, founded on the Revolution, nor aversion to the
Popish line, as to induce them to hear the odium of raising the necessary supplies.

The two mentioned ministers finding themselves under this difficulty,
by the intervention of the late Duke of Montague, applied to some of
the principal lords who had been in business under the late king, and
were of the Whig party, who very willingly undertook to endeavour
the carrying on the Queen's business in Parliament on this very reasonable consideration, that some of the offices of principal trust, if not the
greater part, should be in the hands of their friends, since experience
had shown they had so little deserved to be run down and oppressed
as they had been; that, on the contrary, they were the only persons
who were willing and able to carry the Queen with success through
that just and necessary war; and accordingly, as an earnest of sincerity,
it was insisted that the Great Seal should be put into the hands of
Mr. Cowper, who had steadily adhered to the Revolution interest in
the House of Commons through several successive parliaments.

This alteration was soon after made, and others following in a little
time of the same nature, it was seen which way the Court inclined,
and thereupon in two ensuing parliaments the Whigs had a clear majority, as it will always happen whenever the Court have a mind
to have it so.

I need not tell your Majesty how faithfully the Queen was served by
that ministry and those parliaments, nor with what a prodigious unin-

terrupted course of success, nor to what a degree the credit of the nation was raised abroad and at home, France reduced and the confederacy exalted. These things cannot but be present to your Majesty, and in the clearest light.

The same ministry and parliaments showed also their affection and unwearied zeal to the interest of your Majesty's house, by contriving and passing the act for the further securing the succession to the Crown in the Protestant line; which put it into such a method as was not to be resisted but by open force of arms and a public declaration for the Pretender, and made it high treason for any whose duty it was to be concerned in the proclamation to be so much as negligent in proclaiming the next Protestant successor.

Under the same faithful and happy management passed the acts in England and Scotland for the union of the two kingdoms (the Tories vehemently opposing it), which the Queen always esteemed to be the chief happiness and glory of her reign, as having been often before attempted, but still in vain; and indeed, when the Tories were before commissionated to that end, they treated it as a jest or impossibility, by absenting from all meetings appointed, and so letting it drop; although nothing is more clear than that, among many other self-evident advantages, the settlement of the Crown in your Majesty's house had probably never been obtained in that kingdom by any other means: the evil consequences of which disunion, had it happened, are but too evident to enlarge upon.

I dare not touch upon the particular causes which drew on the disgrace and change of that ministry, nor will venture to say whether it was occasioned at first by any greater design than to change the she-favourite, which unavoidably drew on more, and those still further alterations; it being not my purpose so much to follow the springs and causes of the variations of the Court measures in respect to the parties, as to show your Majesty how they severally behaved themselves, when they got the ascendant in their turns, as to the Protestant succession, the good of the state, and the common cause of Europe.

Your Majesty was so much concerned to attend to our affairs since this last alteration, and they are so fresh in memory, that I need not be particular as to what has passed. It is enough to assert, as I think it may be done with clear truth, that immediately ensued a manifest attempt, by addresses and other occasions encouraged by the Court, to sap the very foundations or principles on which the acts for securing the Protestant succession was built, by decrying all right to the Crown but what was purely hereditary and in the course of descent, according to the common law; that the Papists and Nonjurors were so far encouraged as to grow remarkable for their insolence; that a peace was in effect concluded with France in a clandestine manner, without the privity of the principal confederates, and little or no consideration had of their interests; that this neglect of them was justified by the ministry in public, by saying that the interest of Great Britain was principally aimed at in this peace (though time and experience have shown even that pretence to be untrue); that our trade is almost oppressed in all its branches, and had been entirely ruined if the Bill for confirming the French treaty of commerce had not been successfully opposed; that the credit of the nation at home was sunk as to the public funds, and abroad as to all our good offices or menaces which were equally despised; that our late confederates, except the king of S——, were all more or less disgusted, and distrusted our conduct in every thing, upon the justest grounds; in short, that the power of France, which had been so happily reduced, has been restored to such a degree as to become again formidable to Europe, and consequently, that the fruits of so many glorious victories as the allies had obtained were in a manner deserted and given up.

The hopes of the Pretender rose in proportion as the power of France increased; and this consequence was so natural, that one cannot avoid suspecting all this favour could not be then showed to France without a design of assisting the Pretender by that means. However it was meant, sure it is, nothing could more weaken the Protestant succession than the promoting the interest of France; and yet that was done, not by any accident, inadvertence, or want of conduct, but by a continued series of contrivances, a zealous application, and an unwearied industry.

But after all this mischief the ministry had done, they still persisted to the end in declaring they had promoted and cultivated a good understanding between her late Majesty and your illustrious house. The appearances of things, as far as could be discerned by those who were out of business, seemed quite otherwise. This is a subject unfit, as well as unnecessary, to be further enquired into, since your Majesty must know to a certainty whether their pretences were any better founded in that particular than they were in most other things; although perhaps your Majesty may receive a yet further satisfaction on this head by looking upon the instructions and letters given and sent to the Earl of Clarendon.

If this short deduction or history of the two parties should give your Majesty any clearer notion of them than you had before, I shall then be so fortunate as not to have trespassed on your patience in vain; since nothing can contribute more to the extinguishing them at length, and making a right use of them in the meantime, than a knowledge of their principles and practices.

Your Majesty may be told, and it has been often said, that the only difference is about the places; but this is either a superficial judgment, or a desire to hinder the true causes from being discerned. For if that was true, then the struggle would only be between individuals, and not between two set parties of men, which can only be kept up by some diversity of opinion upon fundamentals, at least points of consequence; and experience shows that many who have no design on preferment either for themselves or friends, but live retired on their estates, are yet as hot or hotter than any in these distinctions: and therefore I take those before stated to be the true causes which divide them, and which I beg leave to recapitulate in a few words,—that as the Whigs always contended for the toleration of the Protestant Dissenters and exclusion of the Popish line from the Crown to be established by law, the Tories did always as earnestly and publicly oppose them till they were enacted. The former are rejoiced at their success in these great points, the latter more or less discontented to see their principles discountenanced, and those of their adversaries succeed. Both, therefore, keep and improve their strength as much as they can—the one to defend their acquisitions, the other to retake them and get rid of both the laws as soon as they safely can. Not that I would have it believed that many of the Tories are not perfectly against restoring the Pretender, by force at least, or that some few of them did not make it appear, by their actions the last year, they would not have concurred to the bringing him in even in a parliamentary way; but the true reason was, they believed their religion and liberties could not be secured if they should; and their consciences not accusing them of having done anything toward the Protestant settlement, they were well contented to enjoy the security arising from the act of others, which, though very useful, had something of unjust in it.

I have sat continually in one or other House of Parliament now about twenty-four years, and observed with as much diligence and indifference as I could, the inclinations and motions of both parties, and I will venture to assure your Majesty as what I am very certain of, that the Whigs would venture all to support the Protestant succession in your Majesty's family; on the other hand, that many of the Tories would rejoice to see Pretender restored, as they call it, even by a French power, much more if by any safer means; that the best of them would hazard nothing to keep him out, though probably do nothing hazardous to bring him in; but that if ever he should declare himself a Protestant, with proper circumstances to make his conversion probable (as after the death of the French King and his mother, it is not unlikely he may do), they would greedily swallow the cheat, and endeavour by all possible means to put in practice again their old notions of divine, hereditary, and indefeazible right, by a restoration of the person in whom by their opinion that right is lodged.

And if any other of the Popish line that are next after the Pretender should, after his decease, play the same part, your Majesty will find the party last mentioned very troublesome, if not dangerous; unless by prudent measures under your Majesty's Government, they shall be brought really and from their hearts, as well as in an outward compliance, to part with those notions which are so inconsistent with a Government founded on the Revolution.

I beg leave further to observe, that when lately some of the heads of the Tory party made it known, both by their words and actions, and I don't doubt sincerely, that they did not intend to concur in the repeal of the Acts limiting the succession of the Crown to your Majesty's house much less to bring in the Pretender with the assistance of France, (which was a very seasonable service, and your Majesty has already shown yourself sensible of it), they could bring very few if any of their party after them into the same honest measures; but, on the contrary, as these leaders above mentioned appeared more zealous for your Majesty's house, so in proportion they visibly lost the affections of their party, and were themselves so sensible of it, that they were forced to bring in the Bill against Schism, only to regain the credit they had lost with their old friends.

It is an old scandal now almost worn out, thrown out by their adversaries on the Whigs, that they are against the prerogative of the crown, which I should not have thought worth mentioning, but that 'tis generally believed to have made some impression on King William in the beginning of his reign, to the irrecoverable detriment of his affairs; but he afterwards found that the Tories, not liking the hand which held the prerogative, were more inclined to straighten it, and the Whigs for the contrary reason to support it. And this false suggestion will certainly have the less weight with your Majesty, when you shall be informed, as the truth is, that the only ground for it was, the Whigs being so zealous for setting aside the Popish line in favour of the Protestant, which the Tories thought an high violation of the rights of Monarchy, and of what they erroneously called the prerogative of the Crown, the descent of which they held to be unalterable by any power on earth, and thence took the liberty of branding all of a contrary opinion as Anti-monarchical, or enemies to the prerogative. But in all other respects the Whigs are as zealous to support the prerogative as the Tories can be, and rather more they are under a government founded on the Revolution.

Having thus stated to your Majesty the practices and dispositions of the parties, I shall only add, that 'tis not to be doubted but your Majesty's known goodness and experienced wisdom will necessarily incline you to such moderate counsels as will render you King of all your divided people. But I humbly conceive it not possible so to distribute your royal favours, but that one or other of the parties will appear to have a superior degree of trust reposed in them: and if such a perfect equality was possible to be observed, perhaps it would follow that an equal degree of power, tending at the same time different ways, would render the operations of the government slow and heavy, if not altogether impracticable.

It remains therefore, in my humble opinion, for your Majesty to determine which of these shall have the chief share in your Majesty's confidence, as most likely to support your title to the Crown with the greatest zeal and most untainted affection to it. For as to their power to do it, give me leave to assure your Majesty, on repeated experience, that the parties are so near an equality, and the generality of the world so much in love with the advantages a King of Great Britain has to bestow, without the least exceeding the bounds of law, that 'tis wholly in your Majesty's power, by showing your favour in due time (before the elections) to one or other of them, to give which of them you please a clear majority in all succeeding parliaments.

It is needless to suggest to your Majesty, but, for method's sake, it ought just to be touched upon, that whichsoever party shall have the lower degree of your Majesty's trust, it ought nevertheless to be used by those in power with very great tenderness and affection while obedient to your Majesty and the laws, and as a father would a child whom he dearly loves, though he does not totally approve, and, to be more particular, should, in my humble opinion, be admitted to a fair share of such places and employments of trust, according to their several qualifications, as are during the pleasure of the Crown, and not attended with the chief dependences.

This would be very far from the usage which the last ministry of her late Majesty bestowed on those who had served the Queen so faithfully and successfully during the war, by turning them out of all places, even

the lowest civil and military, very few excepted; by maintaining libel-
lers, and often writing libels themselves against them; by using their
power and majority in parliament to garble their predecessors' conduct,
and, for want of better matter, to misrepresent and reflect on parts of
it, which were unblameable if not commendable; by proscribing, as
far as they were able, to the contempt and hatred of the people, all
that did not come into their measures, and among these the majority
of the House of Lords (not reckoning those which that ministry plainly
brought in for their own support), in calling them the faction, and
even prevailing with the Queen to brand them plainly enough with the
same name, both in several answers to addresses and speeches from
the Throne, and that for no other reason but their endeavouring, in
a legal parliamentary method, to oblige the ministry to make something a better peace than they were about to make, to hinder the
separation of the confederate army, to rescue the trade and manu-
factures of Great Britain from the French treaty of commerce, and to
make it evident, as they did at length, that the trade of Spain was
become impracticable by the Spanish treaty of commerce.

I have but one thing more humbly to represent to your Majesty, as
the only, and, if I mistake not, a sure means to extinguish the being
and the very name of party amongst us, that your Majesty would be
pleased to use the utmost caution not to prefer any of those ecclesiastics
whose known principles lead them to scruple the validity of a limitation
of the right to the Crown by act of parliament. There is a sufficient
number of the clergy of the Church of England, of the most learned
and best livers, out of whom your Majesty may choose for all preferments that shall fall vacant, who are not the least tainted with those
notions which, while they continue, will ever find matter for discontents
and divisions in your Majesty's kingdoms. But when once it is discerned that, by a steady and uninterrupted administration, no man who
is known to hold opinions inconsistent with the very foundation of your
Majesty's government can get into any of the Crown preferments in
the Church, they who find themselves troubled with these inconvenient
scruples will soon apply their thoughts and studies in good earnest to
satisfy themselves, and then others, of the weakness of those errors,
which will afterwards, in a little time, be confined to a few melancholy
Non-jurors, who are the less dangerous for being known; and when
the clergy are brought to be of one mind as to your Majesty's title,
all differences in opinion among the laity on that head will soon vanish.
But that part of the clergy who have always violently contended against
excluding the next successor, though a Papist, will never own them-

selves to have been in the wrong while they find they have a fair chance for the best of the Church preferments without disavowing those errors, otherwise than by taking the oaths in form.

I have nothing further to importune your Majesty with, nor that good Providence which so visibly has placed you on the throne with anything so earnestly as my hearty prayers that your reign may be long and glorious, and that your posterity to the end of time may rule over an happy and dutiful, and, if it is not too much to ask, an unanimous people."

II

THE PROTAGONISTS

Correspondence dominates this section. Careful consideration of these documents will enable the reader to construct an account of the mounting disagreement among the Whig ministers that led to the resignations of Townshend and Walpole. A variety of political reportage is represented: though the range of political gossip is wide, the protagonists in this struggle focus the contentious issues in their exchange of letters. How much of their motivations do they reveal? It is from such materials as these that the historian must draw his conclusions and develop an interpretation of what in fact happened.

In his work, he is indebted to those who have labored in the muniments rooms—all too often dank and chilly—of English and Scottish castles, collecting and arranging family papers and correspondence that extend over centuries of history. Without the indefatigable archivist the historian would lack access to such revealing sources. Few men combine the two pursuits, and few among them ever excelled William Coxe (1747–1828), an archdeacon of the Church of England who wrote what were in his time and for long after exhaustive biographies of Sir Robert Walpole, the Duke of Marlborough, the Earl of Shrewsbury, and Henry Pelham, men who decisively shaped eighteenth-century English politics. Coxe's studies were soundly based upon documentary materials, which he appended to his accounts. Thus, correspondence and other materials which might have been otherwise lost are preserved through his efforts. This section draws heavily upon the correspondence of Walpole and his associates published in the second volume of Coxe's biography, a work which still merits the serious attention of scholars.

A succession of archivists have labored for the Historical Manuscripts Commission, founded in 1869 and empowered by the government to list and publish periodically important documentary collections held in private hands. Many volumes resulted, and the Commission is active to this day. Among the more important collections is that of the Stuart papers, bought by George III and housed at Windsor Castle. This and other collections are drawn upon to supplement the accounts which the protagonists provide.

Two other selections complete this section. One is drawn from a table compiled in 1719 by Abel Boyer, an industrious writer who published between 1711 and 1729 a monthly periodical, *The Political State of Great Britain*. In the midst of much debate concerning the peerage, he analyzed its change in size since the time of James I, providing a factual base for such discussion.

The other selection, a secondary source, provides for us what Boyer did for his readers, a sound base for discussion of some issues associated with the Peerage Bill. Basil Williams, an outstanding historian of eighteenth-century England, provides in his biography of Stanhope both a sense of continuity and a wealth of details which the student of the Peerage Bill requires. Similarly, the student ought to consult both the note on dates and, at greater length, the list of correspondents that follows.

POLITICAL CORRESPONDENCE, 1716–18

NOTE ON DATES

In the years which this book spans, two calendars were in use in Great Britain. Until 31 January 1751 the Julian or Old Style (O.S.) was the legal calendar, which was at the time eleven days behind the Gregorian or New Style (N.S.) used in all other European countries except Russia—where it survived until the revolution of 1917—and Turkey. Further, until the end of 1751 the legal beginning of the year in Great Britain was the 25th of March rather than the 1st of January. To avoid confusion between the two calendars, often letters were dated in both styles, as

$$\frac{25 \text{ January}}{5 \text{ February}} \quad 1718/19; \; 10/21 \text{ May } 1717.$$

Most dates on the documents in this book are given either in the combined style here illustrated or according to the New Style. Some anomalies may result, however, if a correspondent lapses into the Old Style.

LIST OF CORRESPONDENTS

Note: This list indicates insofar as is possible the locale or interest of each of the correspondents in the various letters printed below, during the years which this problem spans in particular. For purposes of convenience, they are subdivided into three groups—general, Scottish peers resident in the British Isles (and hence not outlawed after the 1715 rebellion), and Jacobites, overt or covert supporters of King James III, as they styled him, serving him in some capacity. In the case of the latter two groups, the category alone serves to define that concern of particular relevance to our problem.

General

George Baillie, son of the famous Scottish patriot, Robert Baillie of Jerviswood. His father, implicated in the Duke of Monmouth's rebellion, was executed in 1684, and George Baillie fled to Holland. He returned with William of Orange in 1688, and the family estates were restored to him.

Andreas Gottlieb Freiherr v. Bernstorff played an important role in the succession of the Hanoverian dynasty to the British throne.

Most influential of the Hanoverian ministers, Bernstorff followed George I to England, where he continued to advise him in matters of state, particularly foreign policy.

Thomas Brereton, a dramatist (*Esther, or Faith Triumphant*) and poet who held a government customs office at Chester.

Thomas Brodrick, brother of Lord Midleton (q.v.).

Earl of Carlisle (1674–1738), twice First Lord of the Treasury, 1701–1702 and 1715, and long-time Lord Lieutenant of Cumberland and Westmoreland.

James Craggs (1686–1721), Member of Parliament from 1713. He succeeded Addison as one of the principal secretaries of state in March 1718 and became a member of the Privy Council at the same time. His career, tarnished by the South Sea scandal, hung in the balance when he died of smallpox early in 1721. Craggs was a great friend of Alexander Pope, who wrote his epitaph.

Charles de la Faye, a London correspondent of Lord Polwarth (q.v.).

Marquess of Granby, son of and heir to the Duke of Rutland.

Edward Harley, only son of Robert Harley, Earl of Oxford (q.v.), whom he succeeded in 1724. Until his death in 1741, Harley was one of the great bibliophiles in England, a close friend of Pope, Swift, Prior, and other writers.

Sir Paul Methuen (1672–1757), diplomatist and long-time M.P.; he served as First Lord of the Admiralty from 1714 to 1717.

Lord Midleton (or Middleton), Irish statesman once dismissed (1711) for "revolutionary principles." Three years later, he was appointed Lord Chancellor of Ireland, a position which he held until 1725.

Lord Mountjoy (Montjoy) before his death in 1721 held extensive Irish estates in counties Donegal and Tyrone. He was a Lt. General in the army and a Master-General of Ordnance.

Duke of Newcastle (1693–1768) adhered at first to Townshend (q.v.) but at the schism of 1717 went over to Sunderland and was made Lord Chamberlain. Subsequently he held many government posts and became the foremost borough-monger of the realm.

Sir John Norris (1660?–1749), Admiral of the Fleet and active in Baltic diplomacy.

Earl of Oxford (Robert Harley, 1661–1724), an important figure in the Tory party from the 1690's, and consequently in the government. He obtained the dismissal of Marlborough and the creation of the twelve peers necessary to carry the peace of Utrecht in 1712, but was himself ousted as head of the Tory party by Bolingbroke in 1714. In 1717 he was impeached and forbidden the court for having concluded Utrecht; further, he was alleged secretly to favor the Old Pretender. He continued to appear in the House of Lords and to correspond with the Pretender, but Oxford refused to lead the Jacobite faction of the Tories.

Stephen Poyntz (1685–1750), tutor to the sons of Lord Townshend (q.v.) and for a time the latter's confidential secretary; in 1716 commissary to Earl Stanhope (q.v.).

Jean de Robethon (d. 1722) was a Huguenot refugee who came to England c. 1689 and was employed by William III. Subsequently he entered the service of George Lewis, later George I, dealing particularly in the latter's correspondence with the English Whigs. In 1715 he accompanied the new monarch to his British domain.

Sir Luke Schaub (d. 1758), diplomatist, headed the British mission in Vienna, 1714–16; in 1717 he served as private secretary to Earl Stanhope (q.v.), and in 1718 as British agent at Madrid.

Duke of Somerset (1662–1748) served as a commissioner for the Union with Scotland and enjoyed the confidence of Queen Anne until 1711; he was reinstated as Master of Horse by George I but was again dismissed in 1716 and lived thereafter in retirement on his estates.

Charles Stanhope (1673–1760), M.P., 1717–41.

James, Earl Stanhope (1673–1721), grandson of the first Earl of Chesterfield, returned to England in 1712 after twenty years abroad in military and diplomatic service, chiefly in the Iberian peninsula, to become a leader of the Whig opposition in the House of Commons. He held major offices of state subsequently, playing a major role in securing the Hanoverian succession and formulating foreign policy.

Colonel William Stanhope (1690?–1756), diplomatist and statesman who served as British ambassador in Spain, 1719–1727, and later created first Earl of Harrington.

Earl of Sunderland (1674–1722), Whig statesman, dismissed by Queen Anne in 1710 at the Tories' urging. Thereafter he was in constant communication with Hanover; in 1715 he was named

Lord Privy Seal, coming into sharp conflict with Townshend (q.v.) and Walpole (q.v.). Upon their dismissal from office, Sunderland became First Lord of the Treasury.

Charles, Viscount Townshend (1674–1738), though bred in the strictest Tory principles, early seceded to the Whigs. Maintaining his connections with Hanover, Townshend was able to play an important role in the accession of George I. In 1716 he fell under the suspicion that he hoped to place George, the Prince of Wales, on the throne; the next year he was exiled to the post of Lord Lieutenant of Ireland, but was once more dismissed on the charge that he was not giving the government his full support.

Horatio (Horace) Walpole, first Baron Walpole of Wolterton, younger brother of Sir Robert (q.v.) and a diplomatist.

Sir Robert Walpole, first Earl of Orford (1676–1745), recognized as a leader of the Whigs as early as 1703, taking an active part in the business of the House of Commons. With great achievements behind him, Walpole was expelled from the Commons and imprisoned in the Tower of London, 1712, by the Tory leadership, upon whom he later revenged himself by bringing impeachment charges. Though an advocate of the Hanoverian succession, Walpole failed to win George I's complete confidence while serving as Chancellor of the Exchequer, 1715–17.

Scottish peers

Lord Balmerino (1652–1736), made a Privy Councillor in 1687, was elected a representative peer in 1710 and 1713. He had, however, opposed the union with England and was stripped of all his offices at the accession of George I; he remained loyal in 1715.

Lord Blantyre (d. 1743) succeeded his brother, who had voted against the union, to the peerage in 1713.

Lord Colville (1689–1741) fought at Malplaquet and aided in the suppression of the Jacobite insurrection in 1715.

Earl of Dundonald (1689–1720) succeeded to the title in 1705, and he served as a representative peer from 1713–15. As Cochrane was his family name, his correspondent is in all likelihood a close relative.

Earl of Eglinton (d. 1729) served as a Privy Councillor both under King William and Queen Anne. Despite his distinct Jacobite sentiments, he fought on the government side in the 1715 rebellion.

Earl of Glencairn (d. 1734) supported the Act of Union and became
     a Privy Councillor.

Earl of Islay (Ilay), younger brother of the Duke of Argyll (Argyle)
     mentioned in the documents, created a Scottish peer in his own
     right in 1705. Both brothers promoted the Act of Union and
     were well rewarded for their efforts; they served in a variety
     of government positions and remained loyal to the Hanoverians
     in 1715, though Argyll lost office between 1716 and 1719.
     Islay succeeded to the dukedom in 1743 and lived until 1761.

Earl of Kellie.

Lord Polwarth (1675–1740), younger son of the Earl of Marchmont,
     who after some Scottish legal experience became envoy to
     Denmark, 1715–21. Those who follow his dispatches closely
     will be relieved to learn that he succeeded to the Earldom in
     1724.

Earl of Ruglen.

Earl of Stair (1673–1747), general and diplomatist, served as British
     Ambassador to France, 1715–20; he secured the expulsion of
     James Edward, the Old Pretender, from Paris.

Jacobites

King James III (James Edward, the Old Pretender, 1688–1766), the
     only son of James II by Mary of Modena, popularly believed
     to be a supposititious child, proclaimed King of England on his
     father's death in 1701 but unable to enforce his claim. After the
     failure of the 1715 rebellion, he finally settled in Rome; his
     tomb is located in St. Peter's.

Lt. General Arthur Dillon (1670–1733) was outlawed as a Jacobite in
     1690. He served as an officer in the French army for twenty
     years; in 1715 he became the Pretender's agent in Paris.

Lewis Inese, a functionary who operated under some dozen pseud-
     onyms; in close contact with the Duke of Mar (q.v.).

Duke of Mar (1675–1732), after serving in a variety of government
     positions and as a Scottish representative peer, was dismissed as
     secretary of state in 1713, despite his professions of loyalty.
     He raised the standard of James III in 1715 and, following his
     defeat, escaped with the Pretender to France. After treating
     with George I for a partial restoration of the Stuarts, in 1717,
     he gradually lost the Pretender's confidence.

John Menzies, agent for the Pretender in London, also operated under
     a variety of pseudonymns.

James Murray, of Stormont, Jacobite agent.

Sir Hugh Paterson, agent (at one point in Rotterdam) for the Pretender, a frequent correspondent of Mar and Menzies.

Bishop of Rochester (Francis Atterbury, 1662–1732), who though taking part in the coronation of George I, inclined toward the Jacobite cause and in 1717 held direct communication with them. Eventually imprisoned, deprived of his offices and banished to the continent, where he entered the service of the Old Pretender.

Hugh Thomas reported to Inese (q.v.) on happenings in London, particularly at Westminster.

Lord Townshend to Bernstorff

Sir,   Whitehall, May 19, 1716

In obedience to his majesty's commands communicated to us by you, we have had a meeting with my lord chancellor, the dukes of Devonshire and Marlborough, and the earl of Sunderland, to consider in what manner it might be most advisable to settle the regency here, in case his majesty should determine to spend some part of the year at Hanover; and as in the course of this deliberation it was impossible for the inconveniences of his majesty's journey not to occur to us in the first place, we think ourselves bound in duty to lay before his majesty with all possible submission the substance of our thoughts on that head; that since we were all unanimously of opinion that his majesty's absence from his British dominions might prove of the utmost prejudice to his interests, his majesty may be apprised of the true reasons which obliged his servants to be of an opinion that cannot but be highly ungrateful to them, while there is a possibility of its being in any respect disagreeable to his majesty. To set their reasons in as clear a light as may be, they beg leave to take a summary view of the present situation of affairs both at home and abroad, that so it may appear what effect his majesty's journey may be likely to have with respect both to the one and the other.

And first it is most apparent that though his majesty's arms have, by the blessing of God been superior to those of the rebels, and though the parliament have in the compass of two sessions done all that was suggested to them, and even more than could be expected towards suppressing the faction of jacobitism, yet the rage and spirit of that

William Coxe, *Memoirs of Sir Robert Walpole*, vol. II, *Original Correspondence* (London, 1798).

party is still very far from being subdued. For having been considerably numerous ever since the revolution, they made such vast accessions of strength under the last four years of the queen, during which time they found means to engage in their interests, not only a great number of private persons, but many of the largest communities (as appears by the conduct of both the universities, and even of London itself till lately) that the confidence of their numbers encouraged them to enter into the rebellion upon their own bottom destitute of all succours from abroad, and still supports them in the same spirit and designs, notwithstanding their late losses and all the endeavours of the parliament. So that it is to be feared the fire of the whole rebellion is rather smothered for a time than totally extinguished, and that it lies ready to catch hold of the first convenient matter that shall be offered it, and may break forth with fresh fury. This is but too evident from the strong disposition in favour of the rebels, which has already shewn itself in different shapes ever since the defeat at Preston, and which appears not only by that open and barefaced obstruction of justice which is at present offered in the trials in the inferiour courts, but likewise by that excess of tenderness which has been expressed for the criminals on every occasion, even in places where his majesty had the least reason to expect it; which shows at once the strength and riches of the faction. The subduing therefore and eradicating of this evil is what ought principally to be aimed at and intended, not so much by violent remedies (which are always dangerous and often fatal) as by a constant steady and uniform application in every branch of the administration towards working out the inmost causes of this distemper, the force of which by this method may in some short time be insensibly dispelled; but such a strict and vigilant application of powers distributed through so many different hands, and in a case where such numerous difficulties are to be struggled with, can hardly be hoped for without the invigorating influence of his majesty's presence and inspection, to quicken the timorous, to strengthen the hands of his servants, and to damp the hopes and expectations of his enemies. Besides which, as the party have all along subsisted on false and scandalous reports, forged without the least colour or shadow of reality, so they will not fail to give the most malicious turn to a step of this nature, and possibly such a one, as may not only make impression on the vulgar (who seem as yet susceptible of the most gross absurdities) but even alienate the minds of many who are at present zealous and entirely well affected to his majesty's service. These we look on to be some of the most natural and obvious consequences of his majesty's going abroad in the present unsettled condition of affairs at home.

And if we proceed to look abroad we humbly apprehend the objections arising thence to hold full as strong against this journey. For his majesty's interest in foreign parts will ever keep pace with the credit and reputation of his affairs at home, so that whatever impairs the latter, will no less certainly affect the former, and accidents may arise by some unforeseen commotion in his absence which may discourage foreign powers from proceeding in those engagements with his majesty which they now are very forward to enter into. For we cannot but observe, that though his majesty's security depends so much on the strength of alliances; and though his endeavours have not been wanting to procure such as might be necessary for his safety, yet the princes with whom we were to negotiate were so cautious of engaging till they should see the fate of the rebellion in some measure decided, that no one treaty for our security is yet perfected, excepting that with the States General. But now that the reputation of his majesty's affairs is so well established that most of the princes in Europe are courting his alliance, we humbly conceive it would be of very dangerous consequence to put it again in the power of fortune and events to hinder his majesty from concluding such treaties as he shall judge necessary; and even though no new disturbances should arise, which doubtless his majesty's enemies will be encouraged to attempt during his absence, yet we are of opinion that if his majesty should fix his residence at Hanover for this summer, so much time would pass in referring matters to his council here, and in receiving their opinion, as joined to the ordinary difficulties incident to all negotiations, would make it impracticable for his majesty to conclude a treaty with the emperor, or any of the northern potentates, before the season of the year returns that will make it requisite for him to meet his people in parliament. Neither can any doubt be made, but that the regent of France, who has hitherto left no engine unemployed to defeat our alliance with the emperor, and whose principal aim seems to be to gain time for putting in execution the designs he has formed against his majesty will eagerly lay hold on such an opportunity to distract the king's affairs, either by encouraging and supporting the jacobites in some attempt here, or by amusing us with specious and insidious proposals at a juncture, when he is sure so much more time than ordinary must be consumed in examining and detecting them, and in advising and returning an answer; and late advices from France, of the most unquestionable credit, do sufficiently justify our apprehensions on this head. But what we take to be the most fatal inconvenience of this journey is, that the Baltic squadron (which alone secures to his majesty the balance and arbitration of the north) must by waiting for his majesty's orders, and by the usual communications to be made hither, lose so much of the season proper for action, as will render that expensive armament wholly fruitless and insignificant, which may not only expose his majesty's dominions in Germany to imminent danger, but likewise administer matter of complaint to such as are upon the watch in parliament, for every handle of traducing and making odious his majesty's administration.

Having thus in discharge of our duty communicated to you these considerations in order to your laying them before his majesty, we proceeded to consider in obedience to his majesty's commands in what manner the regency might be most properly constituted during his absence, and upon a careful perusal of the precedents finding no instance of persons being joined in commission with the prince of Wales, and few if any restrictions upon such commissions, we are of opinion that the constant tenour of ancient practice cannot conveniently be receded from.

James Murray to Mr. Le Brun (the Duke of Mar)

1716, July 12[23]. London . . . In the meantime please receive the following account of your friends. It is impossible for you to imagine the confusion in which Mr. Hannes [King George] has left his family in town, and the disorder in which their friends, relations and servants are at present. His son and he are at the utmost variance. Mr. Ashburnham [Argyle] and his brother have been turned out of the family, notwithstanding their great services to it, with all the circumstances of contempt and ill usage possible, and thus upon the representations of some of their fellow servants over the young gentleman's belly; yea, to that extremity were matters carried that, the son having for some days shewed a desire to continue Ashburnham in his service, he at last received a message, importing little less, as I am credibly informed, than that both should go to gaol if he did not dismiss him. This was not to be withstood, and accordingly he was dismissed, but was to take leave of Mr. Hannes that morning he went out of town. However, it is certain that no person of his name, or who is any ways related to him, will be allowed to serve in any station. He maintains his interest

Historical Manuscripts Commission, *The Stuart Papers*, vol. II (London, 1904).

with the young gentleman, and endeavours with such success to inflame him against those whom he takes to be the authors of his disgrace, that he would certainly at this moment hang some of them, if he could. This they themselves are sensible of, and so you may foresee what good agreement is like to be amongst them. What may be the consequences of these divisions nobody can positively determine, but sure the enemies of the family have reason to rejoice to see things come to this pass, and may expect everything from thence, provided nothing diverts these things from producing their natural effects.

As for news the town is full of it. The King is gone to Hanover without naming any precise time for his return, and the Jacobites have malice enough to say he is so tired of the people of this country that he never will. The regard you know I always had for his Majesty makes me regret an accident which happened the day before he went out of town; which was, that he unluckily met a number of the rebel prisoners going down to receive sentence of death, who stopped his coach, being attended with a numerous mob. The people had an expectation that he would have ordered them to be pardoned, which happened so far other ways, that I have reason to think some of them will be executed to-morrow. I can easily foresee the horror this ill-timed piece of severity will raise and the disservice it will do to the King and royal family, which is a strong reason to make any honest man sorry for it, though he has no concern for the rebels themselves.

The Prince of Wales is to our great joy left guardian of the kingdom and is invested with a full power to govern it, though, it said, this power is limited by instructions in a paper apart. But, as the commission does not relate to these instructions, they cannot invalidate any exercise of the regal power, for they can amount to no more than a trust between his Majesty and the Prince, which the public neither knows nor can take any notice of. General Cadogan at present commands the army under my Lord Marlborough's shadow, but how far he will be able to support himself in the possession of that power is uncertain, for he is without doubt in great disfavour with his Royal Highness. The Earl of Sunderland has got a grant of an employment during life worth at least £ 10,000 a year. This, with my Lord Argyle's removal, sufficiently demonstrates the power my Lord Marlborough or his friends have at Court. My Lord Sunderland is going to the Spa, and the Duke and Duchess of Montagu to Aix. I hear this morning arrived an account that his Majesty was safely landed on t'other side. But what will be the form or spirit of the new administration a little time will inform us. I shall be glad to know if you rightly understood mine of the 6th, because it might be of great use for the future.

Stephen Poyntz to Secretary Stanhope

Sir,   Albermarle Street, 28th July, 1716

It is impossible for me to open the commission I have the honour to be charged with from my lord Townshend and Mr. Methuen to you, without being put in mind of returning you my most humble thanks for your many great favours, and particularly for the part, that you were so kind as to take in that, to which I owe the honour of being now employed in writing to you. Nothing less than the experience of so much goodness could support me under the unequal task that is assigned to me of being regularly to lay before you such occurrences and observations as my lord Townshend and Mr. Secretary Methuen think less proper to be inserted in their public dispatches. I am never to write to you but by the hand of a messenger, and my lord and Mr. Methuen do most earnestly beg, that the letters you shall receive from me may not be communicated to anybody, but to his majesty only, and that with all imaginable precautions of secrecy; and they desire to receive from you by the same conveyance, under cover to me, all such particulars as the king may judge improper and inconvenient to be communicated to the whole cabinet council. I am therefore by their command to acquaint you that hitherto everything goes well, the prince appearing entirely disposed to follow his majesty's directions, and to answer his intentions in every respect. The only apprehension they labour under is least some division should be formed in the army, by the opposition there is between the duke of Argyle and my lord Cadogan, which they desire you to assure his majesty they will labour to prevent with all possible fidelity and application. You will see by my lord Townshend's dispatch, that lord Belhaven makes application to be knight marshall of Scotland; this is one of the places that the prince is at liberty to dispose of without consulting his majesty; however, you will see he chooses to refer it to the king's disposal, and my lord Townshend and Mr. Methuen are humbly of opinion, that his majesty's gratifying his royal highness by conferring it on lord Belhaven will have a good effect at the prince's first setting out, and will tend to confirm his royal highness in the disposition of referring all matters of importance to his Majesty: and though lord Belhaven be a creature of the duke of Argyle's, yet they think they have reason to believe that he will always fix his chief dependance on those who have his fortune in their hands; and he has hitherto behaved himself with such zeal for his majesty's service in parliament as very well to deserve this mark of his royal favour. I am with the most dutiful respect.

What follows is in lord Townshend's hand, and signed by him and Methuen.

Sir,

We are of opinion that the method above mentioned is on several accounts the properest for carrying on a private correspondence with you, and repeat to you as our most humble request, that you would lay this letter, and all other of the same nature before the king, but must at the same time beg that none else may see them.

Robert Walpole to Secretary Stanhope

Dear Sir,   July 30—August 10, 1716

Although you were very sensible how affairs stood among us here at your departure, and were acquainted with the heats and divisions betwixt the king's servants, yet we having picked up some particular accounts which may a little contribute to your better informations, I thought it not improper to write to you a little at large, that you may know in what situation we apprehend our matters stand at present.

We conceive then there is reason to believe that the designs of lord Sunderland, Cadogan, &c. were carried further, and better supported than we did imagine whilst you were here, and that all the foreigners were engaged on their side of the question; and in chief that the dutchess of Munster entered into the dispute with a more than ordinary zeal and resentment against us, insomuch that by an account we have of a conversation with the king at the dutchess of Munster's, they flatter themselves that nothing but the want of time and the hurry the king was in upon his going away, prevented a thorough change of the ministry, which they still proposed to carry on upon the whig foot, exclusive of us, and by the account we have, there was no difficulty at all in removing me; you, it was thought, might be taken care of in the army, but they were at a loss about my lord Townshend. That this was discoursed of, there seems to be no room for doubt; how far the king gave into it is not sufficiently explained, or whether he was more than passive in hearing the conversation; but it seems to me so contradictory to the accounts I always had of the king's behaviour to lord Townshend and you upon this subject, that I am at a loss how to question what is positively affirmed, or to believe what is so very extraordinary and irreconcilable with all other parts of the king's conduct, but now you are informed of this, I think you will be able to learn or guess what foot we stand upon. That the dutchess of Munster was very angry at her not being an English dutchess is most certain, and that she imputes the whole to my lord Townshend, and has expressed a particular resentment against him; I fear old Bernstorff has given into these matters more than we are willing to believe, but yet I cannot be persuaded that he had any thoughts of entering into their thorough scheme, which to me must appear impossible, when I recollect the discourse I had myself with him upon these topicks: Robethon's impertinence is so notorious, that we must depend upon it he does all the mischief he possibly can; but if the heads can be set right, such little creatures must come in in course, or may be despised.

Lord Sunderland talks of leaving England in a fortnight, and to be sure will not be long from you; he seems very pressing to have instructions from us how to behave at Hanover. His professions for an entire reconciliation and a perfect union are as strong as words can express; and you may be sure are reciprocal; and when I consider that common interest should procure sincerity among us, I am astonished to think there is reason to fear the contrary. What to my conception is first and chiefly necessary is the king's return, if practicable, which must determine these doubts one way or other, for nobody can answer for the success of any thing, as long as nobody durst undertake, or knows, he shall be supported in what is found necessary for carrying on the king's business. I find lord Sunderland and they persuade themselves the king will come back before the parliament sits; the prince talks of nothing but holding the parliament. It were very material to us to know which will be the case, because I think a different management will be necessary according to this event, and such measures must be kept with the prince, if he is to hold the parliament, as may perhaps be misrepresented with you, and may be declined if the king comes over himself.

And now I have mentioned the prince, 'tis fit you should know how it stands with him, which is in appearance much better than it was, and instead of pretty extraordinary treatment, we meet civil receptions.

He seems very intent upon holding the parliament, very inquisitive about the revenue, calls daily for papers, which may tend to very particular informations; and I am not sure, they are not more for other people's perusal than his own. By some things that daily drop from him, he seems to be preparing to keep up an interest of his in parliament independent of the king's; but if that part is to be acted, I hope 'tis not impossible to bring him into other and better measures, but for this I do not pretend to answer. As for our behaviour to his highness we take care not to be wanting in duty and respect, not to give any offence or handle to such as are ready to take any opportunity to render business impracticable, and we hope we demean ourselves so, that neither they who would misrepresent us to the king for making our court too much to the prince, nor they who would hurt us with the prince for doing it too little, can have any fair advantage over us, but this is a game not to be managed without difficulty. Lord Townshend goes tomorrow to live at Hampton Court, I shall go twice a week, and on those publick days we both shall keep tables. . . .

This correspondence is a secret to all the world except lord Townshend and Mr. Mettwyn. He is acquainted with every step we take, and has indeed entered into business with us with so much friendship and honour, that we are in the same confidence and intimacy with him, as we were with you: what comes from Mr. Poyntz you are in all respects to treat as from ourselves, and 'tis desired your private letter may for the future be directed to him; this saves the trouble of denying and chicaning about the correspondence both to and from you; and I promise you 'tis necessary to say every post something that shall look like truth upon the subject of the private correspondence. I am ever dear Don, &c.

Robert Walpole to Secretary Stanhope

August 7—18, 1716

By a letter I wrote to you some time since, I gave you the best account I then could of the state of our affairs. What I have now to add from the occurrences that have since happened is to tell you, that not only the duke of Argyle and lord Ilay, &c. but duke of Shrewsbury, Dick Hill, lord Rochester, and their wives and other tories are constant attendants at Hampton Court. They generally choose to come on the private days; but their reception gives great offence to all well wishers, and I assure you, does not a little animate the tories, who generally, I mean such as are near the town, resort to court, and meet all possible encouragement to go on so. I cannot but say, the prince is civil to us, but that is all that I can say, which is now so well known and understood, that the tories take great pains to publish it; that the prince hates us, and at the same time that we are almost lost with the king, having all the foreigners determined against us. This is the situation which the world looks upon us to be in, which, if be true, as far as relates to your side of the water, it is very desireable that we should know it, to take our measures accordingly; and if it is not true. I am sure it is absolutely necessary that some method should be found out to make the contrary known, for no man can serve in this nation, whose credit with the prince is supposed to be lost or declining.

We have very good accounts that the duke of Argyle and his creatures are endeavouring to engage particular persons against next sessions. I think it cannot be doubted from the reception the tories meet at court that there is an understanding betwixt him and them, though the persons he particularly applies to are whigs that he apprehends are disgusted.

Robert Walpole to Secretary Stanhope

Hampton Court, August 9th—20th, 1716

We came hither last night since I wrote to you by Mr. Jennings, and here we find the duke of Shrewsbury upon pretence of the duchess's being in waiting an inhabitant of the place, which by all accounts, his publick as well as private reception and conferences with both prince and princess sufficiently encourage. The duke of Argyle is never absent from hence one day, he is constantly in parties of pleasure with the prince, they have begun little private balls, which 'tis said are to be twice or thrice a week. The company are his highness, his grace, and such of the family as are his grace's humble servants, the women, the maids of honour, and some of the dressers, and no spectators admitted. You can easily conjecture what must be the consequences of these appearances, they have such an effect already, as draws the tories from all parts of the neighbourhood, gives such a disgust to the whigs, as before Michaelmas I may venture to prophesy, the company here will be two to one of the king's enemies.

We are here chained to the oar, and working like slaves, and are looked upon as no other; for not only the behaviour and conduct of the prince are a weight upon us; but the industrious representations that are made of our being lost with the king reduces our credit to nothing. If we are to be the king's servants, and to be supported in serving him as king, our hands must be strengthened. A known division among ourselves, which common danger, if the king pleases, he may remedy, the appearance of a declining interest with the king, and the unalterable resentment of the prince, however at present disguised, against such as he looks upon attached to the service of the king preferable to his interest, leave us in a situation scarce to be weathered through. We know of no remedy to these evils but the king's return, and if he will put his affairs upon the same foot as formerly, there will be no difficulty in serving with the same success. If he is otherwise disposed, and has thoughts of fixing another scheme of ministry, not to advise him to determine one way or other, is to betray him, for in the present state of affairs his business will moulder to nothing, and whilst all the world is in a gaze to see which way the wind will blow and settle, nobody cares to putt to sea in such a storm and hurricane as we are in at present.

Stephen Poyntz to Secretary Stanhope

Hampton Court, August 21—September 1, 1716

. . . As to domestic affairs, they [Townshend and Methuen] command me to acquaint you, that they are well informed the whole body of the tories are promoting addresses from all parts to the prince, the heads of which they hear are already sent down, and that the general tenour of them will be to compliment the prince upon his regency and upon his showing himself disposed to be a common father to all his people, in spite of the artifices and insinuation of such as delight in war or bloodshed; by which it is intended to reflect on his majesty's conduct, and stigmatize such of his servants as were most active in carrying on the late war against France, and in pursuing the measures found necessary for suppressing the rebellion. They are assured that Sir John Packington has undertaken to procure such an address from Worcestershire, and Mr. Bromley another from Warwickshire, and that the same are carrying on in most of the western counties; they likewise hear that some of the discontented whigs are entered into this project, encouraged by the duke of Argyll, Mr. Lechmere and Mr. Hamden, and though they make no doubt but that the main body of the whigs will now be upon their guard, and oppose a design of such pernicious tendency, yet they find that some well-meaning people have been already drawn in to promote congratulatory addresses to the prince. My lord Townshend and Mr. Methuen are of opinion that this is the wisest step the jacobites have yet taken, since it manifestly tends to set up the son against the father, and to lay a lasting foundation of uneasiness and distraction among those who are best affected to the royal family: however they think themselves obliged to do his royal highness the justice to declare, that they neither hear, nor can perceive by any observations they have yet been able to make, that he has given the smallest encouragement to these addresses.

The only remedy they can foresee for this and other growing evils is, what I had the honour to mention to you in my last, that his majesty should take the resolution of coming over to hold the parliament, and that it should be known immediately he has such an intention. They have nothing further to add on this head, but to desire you would manage the intelligence with such caution, that no person living but the king may know it comes from them.

My lord Townshend does most earnestly desire that you would use your utmost endeavours towards getting the duties on the British tobacco imported into Bremen reduced to the ancient foot as soon as possible; since that matter begins to make a great noise already in London, and will probably give a handle to such complaints in parliament as may confound the business of the whole session.

Enclosed are some pieces of intercepted correspondence which I have the honour to transmitt to you by my lord Townshend's command.

Robert Walpole to Secretary Stanhope

Dear Sir,   London, Sept. 28—October 9, 1716
I have received the favour of yours of the 19th instant, and am very glad to hear, that our endeavours to render his majesty the best service we are able is graciously accepted by him; and 'tis a further satisfaction for us to find that though we have no easy game to play here, we are not entirely unsuccessfull; and although it may be possible still to carry

on the king's business here with a constant assiduity, application and careful management, I must confess I was infinitely pleased with that part of the letter which gave us hopes of his majesty's coming over to hold the parliament himself. But I cannot but be concerned at your apprehensions upon this point expressed in your letter to Mr. Poyntz; but in this case next to the want of the king's presence, to be kept in doubt and suspence will be the greatest misfortune.

I have got the prince's leave to go into the country for a month, to try if I can lay in a little stock of health, to enable me to undergo the winter's campaign, and as I may not be in the way to give you my thoughts very suddenly again, I shall take the liberty to tell you my sense very plainly. If 'tis possible to prevail with the king to come over, no endeavours should be wanting to convince his majesty, that it is of the last consequence to his affairs, and indeed almost of such absolute necessity, that nobody dares to answer for success in this businesse in parliament in his majesty's absence; so that if there is any hope of the king's coming over, I think it advisable to defer the meeting of the parliament as long as 'tis possible, which I think may be done till after Christmas. But on the other hand, if his majesty is determined to suffer the prince to hold the parliament, I am of opinion, there should be no thoughts of deferring the sessions any longer than the latter end of November or beginning of December at furthest. For besides the general inconveniencies of a late session, and the particular prejudices that the public suffers in our money matters, you may depend upon it, the prince will soon grow uneasy; and if he once begins to think, that the session is delayed only to defeat him of what he so much desires, this will be imputed entirely to us; and if he at last holds the parliament, his resentment upon this account, may give those that desire to confound the king's affairs such an advantage over us, that we shall feel the effects of it through the whole session; that 'tis plain to me, if the king designs the prince shall hold the parliament, and will thereby put the whole affairs of this winter into his highness's hands and power, it should be done in such a manner as may not engage the prince in measures opposite to the interest of the king. It is easy to see of what use and service it will be, for the king's servants to know his majesty's resolutions upon this head as soon as may be, that they may begin to form the scheme of the session, and take his majesty's pleasure upon the several heads, before they are finally fixed and determined with the prince. . . .

Secretary Stanhope to Lord Townshend

My Lord,   Göhre, October 16, 1716
You will see by my other letters the state of things here; all endeavours
have been used with Prussia, but hitherto to no purpose. Mr. Bernstorff
said today to one who told it me, that if the king were now in England
the exigency of affairs here would make it necessary for him to come
over hither. I must observe to you that as the king is now to make use
of the troops of Munster and Saxe Gotha, he told me with some
warmth that he has hitherto been obliged to pay them himself, notwithstanding what had been promised him in England, and that he
had contracted for them at the request of his council. I must therefore
beg of you to press Mr. Walpole to have that matter settled. I have
more reason to press this than I care to say to you, but I fear some
people do ill offices to Walpole. . . .

Coxe, *Walpole*, vol. II.

Lord Townshend to Secretary Stanhope

Sir,   Hampton Court, Tuesday, October 16—27, 1716
I have received the favour of your private letter of the 16th inst. N.S.
and am sorry to find his majesty should have spoken to you with some
warmth concerning the payment of the Munster and Saxe Gotha
troops. My brother Walpole is at present in Norfolk, so that I cannot
send you his thoughts as to the practicableness of finding some expedient for paying those troops before a parliamentary provision is
made for them; but being able to charge my own memory with the
particular circumstances which have hitherto hindered that payment, I
must beg leave to give you a short deduction of that matter, leaving
it to you to trouble his majesty with as much or as little of it as you
shall think proper.

You must, I am persuaded, remember as well as I, that upon the
Pretender's landing in Scotland, no one imagining he would have
engaged in such an undertaking without foreign assistance, the parliament gave the king unlimited power to raise what number of men he
should think fit for the defence of the kingdom, and farther the lords

Coxe, *Walpole*, vol. II.

of the Cabinet Council, his majesty being present, did unanimously advise and desire him to secure and take into his service a body of troops from abroad, and orders were accordingly given to the king's German ministers to hire the troops above-mentioned. The precipitate retreat of the pretender having afterwards made it unnecessary for his majesty to increase the number of troops within the kingdom was as intended, and it being thereupon judged adviseable for his majesty to mention to the parliament this instance of the good use made of the trust reposed in him, it was thought very inconsistent after such a step to retain a body of foreign forces in pay; accordingly orders were given for stopping the conventions with Munster and Saxe Gotha, in case they were not finally concluded. But those orders coming too late, it happened that the treaties were (according to the report of Messrs. Bernstorff and Bothmar) actually signed; however we were assured that in consideration of the troops not being made use of, endeavours should be used to get a new convention, by which part of the charge should be mitigated, which convention I am told has since been perfected. These first treaties did not come over till late in the session, while my brother Walpole lay so ill that his life was despaired of, and as soon as ever he recovered Messrs. Bernstorff and Bothmar and I had a conference with him about settling this affair in order to lay the said treaties before the parliament that the necessary provision might be made for this service. But upon perusal of the papers brought us by Messrs. Bernstorff and Bothmar we found they were only copies of the treaties, and that the originals were not sent over. This made it impracticable to have them laid before the house of commons, to whom either the original conventions or authentic copies attested by one of the secretaries of state must always be produced; besides which, one of these conventions was drawn in such loose terms as seemed to imply that if the troops were not demanded within a certain time, the agreement was void, which however Messrs. Bernstorff and Bothmar assured us was not the intent and meaning of it. For these reasons it was judged improper to bring this matter before the parliament at that time for fear the want of an authentic instrument, and the loose wording of the treaty should have given a handle for putting a negative on this demand, and thereby have precluded us from ever bringing it into the house again; and it was agreed to defer moving that matter till the new conventions could be finished, and authentic acts of them be got ready to lay before the parliament, which conventions were not perfected and sent hither till since the end of the session. So that the soonest this money can be paid in a regular way will be some time after the opening of the next session; but if it is the king's pleasure some extraordinary method should be found out for furnishing this sum immediately, I own freely to you, were I in Mr. Walpole's case, I should expect his majesty's commands for laying that matter at least before the Cabinet Council; it being in my opinion too great a weight for Mr. Walpole to take upon himself.

In the meantime it is a very melancholy reflection, that our best endeavours for his majesty's service are liable to be thus interpreted; and I am sorry I have this occasion to be confirmed in my opinion, that no services which Mr. Walpole, or you, or I, can ever render to his majesty, will be sufficient to screen and support us against the false and malicious suggestions of our enemies. The success with which our endeavours have hitherto been crowned is such, as it would look like vanity even to mention, and since the only aim of my ambition and the reward of all my labours is now attained by seeing his majesty firmly seated in the throne; I can struggle no longer against the difficulties which our enemies about the king create us every day, and shall therefore most earnestly beg leave to resign my employment and to retire into the country as soon as the king returns, and his majesty may depend upon my not behaving myself in the manner others have done after quitting his service. But I shall, I hope, by the steadiness of my conduct, and by doing the duties of a good subject in a private station, efface those ill impressions which have been given him of me. . . .

The miserable and distracted condition into which the northern affairs are plunged gives the discontented and enemies of the king's government hopes, that they may be able to raise some disturbances in parliament on that head, which they flatter themselves may be managed so as to affect the king's affairs in general; and indeed I cannot but own their expectations in this particular to be better founded and their schemes more wisely laid than they used to be. . . .

P. S. I am very sure that all these malicious insinuations to Walpole's and our prejudice arise from Bothmar, who has every day some infamous project or other on foot to get money; and his disappointments in these particulars are what he cannot bear, having nothing in his view but raising a vast estate to himself; and therefore he will never be satisfied till he has got the Ministry and Treasury into such hands as will satiate his avarice, at the expence of the king's credit, interest and service.

Secretary Stanhope to Lord Townshend

My Lord,   Göhre, November 6, 1716

I am to acknowledge the honour of your letter of the 12th and 16th of October. I do not yet know whether baron Gortz's letter will be deciphered, but if it be, I will not fail to send you a copy of it. I think there is no reason to doubt from the king of Sweden's temper, but that he may be prevailed upon to undertake anything. I have laid before his majesty all these intercepted letters, and have communicated to him good part of the contents of both your lordship's of the dates above-mentioned. I think the latter of them is come very seasonably; for the king being upon the point to take his final resolution touching his holding the session of parliament in person or not; it hath given me an opportunity to show his majesty, that his servants in England did not think it possible to carry those things in parliament, which seem absolutely necessary, unless countenanced and supported by his presence. I very believe this will determine him to take the resolution we all wish, and that his presence will enable us to deal with Mr. Lechmere and his followers. It was never imagined, that any supply should be asked of the parliament, immediately, on account of the northern affairs: but it will certainly become the parliament to address the king to form in concert with such other powers, as your lordship names, such alliances, in order to force a good peace there, as shall be judged necessary, and to promise the parliament's support for such engagements; otherwise I know not what minister can make a step with safety towards forming any plan. Whether the disbanding forces, while these matters are pending, will enable the king to treat with advantage, I beg may be considered. . . .

I have represented therefore to the king, the sentiments expressed in your letter on this head, as proceeding from the apprehensions you were under of difficulties, in case his majesty should not come in person to give life and vigour to all his business. You may imagine I said nothing of that part of your letter where you talked of laying down: for if you knew how thoroughly well the king thinks of your lordship, and how often he upon all occasions expresses it, I am sure you would not have said it yourself. It is very likely that Bothmar may have done ill offices to Mr. Walpole: but the king upon that subject tells me, that he spoke himself with Mr. Walpole about it before he left England. It is very possible the king and Mr. Walpole might mistake one another. But the king says, he did apprehend, that Mr.

Coxe, *Walpole*, vol. II.

Walpole had told him a way would be found to pay that money: he says he hath in fact advanced the money. I do therefore beg, that Mr. Walpole and you will think of this matter. If it be necessary that I write a letter to be laid before the cabinet council, let him tell me in what manner he would have me write, and I will immediately send a letter, if he would have it, and do every thing that he and you will let me know of for your service. The concern I have for him makes me wish most earnestly, that he will find some way to make this matter easy, which may, and will otherwise, give his enemies an opportunity of hurting him. I am sure I have stayed in this office much longer than I would have done, for your sake and his; and whenever we are to go out of place, let it not be upon such a foot, that the king shall say Mr. Walpole hath promised such a thing, and that Mr. Walpole shall say otherwise. I vent my thoughts very freely to you, and will do so, while I am in business. You will easily believe me, when I tell you, that considering the present situation I am in, I do not wish that may be long. In all states and conditions I shall ever be, &c.

The Earl of Sunderland to Lord Townshend

My Lord,   Göhre, November 11, 1716
My giving your Lordship this trouble, is occasioned by Mr. Stanhope's having shown me a letter he has written to you, by the king's express command upon the subject of the French treaty, and the delays in the signing of it. Your Lordship may remember, that at the beginning of this negotiation with France, I was very much against it, apprehending it was an artifice only of the French party in Holland to avoid the treaty with the emperor, and to sow disunion among the allies. However, when I left England, I saw plainly the torrent was for carrying on the negotiation. I knew no more till I came hither of this affair, but what I had from the common news and reports in the Low Countries; and therefore, upon the same general notion, I wrote my opinion to your Lordship in general, still to the same effect, while I was at Aix. But upon my arrival there, and Mr. Secretary Stanhope's having acquainted me with the treaty itself, and every step that had been taken in it, I was entirely convinced that no negotiation had ever been managed with more pains and prudence, nor no treaty ever brought to a conclusion more glorious nor more advantageous to the king of England: especially, under the circumstances Europe is like to be in by

Coxe, *Walpole*, vol. II.

these proceedings of the czar, the king of Prussia, &c. which very probably may make France take a pretence, from these delays, to avoid signing at last; and, what is worse yet, is, that the occasions of this delay leave it in the power of France to say it is not their fault.

I am sincerely concerned at anything that may be prejudicial to the king's service, and particularly at anything that happens, that may not rightly be understood among those in his service, that always have, and always ought to act cordially together: and that is the single reason why I say anything upon so unpleasant a subject. I must therefore be so plain as to tell you, that I never saw the king resent anything so much, as this affair, in which he thinks not only Mr. Secretary Stanhope but himself not well used; and indeed, I think it wants to be explained.

I must not omit too acquainting your Lordship, that the king is very much surprised at the strange notion that seems at present to prevail, as if the Parliament was not to concern themselves in anything that happens in these parts of the world, which he looks upon not only as exposing him to all kinds of affronts, but even to ruin: and indeed this notion is nothing but the old Tory one, that England can subsist by itself, whatever becomes of the rest of Europe, which has been so justly exploded ever since the revolution.

I am very sensible, that upon many accounts, it might have been more prudent in me, not to have mentioned these things; but the king's service, and the supporting of the right interest, and the union of those in his service depend so much upon these things being rightly understood, that I could not have answered it to myself, if I had not troubled you with this letter. You will take it, as I am sure it is sincerely meant by him, that is with the greatest truth and respect, &c.

Lord Townshend to Secretary Stanhope

(November 11, 1716.) The enclosed is a copy of my letter to the king; my heart is so full with the thoughts of having received this usage from you, to whom I have always been so faithful a friend, that you will excuse my not saying any more at this time. I pray God forgive you; I do.

P. S. Lord Sunderland will, I am persuaded, excuse my not answering his letter.

May it please your Majesty,   November 11–22, 1716
It is with the utmost surprise and concern that I received yester-

day your majesty's letter of the 1–12 instant, together with one from Mr. Secretary Stanhope, written by your majesty's express command.

I was in hopes the frankness and openness of my temper, might among several inconveniencies, at least have had this one good effect with respect to myself, that I might thereby have been secured against the suspicion of being likely to have recourse at any time to artifice and evasion, in order to conceal my real sentiments, or to decline by indirect methods what I had not the courage openly to declare against and oppose. However, since it has been my misfortune to fall under the suspicion of such a weakness, it is at least some comfort to me, that the instance given, is such, that your majesty upon a fair representation of what has passed, must be convinced from the facts themselves, that I am entirely innocent of the crime insinuated against me.

Your majesty will do me the justice to remember, that ever since the regent first gave reason to believe he was sincere in desiring this alliance, by his sending the abbot du Bois to the Hague, I have all along been one of the forwardest in pressing and soliciting the advancement of this treaty, even at a time when I had some grounds to doubt, whether your majesty entered with equal conviction into the reasons which induced me to represent this alliance as most advantageous for your kingdoms.

As soon as the article of Mardyk was referred hither, the British engineers, the minister of France, the committee of council, and his royal highness the prince himself, will all witness with what earnestness and application Mr. Methuen and I laboured to bring this point to a happy and speedy conclusion. I have since countersigned two warrants from his royal highness to my lord chancellor, for causing the great seal to be appended to lord Cadogan's full powers, by which he is authorised to sign this treaty, either jointly with the Dutch or separately; and I beg leave to say, with all submission, that after all that has passed on this occasion, I never expected to be accused of want of zeal for the perfecting this treaty. I own, that I was under an error in thinking Mr. Walpole's first full powers were sufficient to authorise him to sign with France separately; but as soon as ever I was sensible of this mistake, without expecting your majesty's particular commands, I immediately obtained a warrant from his royal highness for a new full power to lord Cadogan and Mr. Walpole jointly, which warrant I countersigned, and got the full powers passed through the several forms, and dispatched to Holland with as much expedition, as was at that time possible; the court being at Hampton Court, and most of the lords out of town.

This full power was, it is true, conceived in general terms, including all particulars, and consequently (as was thought here) the better fitted to suit all unforeseen circumstances that might arise. And it is no less true, that full powers in the same general form have ever been, and are daily given to all the plenipotentiaries, whom your majesty or your predecessors have sent into foreign courts. Mr. Methuen himself concluded the treaty of Portugal, in virtue of such a full power, and several others have done the like, without anyone's making the objection now started by the abbé du Bois; and it is certain, that your majesty might, by one single full power, authorise one and the same person to negotiate with all the princes in Europe. My lord Cadogan's letters to me, show him to be of this opinion; and M. d'Iberville is so much of the same sentiment, that when Mr. Methuen stated the abbé's difficulty to him, he said the abbé was but a novice in this sort of business; and that there was not the least weight in this objection.

But to convince your majesty, that I had no intention to delay this great affair, and that it never was in my thoughts to make use of any artifice to avoid having my hand appear to the orders for my lord Cadogan's signing this treaty separately without the Dutch, the very moment that I received notice from him of the Abbé's objection, I obtained a warrant from his royal highness (and countersigned it myself, a copy of which, I take the liberty to enclose to your majesty) for passing a second full power to lord Cadogan in the form prescribed by the abbé; and the court being then returned to town, I got it dispatched with so much expedition, that though lord Cadogan's letter was not received till the 29th of October in the morning, the messenger set out with it the same night at 12 o'clock, with orders to the postmaster to furnish him with a boat express to Calais, the winds being then contrary for sailing to Holland. The dispatching these full powers, with so much diligence, and in such explicit terms, before I had the honour to receive your majesty's commands, will, I hope, convince your majesty of the fairness of my intentions, and how far I was from having the design with which I am charged.

I am equally surprised and concerned to find, that notwithstanding the arrival of these powers, the abbé still persists to form new pretences of delay; alleging now, that these full powers ought to have been countersigned by me. The warrants by virtue of which the great seal was appended to both the powers were (as I have already had the honour to acquaint your majesty) countersigned by me, according to what is usually practised here, in the like cases; but having examined the registers of the office, and caused an extract to be made of the manner of signing the full powers for almost an age back (a copy of which extract, I have sent to lord Cadogan) it appears, that it is not the custom for secretaries of state to countersign instruments of that nature. And the lords of the committee, having read my lord Cadogan's letter, were of opinion, that it was not convenient in the present case to recede from the usual practice on the like occasions, lest a handle should be taken from thence to invalidate all that was transmitted by the English ministers at the treaties of Utrecht, of Riswick, of Nimeguen, and higher up, at all which negotiations, the ministers of France and other courts signed with ours, upon the credit of full powers, not countersigned by any of our secretarys of state. But as the abbé du Bois signified to lord Cadogan, that he should be contented with a declaration on this head, I sent my lord Cadogan such a declaration last night by an express.

As for Mr. Walpole's declining to assist at the signing this treaty (which I perceive has helped to mislead Mr. Stanhope into these undeserved suspicions of me) is what I was so far from being accessory to, that upon his applying to the prince by me for leave of absence, I sent him a positive refusal, and advised him to let no private reasons of his own interfere with your majesty's express commands.

Having thus laid the real facts before your majesty, without any colouring or disguise, I have nothing more to add, but most humbly to beg pardon for the tediousness of this relation, and to assure your majesty, that I am with the utmost submission and duty, &c.

Robert Walpole to Secretary Stanhope

Dear Sir,   London, November 11—22, 1716

At my return from the country, lord Townshend communicated to me the contents of both your letters, which so nearly concern me, as everything must needs do, that gives me reason to believe I suffer in his majesty's good opinion. There can be no greater misfortune, than to incur blame and displeasure for those very things, which a man thinks he has deserved well in; but this seems to be the fate of those who have the honour to serve at a distance. As to the business of St. Christopher's, I am sure I have done nothing in it yet, wherein 'tis possible for me to offend; and I have already written to you my sentiments so fully, that I can say no more upon it, unless in a conference which count Bothmar has desired with me on Tuesday morning, something shall occur that I may think proper to give you an account of; and I must beg leave to defer entering into any particulars relating to the payment of the troops of Saxe Gotha and Munster, till after that time, because I am sure count Bothmar dares not deny to me, but that I have shown a more than ordinary readiness to facilitate that matter; and this I am confident I shall be able to tell you, he has confessed to me. I must only add one thing, that I am at a loss what to say, when I am told, I promised the king a method should be found out to pay this money. I do not presume to enter into this dispute, but I hope I shall be thought more excusable, when I protest before God, that I cannot recollect, that ever the king mentioned one syllable of this to me, or I to him; but my memory must fail me, when his majesty says the contrary.

By your letter to lord Townshend, received this day, I understand 'tis his majesty's pleasure that the parliament should not meet before the eighth of January. I think it my duty to suggest to you, that 'tis to be remembered, that the parliament left last year above six hundred thousand pounds of the supply unraised; notwithstanding which, it has been so ordered, that we shall be able to subsist the forces till the latter end of January, by throwing the deficiency upon such parts of the service as were best able to bear it, but this not without great inconveniencies; and if his majesty should have any thoughts of a further prorogation, I beg this may be considered, and we may timely know, what is to be expected, that all possible care be taken; though I am sensible, it must be done with the greatest difficulty, if at all practicable; and the methods we shall be obliged to take, will in some measure, I fear, affect our creditt, which at this time proves very unfortunate. I am, &c.

Lord Townshend to the King

December 11—22, 1716

I have received with deference, and with the utmost submission, your majesty's commands, intimated by M. secretary Methuen, depriving me of the office of secretary of state. I most humbly demand permission to remind your majesty of what I said, when you did me

This letter to the king is taken from the second edition (1800) of Coxe's *Walpole.*—Ed.

the honour to confer on me that employment; that I should esteem myself happy, if I had as much capacity as zeal and affection for your majesty's service, in which case I am sure that your majesty would have every reason to be satisfied with my services. I can venture to affirm with truth, that the desire of testifying my gratitude has been the only motive capable of hitherto supporting me under the fatigues of my employment. I am highly sensible of the honour which your majesty confers on me, by condescending to appoint me lord lieutenant of Ireland. But as my domestic affairs do not permit me to reside out of England, I should hold myself to be totally unworthy of the choice which your majesty has been pleased to make, if I were capable of enjoying the large appointments annexed to that honourable office, without doing the duty of it. I trust that your majesty will grant me the permission to attend to the private affairs of my family, which I have too much neglected. Yet I will venture to assure your majesty, that whatever may be my situation, your majesty will always find me a faithful and grateful servant, anxious to promote, with all his power, your majesty's service; having the honour of being, with the most inviolable attachment, sire, your majesty's most humble, most obedient, and most faithful subject and servant.

Robert Walpole to Secretary Stanhope

Dear Sir,   December 12—23, 1716
Your private letter to me, I have not let one mortal see. I never read it, but some parts of it astonish me so much, that I know not what to say or think. What could prevail on you to enter into such a scheme as this, and appear to be chief actor in it, and undertake to carry it through in all events, without which it could not have been undertaken, is unaccountable. I do swear, to you, that lord Townshend has no way deserved it of you; and even after the letter that came with the king's, I do protest to you, he never treated your conduct in that matter, but as a mistake; which, when you were sensible of, your friendship for him would easily prevail upon you to retract. Believe me, Stanhope, he never thought you could enter into a combination with his enemies against him.

I find you are all persuaded, the scheme is so adjusted, that it can meet with no objection from the whigs. Believe me, you will find the direct contrary true, with every unprejudiced whig of any consequence

Coxe, *Walpole*, vol. II.

or consideration. I, perhaps, am too nearly concerned in the consequences to gain any credit with you. However, I can't help telling you, you don't know what you are doing. 'Tis very hard to treat my lord Townshend in the manner you have done, but 'tis more unjust to load him with imputations to justify such ill treatment. Such sudden changes to old sworn friends, are seldom looked upon in the world with a favourable eye. What is given out here and published, from letters from among you, in regard to the prince, I cannot but take notice of, and will stake my all upon this single issue, if one instance can be given of our behaviour to the prince, but what was necessary to carry on the king's service; and we never had a thought, but with a just and due regard to the king as our king and master; and as for any secret intimacies or management undertaken with the two brothers, if there be the least handle, or one instance can be given of it, call me for ever *villain*; if not, think as you please of those that say or write this.

I will say no more, but give you one piece of advice. Stop your hand till you come over, and can see and hear, how that you have already done, is resented here. I am very sensible in what a manner lord Townshend's refusal may be represented to the king. Think a little coolly, and consider how possible it is for men in a passion to do things, which they may heartily wish undone. I write this as an old acquaintance, that still desires to live in as much friendship, as you will make it possible or practicable for me. And lett me once more beg of you to recollect yourself, and lay aside that passion, which seems to be so predominant in all your actions. I have heard old friends were to be valued like old gold. I never wished anything more sincerely than to bear that title, and to preserve it with you.

Robert Walpole to Secretary Stanhope

December 12—23, 1716

I have received the favour of yours of the 3d instant, N. S. by my brother, and very soon after had what you sent by Mr. Brereton of the 15th. What could possibly create so great an alteration among you in the space of twelve days is in vain to guess, and impossible to determine. But I suppose I am mistaken, when I think there was any change in the measures, except in the time of execution. I think I have no commands at present from his majesty to you, but in relation

Coxe, *Walpole*, vol. II.

to the payment of the Saxe Gotha and Munster troops, which I hope
will be no longer thought to stand at my door: since after all that has
been said about this affair, there are at this hour no powers from Saxe
Gotha to receive the money; and as M. Hallangius tells me, his master
will give no powers but to him; and count Bothmar tells me this
morning, what was agreed upon betwixt us to be sent from your side
of the water, in order to be laid before the cabinet council, is come
so imperfect, that 'tis not fit to be produced. He has desired however,
that six or seven thousand pounds may be paid upon account of the
troops of Munster, which shall be laid before the cabinet council at
their first meeting.

When you desired me to prevail with my lord Townshend to acquiesce in what is carved out for him, I cannot but say you desired
an impossibility; and 'tis fit you should know, that there is not one of
the cabinet council, with whom you and lord Sunderland have agreed
in all things for so many years, but think, that considering all the
circumstances and manner of doing this, nobody could advise him to
accept of the lieutenancy of Ireland; and that it cannot be supposed,
that the authors of this scheme either thought he would, or desired he
should. And believe me, when I tell you, this matter is universally
received here by all men of sense, and well wishers to the king, in
another manner than you could imagine, when you gave into the
measure. And be assured, that whoever sent over the accounts of any
intrigues or private correspondence betwixt us and the two [The duke
of Argyle and the earl of Ilay] brothers, or any management in the
least tending to any view or purpose, but the service, honour, and interest of the king, I must repeat it, be assured, they will be found,
pardon the expression, confounded liars, from the beginning to the
end.

Whilst we write at this distance, and think so widely different of all
things transacting, 'tis labour lost to enlarge; so that I will give you
no further trouble till we meet, but to assure you, that I am very
sincerely, dear sir, your most faithful humble servant.

The Duke of Somerset to the Earl of Ilay

My Lord,   Petworth, December 13—24, 1716
I think lord Townshend is very rightly kicked out from being our first
minister and governour in Great Britain, into a second governour in

Ireland; and lord Sunderland, who has been false even to his best friends, will now fall unpitied. Stanhope has no interest in the nation; he is to make friends, when he is made a lord; for that part of the scheme one may dive into, that he is no more to expose himself to the contempt of the house of commons. I long to know the parts which Lord Cowper, and my friend Parker will act in this jumble; for if they are not lett more into in the secrets, than hitherto they have been, or at least as they say, they have not been; neither the duke of Grafton, duke of Kingston, duke of Roxburgh, nor lord Polwarth's interest in parliament will be any help, especially if Walpole does either lay down or become silent, or one would think there is a great deal more still to be done; or they had better not have done so much, though I am in high delight with what these things will produce, good for us all at last.

Yet what distracts my thoughts, are the king's orders to the prince to give away the duke of Argyle's regiment and groom of stole. The first is in the king to do as he pleases, and the other as much in his royal highness; this is very hard to be acted by the prince. Will it hurt the prince to let his father know, that he takes a groom of the stole's place to be useless as his majesty does, therefore he desires that expence to be saved, and to be sunk in his family too. But as you and your brother are much better judges than I can pretend, I do submit. This is the only alloy to the joy I have, that our wrongs are thus revenged on those two last of ministers. Forgive these rough thoughts, so suddenly written on paper: they are written in confidence to a friend, who I have all the value and esteem for, that man can have. Ten thousand thanks for your lordship's letter. I beg my very humble service to your brother and my lord Orrery.

Secretary Stanhope to Lord Townshend

My Lord,   Hanover, December 15, 1716
The enclosed copy of my dispatch to Mr. secretary Methuen, [The dispatch to secretary Methuen, which announced the removal of lord Townshend, and his appointment to act as the secretary of state in England, is missing.] will inform your lordship of the great regard which his majesty has thought fit, upon this occasion, to express for your eminent services; which, as they have very justly entitled your lordship to the greatest employment a king of England has to give, so

I am persuaded the services you will do his majesty in this station, will be no less advantageous to the public, and will, if possible, increase your lordship's own reputation. That it may be so, is most sincerely wished by, &c.

Secretary Stanhope to Robert Walpole

Dear Sir,   Hanover, December 15, 1716

You will see by my dispatch to Mr. Secretary Methuen, of which I send you enclosed a copy, the alteration which his majesty has judged necessary for his service to be made in the ministry. If I could possibly have an hour's discourse with you, I am sure I should make you sensible, that the part I have had in the last step hath been for my lord Townshend's service. Every circumstance considered, I do in my conscience believe, this was the only measure which could secure the continuance of a whig administration with any ease to the king. His majesty has been more uneasy of late, than I care to say; and I must own, I think he has reason, even though I don't pretend to know so much of the matter as the king does; his majesty receiving many advices, which come neither through my hands nor my lord Sunderland's. But I cannot help observing to you, that he is jealous of certain intimacies with the two brothers. I hope his majesty's presence in England, and the behaviour of our friends in the cabinet, will remove these jealousies. No one man can contribute more to this than yourself; and I must tell you, that my lord Sunderland, as well as myself, have assured the king that you will do so. You know that ill offices had been done you here, which might have made some impression, if my lord Sunderland and I had not in good earnest endeavoured to prevent it.

You will, I am persuaded, believe that our endeavours were sincere, when I shall have told you with the frankness I am going to do, what our scheme is here for the ministry. In case my lord Townshend accepts of Ireland, which for a thousand reasons, he ought to do, the cabinet council will remain just as it was, with the addition of the duke of Kingston as privy seal. Mr. Methuen and I shall continue secretaries. But if my lord Townshend shall decline Ireland; and if, which by some has been suggested, but which I cannot think possible, he should prevail upon you to offer to quit your employments, the king in this case, has engaged my lord Sunderland and myself to promise,

Coxe, *Walpole*, vol. II.

that his lordship will be secretary; and that I, unable and unequal as I am every way, should be chancellor of the exchequer for this sessions; the king declaring, that as long as he can find whigs that will serve him, he will be served by them. Which good disposition his majesty shall not have reason to alter, by any backwardness in me to expose myself to any trouble or hazard. You know as much of our plan now, as I do, and are, I dare say, fully satisfied, that I think it highly concerns me, that you should stay where you are. I am very sorry that my lord Townshend's temper hath made it impracticable for him to continue secretary. The king will not bear him in that office, be the consequence what it will. This being the case, I hope and desire that you will endeavour to reconcile him to Ireland, which I once thought he did not dislike; and which, I think, he cannot now refuse, without declaring to the world, that he will serve upon no other terms, than being viceroy over father, son, and their three kingdoms. Is the whig interest to be staked in defence of such a pretension? or is the difference to the whig party, whether lord Townshend be secretary or lord lieutenant of Ireland? I hope this letter will convince you of the confidence in which I desire we may live and act; and am ever with great truth, &c.

The present dispatch leaves, you see, a commissioner's place vacant at your board, touching the filling up which, I should be glad to have your sentiments as soon as may be. I believe the king will leave Hanover as soon as he has advice, that the yachts are in Holland. Judging that it may be very much for my lord Townshend's service and for yours, that you should receive this letter as soon as may be, I send it by your friend Brereton, who is a very sensible young man, and I have ordered him to manage it so, that this letter be delivered to you four and twenty hours, before the messenger who goes along with him, delivers my dispatch to Mr. secretary Methuen, that you may have so much time to reason with my lord Townshend.

Thomas Brereton to Charles Stanhope

Dear Sir,   London, December, 1716
By Friday's post, I acquainted you with my safe arrival here, with my having delivered the dispatches with which I was charged, and slightly hinted the confusion I found everybody in at the contents of them: I have since, by going to the court and city, had opportunities more

Coxe, *Walpole*, vol. II.

particularly to observe the temper of those who make up these two
different parts of the town; and as I have the greatest reason to have
a perfect esteem for the secretary, you will give me leave to trouble you
a second time with the sentiments of those, who have his majesty's
interest entirely at heart, and who wish him also the greatest prosperity.
I told you in my last, the turn I gave to the surprising news I brought
was, that to prevent the further torrent of the German interest, the
secretary found himself for the present obliged to come into their
measures so disagreeable to himself, which was relished by some
persons pretty well, and I don't know, but thereby a stop was put for
a while to the sinking credit of the stocks: but those transacting that
way, since fearing the certainty of it, and seriously reflecting on the
fatal consequences of the removal of so great a man as lord Townshend, and that that must necessarily be attended with further alterations, I will venture to say, the town is in greater confusion now, than
it was in any part, or at any alterations whatsover made in the late
queen's reign, and that all public credit will continue daily to sink
till his majesty's arrival, or a further prospect that the true and honest
interest of the nation will still be preserved and restored. Perhaps it
may be disagreeable, that I tell you, when I go into the citty, all the
considerable men there crowd about me, and press me in the most
earnest manner to give some reasons for these sudden and unexpected
resolutions, to tell them who I thought the advisers and contrivers of
them. When I go to the court, the very great ones there, to whom I
had scarce the honour of being known before, salute me, and are
also very solicitous to find out the true springs and causes of what they
don't scruple aloud to call these extraordinary proceedings. Nay, it
has there been said already, that never was anything more unprecedented, than for his majesty, when out of the nation, with the
council of one single minister only, to make so prodigious a change
in his ministry, just before the meeting of his parliament: a parliament, which 'twas to be hoped, by their unanimity and steadiness,
might have brought about not only the reduction of interest upon
public funds, but several other matters of the greatest importance, to
the further security and quiet of his majesty's government, the very
prospect of which had raised your credit to such a pitch of glory; and
all these good projects, I will take upon me to pronounce, cannot even
be proposed, unless the ministry is continued, and lord Townshend
restored.

I still flatter myself I am right in my notions of Mr. Stanhope, and
that he will preserve the ancient friendship he has professed to lord

Townshend and Mr. Walpole. If he does not, give me leave to say you will see the most valuable part of his majesty's friends show their resentment in a most generous manner. For I have reason to know not only the ministry, but the most wealthy in this metropolis, have been to intercede with Mr. Walpole not to resign his office, and have given him the strongest instances of their support and friendship; and that if he should find it consistent with his honour so to do, his example will be followed by the strongest body of the greatest subjects that ever prince had. How often dear sir, have I said to you, that the greatest bulwark against the foreign and home enemies, was the everlasting unity of lord Townshend, the secretary, and Mr. Walpole, that whilst they went hand in hand, the expectations of both were equally absurd and ridiculous, and the jacobites had very little to hope. This already appears by the gayness of the disaffected, who though silent ten days ago, are now as loud as ever in the coffeehouses; and I saw twenty guineas given, to be repaid with ten times the sum, when baron Price is chancellor.

Forgive me for letting you know these particulars, and impute it to my zeal for my country and my extraordinary veneration for the secretary: I must take the liberty to let you know the world cries aloud against him, and if his correspondents from hence be faithful, he must be sensible of it. All I am able to say in his vindication, avails but little, yet I require some further proofs, before I can give into opinion, that he will be guilty of that faithlessness with which he is charged: for God's sake, won't he consider, he not only forfeits his private honour, but will draw upon himself a number of enemies, which he will find it impossible to subsist against. The ministry looks upon this juncture as a trial between the English and German councils, and will no doubt exert themselves in a manner becoming Englishmen; and I should be very sorry indeed, to find him that has preserved so steady a character hitherto, forfeit it by adhering to a new interest in opposition to those who have I will say promoted his equally with their own. I delivered the message he commanded me to Mr. Walpole. I wish I could assure myself, 'twas received with that confidence that heretofore such a message would have been received. Several conjectures are made from my being sent express with this unwelcome alteration, (I may boldly so call it, since the whole body of the king's friends are displeased at it) but most agree that 'twas to hinder me from knowing by what councils these measures were pursued, and from having opportunities of learning what is yet intended. But my friend will permit me to say, notwithstanding the great care that was taken by him to prevent my knowledge of any of these matters, I was not so altogether ignorant of them as he may imagine; but I all along depended upon the secretary's integrity, and that another expedient was forming which would have been much more consistent with his honour and profit; and you may remember, that when I was apprehensive of lord Townshend's being sent to Ireland, I expressed my concern, and hoped the secretary would never be the adviser of it. All I shall say further is, that I am afraid he will find himself tricked by a man, who though so unreasonable in his pretensions, has the smallest interest of anyone that's admitted to his majesty's council board. Forgive me dear sir, for taking up so much of your time; but I should think myself unworthy the future favour of Mr. Stanhope, if I flattered him, or forbore to let him know things as they are; perhaps those who have greater expectations from him, will be cautious how they do this; but I shall always choose to give a faithful account of things, though disagreeable, rather than one filled with falsehood and flattery. One thing I must not omit, which is, that Mr. Micklethwaite has offered wagers, that Mr. Walpole will be out in thirty days; but notwithstanding his imprudence, I will pray that he, lord Townshend, and Mr. Stanhope may unite and remain what they have long been, a terror to king George's enemies; if they do not, I shall expect a long continuance of the present disorder and discontent, though, I assure you, that will be to no one upon earth more disagreeable than to dear sir, &c.

Secretary Stanhope to Robert Walpole

Dear Sir,   Hanover, January 1, 1717
I have received the favour of your two letters of the 12th of December, and am very sorry to find, that what I judged and meant as a service to my lord Townshend, is resented in the manner it is. I delivered my lord Townshend's letter to the king; and instead of representing his lordship's refusal to his prejudice, I have procured his majesty's commands to repeat this offer to his lordship, and I rather choose to mention it to you, than to write directly to his lordship as yet. In the meantime I am commanded to acquaint you, that Ireland will be kept open till the king comes to England, and I cannot help telling you, that I think you cannot do your king, your country, and my lord Townshend a more signal service, than by prevailing with his lordship to accept of it. If you can suggest to me any method by which it may still more plainly

and evidently appear, that the king's intention and desire was, that he should be lord lieutenant of Ireland; I shall be obliged to you, and will certainly convince you, that you have judged hardly of your humble servant, in supposing it was not meant so. I do not write to my lord, because I fear, that anything which comes from me, at this time, will only irritate. But I do pray you to communicate to him, what I have in command from his majesty, in relation to this business. I have as just a value for old friends as is possible, and I cannot, I confess, discover that I have been guilty of a breach of friendship, in procuring the offer of Ireland, at a time when the king was determined he should not be secretary.

I wish it had been as easy for me to have got rid of my office of secretary, as I will venture to affirm, it was impossible to have kept lord Townshend so. Ought I, either in my own name or in the name of the whiggish party, to have told the king, that my lord Townshend must continue to be secretary of state, or that I, nor any other of our friends, would have anything to do. I really have not yet learned to speak such language to my master; and I think a king is very unhappy, if he is the only man in the nation, who cannot challenge any friendship from those of his subjects, whom he thinks fit to employ. I think more is not required from a man in behalf of his friend, than in behalf of himself. And I can assure you, that it would be impossible for me to bring myself to tell the king I won't serve him, unless he give me just the employment which I like best, though at the same time he either gives or continues to me an employment much more honourable and beneficial than that which I had a fancy for. You alarm me, and I fear with too much truth, with the consequences of this step, which may prove very fatal, and create a division amongst the whigs. But pray, at whose door must this resentment be laid? I hope that you will grow cooler on your side; that even my lord Townshend will sacrifice his resentment to the public good. And I would then gladly know what cause or colour of uneasiness there can be to any honest man. I heartily wish you may well consider all circumstances, and promote that union amongst well meaning men, which is necessary. No one man in the world can do so much good as yourself; and give me leave to say, no one man will, I think, have more to answer for to his country, if you do not heartily endeavour to make up these breaches. That I have never been wanting in any kind of friendly office to you, I am perfectly conscious to myself; and I am sure, that my interest, as well as inclination, lead me to wish the continuance of a friendship

I ever valued. Pray excuse me to your brother Horace, to whom I am sincerely a well wisher, though he be very angry with me. I am, &c.

Secretary Stanhope to Robert Walpole

Dear Sir,   Hanover, January 3, 1716–17
Having sent by last post an answer to your letters of the 12th instant; this serves chiefly to cover a duplicate of the same letter which goes by a messenger for fear of accidents. Upon reading over your letters again I wonder what could induce you to make use of one expression. You caution us to stop our hands, and to proceed no further in changes, when both lord Sunderland and I had told you in the strongest terms we could, that no other alteration was thought of, or intended; unless your quitting your employment should have made it absolutely necessary to fill it. At the same time, I think I could not express in words more strong than I did, how much I desired that might not happen. Notwithstanding the passion you were in when you wrote, I am very glad you expressed no thoughts of leaving the king's service, and I will even flatter myself that you will still prevail upon lord Townshend to accept Ireland, and that we may continue to live and act for the king's service, with the same friendship and union which has been. I think it more respectfull to my lord Townshend, that I should not write to him to acquaint him with the king's repeating the offer of Ireland, till I hear from you, who are more likely to prevail. I am, &c.

Coxe, *Walpole*, vol. II.

Robert Walpole to Secretary Stanhope

Dear Sir,   London, January 1—12, 1716—17
I have the favour of yours of the 1st instant, N.S. and am glad to find you seem to be in a little better temper than you were, and believe me, if you were here, you would be ten times more sensible, than any representations from hence can possibly make of the ill effects of what is doing. The universal discontent and apprehensions of all that wish well, is more than can be expected, and I do assure you, this is not owing to any industry or endeavours of those that may be thought

Coxe, *Walpole*, vol. II.

more nearly concerned. The spiritt of the tories and jacobites is at the same time revived beyond measure, and has had this effect already, that summonses are sent into all parts of England to make a general muster, when 'tis certain they had no thoughts before of giving any trouble this sessions; I must farther acquaint you, that the discontented whigs flatter themselves, that the game is now their own, and are disposing and dividing of all the employments with an air of authority, which you may easily imagine, gives great credit and weight to those in possession. I cannot forbear telling you, that some immediate creatures and dependants of yours, are the most busy and impertinent in all parts of the town; I have said thus much in short, that you may be truely informed of the state of affairs. If you have any other accounts from hence, you are abused, and depend upon it, you will find the sense of every man in England of any consideration, that you ever had any esteem for, or that deserves the least regard, to be the same.

When I have said this, I will not enter into any reasoning or argumentation with you at this distance, but think, you must be sensible, that a great deal of what you say, is not to be supported in a conversation betwixt old friends. We very well understand the language of ministers, but when this matter comes to be canvassed with freedom and liberty, you will be sensible of more than 'tis proper to write.

In the meantime, as to what immediately concerns my lord Townshend, I must only beg at present, that you will prevent a second hardship being put upon him, by a second offer of the lieutenancy of Ireland, and since you say, that the king commanded you to acquaint me, that Ireland shall be kept open till his majesty comes into England, there can be no difficulty in this, or at least no necessity of doing anything till his Majesty's arrival.

You will give me leave to think it a little hard when you say, no one man will have more to answer for to his country, than I may have. I agree with you, if I do not honestly endeavour to make up these breaches, I shall be very much to blame; but if what has been done, or is still to be feared, have or shall make that impossible, the weight will fall elsewhere, and be a burden too heavy to bear. Let me use your own words; you must grow cooler on your side, consider all circumstances, and remember that in England, the manner of doing things is often more to be regarded than the thing is itself, and I am confident I shall be able to convince you when we meet, that my lord Townshend's case can be considered in no other light. I can give no advice, but repeat what I said before; take care that nothing more be done, till you are upon the spott: I think you will alter your sentiments with the climate, if you have not drunk deeper of the bowl than I am willing to believe. For as I lived with you so many years in intimacy and friendship, I shall be glad still to live and die upon that foot, and shall with great pleasure see you delivered from imputations, it would grieve you to think of. I will do my part, and if you will do yours, it seems possible to retrieve the most fatal step, that ever was taken: that all may go well, is my sincere wishes, and I am, with all possible truth dear sir, your most faithful humble servant.

Secretary Stanhope to Robert Walpole

Dear Sir,   Hague, January the 16th, 1717
I have received this morning the favour of yours of the 1st instant, O.S. and I shall follow the advice you are pleased to give me, of writing nothing to lord Townshend touching Ireland, which as I told you, his majesty will keep open till his arrival. Since you seem to lay a greater stress upon the manner in which this offer was made than upon the thing itself, I hope you have been turning it in your thoughts, how anything which may have been taken amiss in the manner, may be set right; and whenever you will be pleased to suggest anything of that kind, which may be consistent with the king's dignity, and the firm resolution he has taken of supporting what he has done, I shall most willingly and heartily employ my best endeavours to make my lord Townshend easy, and so will my lord Sunderland. But though I will not repeat to my lord Townshend, in the king's name, the offer of Ireland, till you allow me so to do, I must, and do for the king's sake, for that of the whigs, and of my lord Townshend himself, most earnestly repeat to you my entreaties, that you will dispose my lord Townshend to accept of it. I am at liberty to assure you, in the king's name, that when my lord Townshend shall have accepted of Ireland, if in six months or in a twelvemonth, he should like better some other post at home in the cabinet council, that his majesty will very readily approve of any scheme that his servants shall concert for placing my lord Townshend where he shall like. At the same time, I have procured liberty from the king, to declare thus much to you. Believe me dear Walpole, when I swear it to you, that I do not think it possible for all the men in England to prevail upon the king to readmit my lord Townshend into his service, upon any other terms than of complying with the offer made of

Coxe, *Walpole*, vol. II.

Ireland. The king will exact from him this mark of duty and obedience. I do assure you, that I am not at present in a passion, I tell you very coolly what in my conscience I think, I leave it to you to make such use as you shall think fit of this very true information; and I will hope, that being thus informed, you will prevent things from being pushed to extremities, which I dread to think of.

For God's sake, is not a lord lieutenant of Ireland of the cabinet council? has he not the same access to the king, whenever he pleases, as any other minister whatsoever? will not my lord Townshend's talents, and the just esteem which everybody in the council, must have for him, give him a share in business, for ought I know greater, I am sure at least, less invidious than he had before? will not he be constantly in the way of effacing, by his behaviour, any impressions made to his prejudice? if I were not still sincerely a well wisher to his lordship, and did not think it probable, that I should again live well with him, I would not press you at this rate upon this point; I would quietly suffer him to indulge his resentment, which must end in the ruin of his and his friends' interest at court, as long as this king lives, which, give me leave to tell you, he is like to do many years.

As to the apprehensions you mention, to have been very general of a change, you know as well as I, what foundation there has been for them, and whether the refusal of my lord Townshend has not given occasion to them. I will not imagine, since you say it, that any of your friends have used any industry or endeavours to beget such a ferment. I will rather hope, that you, knowing with so much certainty, that not one remove was intended by the king, will have endeavoured to quiet and calm this ill grounded jealousy. I do not know that I have any creatures or dependants, whose behaviour I can govern, or be answerable for, but this I know, that I have not directly or indirectly, either myself or by any other person, wrote or caused to be written one syllable since this business has been on foot, except to yourself, and once to Mr. Methuen. I know not what you mean by having drunk deep of the bowl, I have already acquainted you with what I judge and know to be the king's sentiments upon this business. Whilst I am his servant, I will, to the utmost of my ability, support his dignity, which, amongst many other good things, I have learned to do from lord Townshend; and I shall not in so doing, value or fear any imputation. It will appear to the world in due time, whether any motive of ambition or interest has governed me in this business, and whether I had not most effectually served those who are at present most angry with me, if their own passion did not hinder the good effects of what was well

designed. I have, dear Walpole, a very clear conscience, and whilst
I am conscious to myself of well doing, I have learnt to be very easy
in mind, whatever other people think of me. I am, with great truth,
&c.

Secretary Stanhope to Lord Townshend

My Lord,   Cock-Pitt, April 9, 1717
The king, judging it for his service to dispense with your lordship's
service, as lord lieutenant of Ireland, I am commanded to signify his
majesty's pleasure to your lordship upon it. His majesty is sorry that
many circumstances render this alteration necessary at present; he
commands me to assure your lordship, that he will never forget your
past services; and you'll give me leave to say, that I shall be very glad
of an occasion of writing to your lordship upon a more agreeable subject, as being with great respect, &c.

Coxe, *Walpole*, vol. II.

Horace Walpole to the Rev. H. Etough

Anecdote of Sir Robert Walpole on his resignation in 1717

Dear Etough,   Wolterton, October 12, 1751
I am obliged to you for your favour of the 2d instant; and entirely
agree with you, that your opinion of the possibility, or if you please,
the probability of my late brother's removal, had the late king lived,
is very excusable, and could be no dishonour to him; and I should not
have mentioned this trifle anymore, had it not been to set you right
in one of your arguments, wherein you are mistaken, and there is an
anecdote of some curiosity relating to it. You say that, *He that could
be worked upon to turn him out, immediately after his services, in and
consequent to the rebellion of* 1715, *was capable of being again disposed to exchange the best for the worst of servants.* The fact is this,
that profligate minister, the late lord Sunderland, had engaged those
of Hanover (disappointed in their ambitious and lucrative views by the
non-compliance of lord Townshend and my brother) in an intrigue to
get them removed, and had gained the lady [the duchess of Kendal]
on their side. They at last made an impression upon his majesty, by
insinuations notoriously false, to the prejudice of lord Townshend, but

Coxe, *Walpole*, vol. II.

could not prevail with the king to remove him, until they had made his majesty believe, that my brother would not resign on that account; and accordingly when lord Townshend was (after he had been made lord lieutenant of Ireland at Hanover, instead of secretary of state) upon his majesty's return to England, entirely dismissed, my brother waited upon the king the next day, to give up the seal as chancellor of the exchequer, at which his majesty seemed extremely surprised, and absolutely refused to accept it, expressing himself in the the kindest and strongest terms, that he had no thoughts of parting with him; and in a manner begging him not to leave his service, returned the seal, which my brother had laid upon the table in the closet, into his hat, as well as I can remember, ten times. His majesty took it at last, not without expressing great concern, as well as resentment at my brother's perseverance: in which contest, among other things, he told his majesty, that, were he ever so well inclined, it was impossible to serve him faithfully with those ministers, to whom he had lately given his favor and credit. For that they would propose to him as chancellor of the exchequer, as well as in parliament, such things, that if he should agree to and support, he should lose his credit and reputation in the world; and should he not approve, or oppose them, he should lose his majesty's favor. For he, in his station, though not the author, must be answerable to his king and country for any extraordinary measure. To conclude this remarkable event, I was in the room next to the closet, waiting for my brother, and when he came out, the heat, flame, and agitation, with the water standing in his eyes, appeared so strongly in his face, and indeed all over him, that he affected everybody in the room; and 'tis said, that they, that went into the closet immediately, found the king no less disordered: and therefore, my good friend, it was no wonder, as I told you before, that when lord Sunderland proposed the laying aside my brother, after he had been employed again, his majesty should say, he would never part with Sir Robert Walpole, as long as he was willing to serve him.

L. Inese to James III

1717, Tuesday, 26 Oct.—This morning Abbé Gaultier, whom I had not seen for several months, "called at my lodgings, and, after a preamble of the danger it was for him, who was a Frenchman, to meddle in any matter that related to the King's affairs, he told me that his zeal for the King was still such that he could not but impart to me a matter he thought might be very much for the King's service, but this upon condition he should not be named to any without exception, except to the King himself and Queen Mary. After I had satisfied him that he should not be named to any other, he told me that a friend of his, a Frenchman, whom he did not name, who had lived long in England, was lately come from thence, and was very soon to return. That this friend had told him in great confidence that, being intimately acquainted with Walpole, he found that Walpole was absolutely re-solved to overturn the present Government, and that he with his friends, who were many and powerful, are now upon measures of compassing what they intend. That Walpole had told him that, though he and his friends had received many affronts and injustices from King George and his factors, yet it was not upon that account, but merely because they now saw plainly that King George and his factors were resolved to alter and overturn liberty and all that had any relation to it; and that he, Walpole, and his friends were resolved to be before hand with him, and to hazard their all rather than liberty should perish. This being the case, that friend asked Abbé Gualtier whether he had any commerce with the King, because, said he, if an application were made by the King to Walpole, I have reason to believe it would be well received, and might turn to his account, in case at the same time great offers were made to Walpole, who was not rich, but very am-bitious. To this Abbé Gualtier said he answered, that he had no cor-respondence at present with the King, but that he would think of the matter and give his friend an answer in a few days. That upon this he spoke of the matter only in general to Father Gaillard, who advised him to propose it to Inese, as accordingly he did, and then asked him what he thought of the proposal. Inese told him he could give no positive answer until he had spoke to Queen Mary, but that what occurred to him in the meantime was, that, as Abbé Gualtier himself could not but know, there were many of England's family that were upon different motives violent enemies to King George, who were not therefore friends to the King, and that perhaps Walpole might be of that number. That Walpole was known to be a man of great parts and credit, and therefore it could not but be of great importance for the King to have him in his interest, and that, if he would sincerely and heartily enter into it, there was no doubt but he would give him all the encouragement his services could deserve or his own heart desire. That, if Abbé Gualtier's friend could so contrive that the motion came first from Walpole to the King, that would be much more natural, than for him to make application to a person who hitherto has ever shown himself to be his mortal enemy. That the least that could be expected were that Abbé Gualtier's friend should begin of himself and merely from himself, to feel Walpole's pulse upon that subject, and try to find out how he is affected to the King, and whether he would receive an application from him in case any were made; and then give notice to Abbé Gualtier, his correspondent, how he found Walpole disposed, and accordingly the King would advance as prudence directed. Inese concluded that these were only his own private thoughts, upon which he, Abbé Gualtier, was to lay no further stress than in so far as he should find they agreed with Queen Mary's sentiments upon the matter, Abbé Gualtier being to see Queen Mary on Thursday and to go to Paris to see his friend upon Friday. Meantime Inese promised to give Queen Mary an account of this conversation, as accordingly he did that same evening. I forgot to mention that Inese asked Abbé Gualtier whether Walpole's intention might not be to lay aside King George and set up his son in his place. To which Abbé Gualtier answered that he had asked his friend the very same question, and that his friend had assured him Walpole and his partners had no such thought, that they knew the son had less sense and much more fire than the father, and consequently that they would be in much worse hands by the change; that they had indeed encouraged the division of the family by seeming to side with the son, but that their design in that was to expose both."

J. Menzies to L. Inese

1717, Monday, Dec. 2[13]. London.—On Thursday I gave you a plain though hasty account of our Parliament matters then. By the order observed in the estimates the Navy was the first, which nobody thought would create any struggle, because some fleet and a competent one we must still have. The next is the Army. You have seen the King's speech and how he lays it down as indisputable that the present force, 16,000 men, is the least, consistent with the people's safety. Many malcontents, Whig and Tory, grumbled extremely at this eternal army.

If the Parliament give a supply suitable to this number this year, then they cannot move to have it diminished. It was expected this question would be in on Friday. But, when the time was coming, the seemingly greatest number of the House seemed to be for gaining time and to go on in a slow method. Several members, one after another, proposed some more papers and accounts to be laid before the House, without which they could not well go on the matter of the Supply at all. The courtiers were a little surprised at this, and seemed in disorder, for they did not expect any opposition, so they dropped their design and said nothing. But they had at bottom another reason of their disorder, which was not then known in the House, which proves to be such as now astonishes everybody. In short that day about noon the Prince of Wales was taken into custody, that is, committed prisoner to his own apartment and to see nobody but his own servants.

It was expected the Prince's arrest would have been laid before Parliament to-day by one side or other. But neither did, and the House of Lords are adjourned till Wednesday. The moment I write, about 11 at night, it is said he is removed out of St. James' and gone in a hackney chair to Berkeley House, which is Devonshire House, others say, to Lord Grantham's in Albemarle Street. But that's no matter, it is a private house, which we shall know to-morrow morning with the other particulars. You may guess what a strange phenomenon this is in England, and will be in all Europe, a Prince of Wales in prison. All the foreign ministers on Saturday sent expresses to all their principals, and you will hear it far and wide. The consequences must be extraordinary some way or other, but that we must leave to time and chance and conduct. I shall only say that this great event draws our attention entirely to it, and supersedes in a great measure all other things. Yet the House of Commons met to-day, gave a supply for the Navy, and are to go on that for the Army on Friday, where the grand question before mentioned must come in. By the air and talk in general of the members to-day there appeared to be an inclination to reduce the Army to 10,000 men, but of this you shall hear when it comes to be debated, and he is too wise that pretends to foretell.

The Tories begin to come up more numerous. What the refining and hot metaphysical heads had neglected, the cooler and solider have endeavoured to repair, and have exerted themselves to the utmost to bring all to town. Mr. Walpole and those that stick to him seem very vigorous to reduce the Army. The wiser Tories have a value for his help.

James Murray to Lieut.-General Dillon

1717, Monday, Dec. 2[13].—I had yours of the 6th this evening, which was a pleasure to me, because I began to be afraid that my letters to you, since I have been in town, had miscarried. "But, since this is to inform you of a fact the most extraordinary that has happened in this kingdom for many years, lest it should be intercepted, I have transmitted the contents to you in another manner, which, I am confident, will come to your hands.

I have formerly acquainted you and with that concern you could expect from one of my principles, that there had been great disputes at Court between his Majesty and his Royal Highness about the christening of the young Prince, his Highness and the Princess having made it their request to the King that the Duke of York should stand godfather with his Majesty, and the Queen of Prussia godmother, and the King on the other hand having been positive (at the Duke of Newcastle's desire as 'tis thought) that the Duke of Newcastle should stand godfather with him, and the Duchess of St. Albans godmother, the matter was at last settled by the Prince submitting to his father's pleasure, after many messages which the said Duke brought them from him, and which people say he delivered in a way not so respectful as could have been wished, so that at last the young Prince was christened last Thursday night. Immediately after the ceremony was over the Prince came up to the Duke of Newcastle and spoke to him in the following manner. My Lord, said he, you see that I have submitted to my father's humour in all this affair, but I must let you know that I am sensible that all the uneasiness I have suffered and the ill blood which has been created between us, is owing to you, for which reason you are a rascal, and be assured that one day I shall be able to revenge your insolence, having at the same time trod upon his toes. The Duke made a complaint of this treatment to the King, upon which a cabinet was called next morning; the result of which meeting was in the first place a message from his Majesty to the Prince to know if he owned the fact. This message was carried by the Duke of Roxburgh and some other Lords of the Cabinet. His Highness made no scruple immediately to acknowledge that it was true, and, when the Duke of Roxburgh took occasion to say that he was sorry the Duke of Newcastle had incurred his Royal Highness' displeasure, and as to his standing godfather, he could assure them that it was not a thing his Grace had courted, but that what he had done in that matter was purely in obedience to his Majesty's commands, the Prince told him he did not believe one word he said. A report being made of this, the King wrote immediately with his own hand an order to him to remain prisoner in his own apartment till he should know his pleasure further. This order was delivered last Friday about two o'clock, and he has been prisoner accordingly ever since with a yeoman of the Guards without the door, who denies access to all but his own servants. It is said he has written two several letters to the King full of the most respectful expressions, but that he made no mention of giving the Duke any satisfaction for the indignity done him, and for this reason his letters have not produced any effect. What will next be done, no mortal can imagine; some talk of his being sent to the Tower, but that is inconsistent with the privileges of an English peer now that the Habeas Corpus Act is in force. In short this is the present situation. You may believe our friends are embarrassed to the last degree, but in what manner the scene may change is more than I am able to inform you. In the meantime you may imagine how uppish the Jacobites are upon this disaster, and it must be owned they never had so much reason. For now the Ministry and in particular the Cabinet Council are so dipped in this affair against the Prince that it is hard to say what they have to expect from him. Mr. Walpole did this day make a speech against the Army, and it is thought that matter will be settled one way or other this week. The Bishop of Rochester is still ill and keeps his bed which renders him incapable of doing anything.

Postscript.—The Prince and Princess are turned out of St. James' House and are forbid the Court. She is very ill, having been obliged to come too soon abroad.

J. Menzies to [Sir H. Paterson]

1717, Tuesday, Dec. 3[14].—Our breaches grow wider every day. The Prince, after 4 days imprisonment was last night about 6 set at liberty, and being turned out of St. James' went with the Princess, though she was not recovered, to Lord Grantham's in Albemarle Street without guards or coaches or anything. Not a farthing of money. The Duke of Devonshire has offered him his house, which is much better. The breach and animosity grows very high. All, who have places both from the father and the son, are to reside on one side and give up the other. Nay, if any lady that serves the Princess has a husband that enjoys any place from the father, he must give up one or t'other. So the Duchess of St. Albans surrendered yesterday to let her husband continue in the father's family. Several others are doing the same daily, and it's said that Lord Hertford and all others must. Yea, Lord Berkeley, that's in waiting, Bedchamber to the father, intimated to-day to the Court at St. James' that whoever went to the Prince must not come there. Such a scene was never seen here. In the House of Commons there seems an intention to break yet more troops and to reduce them to 10,000 men in the island and foreign garrisons. This comes on on Friday.

J. Menzies to L. Inese

1717, Thursday, Dec. 12[23].—We have had so many and so strong reports of the stopping of letters since this affair of the Prince that it seems most uncertain if anything by the common post shall come to your hands. But, since our correspondence consists only in matters of our own particular private affairs or in the public news, our letters can neither hurt nor offend anybody, and so perhaps they may pass.

As to the public, the King's own friends or party have got an entire victory at present over all opposition, for, after some light skirmishes in parliament and some hot speeches, wherein the Tories and the Walpole men have shown themselves very shallow and continued disjointed, the Court has in spite of both found a majority. And now, since the Walpole men have considered the Prince as submitting, and consequently that their support failed, and their further danger was certain, and complaining likewise that they were neglected by the Tories, they have made a sudden and thorough turn, and have run *in tête baissée* [with bowed heads] to the Court, so that in yesterday's vote in the Committee, and to-day in the full House for 3 shillings in the pound Land Tax, the Tories stood alone to the number of 80 or 90, and very hard to get so many of them to attend, even of those who are to come to town, but about 70 are not come at all. And now indeed they may stay at home, for the principal points of fleet, army and money are already voted and settled, which are the great business of the session, the fleet entirely as last year, the Army 16,000 men, without breaking of regiments or corps, and for this army 650 odd thousand pounds, which, if well managed, will maintain 25,000 men, if the Court has a mind to. The day this was voted in the full House many of the Tories were abed, and near a dozen of them went to dine and drink with Mr. Shippen in the Tower, who for a hot speech is thus not only punished, but disabled for this Session.

In short their behaviour this Session is generally compared to the whole affair of Preston, strange commanders, and strange conduct, etc.

The Prince's affair is variously believed and asserted. It is generally said, and by those who should know very well, that he entirely submits *carte blanche* and the particulars are very oddly talked of.

The order for his first confinement, and that for his getting him out of St. James' with his three letters to the King and the papers given to the foreign ministers by way of manifesto, of which there were two, you will see in print and in the public news in a little time, so I need not trouble you with them at present, not knowing either, if it be fit for a private man yet to meddle with them.

Though generally this entire submission is talked of and believed, yet others positively deny it and believe the contrary.

Memorial containing an account of the present state of affairs in England, sent by the Bishop of Rochester

1717, Dec. 14[25].—(Beginning with an account of the quarrel between the King and the Prince of Wales, of the orders to those who held offices under both of them, and of the letters to the foreign ministers as in other letters and papers.)

In this condition it is a particular worthy to be remarked that some people who have gone to see the Prince and Princess, who are neither in the service of the father or the son, have been desired not to appear at Court, and, when they did appear, they have been desired to withdraw.

How and with what view things have been brought to this pass shall be mentioned hereafter, but 'tis certain nothing in the universe could have exposed both father and son so much to the contempt of all rational men in this kingdom, or have weakened their interest more effectually, which according to common reason ought also to produce very good effects abroad.

Everybody sees what degrees of wisdom and good nature they are to expect from a Government, where the next heir, his wife and family are treated in so outrageous and unprecedented a manner at

Stuart Papers, vol. V.

the time when the birth of a new Prince had just strengthened their common interest here, and disposed people more and more to unite in their adherence to them, and when it behoved them by all possible methods to have prevented such an open rupture among themselves, but the advice of the D[uke] of Ma[rlborou]gh and the Ministry, applied to the weakness and resentments of the father, prevailed against all the rules of prudence and pushed him on to a step from the ill consequences of which he can never deliver himself.

No longer is the Kingdom divided only into those who are friends to the King and those who are friends to the Hanover family, but now we find the last party sub-divided into those who are for the father and those who are for the son. And, should the wound be ever in appearance healed between the Prince and his father, yet those who have sided with the Prince and been his advisers before and since the rupture (particularly Devonshire, Compton, Townshend, Walpole, and their followers) will never come into the father's measures whilst he governs by this Ministry, but will keep up a separate party of Whigs in opposition to the Court, and, being not considerable enough of themselves, must at last fall in with the Tories, and perhaps be driven to help forward what they never intended.

The Prince without doubt looks upon the Ministry, who have used him in so strange a manner, as his mortal enemies, and, as they have no mercy to expect from him after such indignities, it is rational to think they either are, or will soon be so. On the contrary it's obvious what opinion the father must have of the discontented Whigs, who, without regard to his inclinations, have continued to make their court to the son, and have opposed with all their might his darling project of continuing the standing army in that number and upon the footing he desired it.

Now as to the motives which have induced the Ministry to bring matters to this extremity between the father and son, it cannot in reason be believed that it is occasioned by the warm expression used by the Prince to the D[uke] of New[castle]le, on the contrary from the several circumstances of that whole story, it seems rather probable that he was ill used and provoked on purpose, in hopes to find some handle for treating him yet worse than they had hitherto done, and the eagerness with which they laid hold on this occasion, the immediate and unaccountable use they made of it, the orders after orders which they soon procured to mortify him, and the affronts upon affronts with which they presently pursued him are sure proofs that they had long designed what they now accomplished, and were resolved to push matters so far upon this advantage gained as, if possible, to prevent a reconciliation, in which they have been encouraged by observing that they could not go too fast for the father into whatsoever measures they hurried him, he having showed himself more satisfied and pleased since this incident and the several steps taken upon it than in any other part of his reign.

The Prince has for above 12 months past used Sun[derlan]d Ca[doga]n and Ma[rlborou]gh himself with very great contempt, and has been a kind of head for their enemies, the discontented Whigs, to go to, the father will in all appearance go to Hanover in the spring, and they have a mind to be in full possession of the Government in his absence, in order to which it was necessary to put the son out of a capacity of being named Regent. This they have now accomplished, and it seems to be one good account of the reasonableness of their proceedings on this occasion.

It is in the next place fit it should be known that a reconciliation has been talked of for some days past, for which hitherto no good authority has appeared, what is in this, time will discover, but it is very plain that such a measure can never answer the designs and views of the Ministers as they are above stated, unless the Prince should submit to such terms as would make him a cipher for the future, which would reduce him to the lowest degree of contempt and therefore be equally for the King's advantage, for then (as was above said) the discontented Whigs (who are for ever severed from the present Ministry) must be a direct faction against the Court, and, whether they will or no, must join at last in promoting the Tory views and designs. Nor it is possible for the Prince to forgive the Ministers, or for them to really believe he did so, should he make a profession of it, so that the consequences of this quarrel would still remain.

For these reasons, whatever may be the projects of this Ministry, it is not natural to believe that they intend the Prince should ever be King of Great Britain, for they must in that event resolve to leave their estates and fly their country or to suffer in it, which can be no comfortable prospect to the Duke of New[cast]le (who has spent £ 100,000 in the service of the family) or to any other concerned in this administration.

As to the affair of the standing Army and the opposition given to it by the discontented Whigs, you are to be informed that, though they were zealous in that measure, yet they joined with the Court in sending Mr. Shippen to the Tower upon some words of his which they voted to contain a reflection upon the Duke of Brunswick. And it will easily be believed that he gave no real occasion for such a step, when it is known that they came that day into the House resolved to send him to the Tower, which design they afterwards executed.

This incident delayed the business of the Army, and at the same time disunited more than ever the discontented Whigs and the Tories. Next day, when the army came to be debated after a long struggle, the Court carried by a majority of 45 that 16,000 men should be allowed for the service of the year 1718. But, a fresh contest having arisen, and several leading Whigs (as Mr. Smith, Sir Jo[seph] Jekyll) who voted for the Court in the former question for the 16,000 men, objected to the manner in which they are now established, to wit, that there are double the number of regiments both of foot and dragoons subsisting of what is necessary to make 16,000 men, if the companies and troops were completed as they used to be, the consequences of which were said to be: 1st, an extraordinary charge to the public of above £ 130,000, and 2nd, that under pretence of necessary recruits the Ministry might upon any design whether good or bad make the 16,000 up five and twenty thousand, which could not be done without alarming the Kingdom, if new regiments were to be levied.

This appeared to be matter of a good deal of consequence both to the Court and those who opposed them, and therefore the debate was managed with zeal on both sides. But at last the Ministry, being afraid of losing it upon a division, by concert gave up the matter and another day was appointed for settling a new establishment for the sixteen thousand men which had been voted. But the next day they resumed what they had in appearance given up, and then the same Whigs with their followers still pressed the disbanding the corps and persisted so firmly in their opposition that (notwithstanding all the closetting work which had preceded) upon a division in the Commons, the Court carried the main point but by 14, there being 158 against it and 172 for it. Upon the report next day to the House, the Court gained a little ground, as 'twas natural to expect they should, when the Whigs who opposed their measures saw they were like to lose their point. However, this struggle has created a new uneasiness amongst the Whigs, and perhaps sowed the seed of farther dissensions, and it cannot but give a great and just alarm to the Court to observe that in so darling a point, upon which they placed all their stress, they were so near miscarrying, especially since they were forced to purchase the vote by giving up another which they had resolved on, whereby £ 30,000 was to have been allowed for the staff officers of the Army. But, since so considerable an Army is continued, it will be sufficient to hinder the affections and aversions of the people (which increase every day) from producing any great effect of themselves.

The Clergy are confirmed in their aversion to the Court by their continuing their unaccountable measures for the protection of the Bishop of B[ango]r, who, though their favourite, is the most detested clergyman in England.

It is observable that the persons in power are not so watchful as to the motions of our friends abroad as their predecessors formerly have been, which may proceed from their being in a most perfect security and wholly taken up with the difficulties they lie under from their own divisions at home, or from some other reason which cannot so easily be imagined, though, as to the main points, they seem firmly to design the sending a squadron to the Baltic and another to the Mediterranean.

From all which it may be naturally inferred that next spring is the most lucky time that Providence could possibly contrive for an undertaking in the King's favour, when George will be in Han[ove]r and the son (whether he goes with him upon a reconciliation or stays here as a cipher) in no condition to do anything, while those to be employed as Regents are his avowed enemies.

There seems nothing further necessary to be mentioned, but to let you know that, as to that affair of the money trade which has been so often recommended as a thing of the last importance, the person who carries this will be able to tell you what you are to expect in that matter.

Postscript.—Nothing material has happened in either House of Parliament since the date of what is above written.

"The Prince and Princess remain in the same situation, and have been and are the most disconsolate creatures ever were known. His behaviour is the most abject and shows the meanest spirit ever known in a man of his birth. He passes his time in tears with his wife, and has sent by Bernstorff to acquaint his father that he is willing to submit to any terms he shall please to impose upon him.

The terms which have been talked of in town (by what authority is not pretended to be said) are: 1st, that he shall consent to go to H[anove]r with his father in the spring; 2ndly, that he shall inform who has advised him to oppose the Court in the manner he has done; 3rdly, that he shall give up the grant he has of £ 100,000 upon the civil list during his father's life, and 4thly, that the father shall have the power of placing and displacing his servants and that the son shall never more presume to meddle in public affairs.

The offer the son has made of a *carte blanche* by Bernstorff is supposed to contain all these particulars and even more if they could be thought of, yet this hitherto has produced no manner of effect on the father or the Ministry, so that as to them the son remains in the same state he was before this offer was made. But is not so with regard to those Whigs or the few Tories who had for some time shown an attachment to him; they, who expected to have been able to have supported both him and themselves, do now find they are given up by this creature's cowardly behaviour, and are at this time as forward to call him a mean-spirited scoundrel as the Tories or the people of the Court, which is to come a great length all of a sudden.

One consequence of his being reduced to such a degree of contempt with people of all ranks and parties is obvious, to wit, that the Ministry will be able with less difficulty to execute their designs against him.

News Letter

[Note: The circulation of News Letters was a profitable journalistic enterprise well into the eighteenth century. Though one cannot say with certainty, it is possible that the origin of the many News Letters found among the *Portland Papers* is explained in this letter from Thomas Jones to Robert Harley: "1689, April 30. At the Pewter Platter, without Temple Bar—Offering to send him the news letters. His terms are, to send once a week for £ 2, twice a week for £ 3 and thrice a week for £ 4; to be paid every year." *Portland Papers*, III, 437.—Ed.]

1717, December 3. London—Statement in French, drawn up by direction of the King, of the matters in dispute between him and the Prince of Wales. At foot of this is written in English:—

The Secretaries are to send the above to the several ministers at the Courts of their respective provinces. Mr. Shippen was voted to the Tower yesterday for words to this purpose that the paragraph on which the motion had been made about the reduction of the army was more calculated for the meridian of Germany than of Great Britain, and that the only infelicity was that the King was a stranger to the language and constitution of the kingdoms. This day, the House of Commons was upon the army. The Lords yesterday received an appeal, and adjourned to Friday. They say the Prince and Princess sent for Baron Bernstorff yesterday morning, and that he came to them yesternight, which makes some hope there may [be] an accommodation. The Princess had been ill, and subject to fainting fits, but yesterday afternoon was better, and rested better last night. Lord Lumley has resigned the horse grénadiers, and it is said Lords Stanhope, Herbert, and Mr. Paget have resigned their posts in the army. Colonel Oughton, and as said the Marquis of Hertford have resigned their places about the Prince. The Duchesses of St. Albans and Montague, the Ladies Hinchinbrook and Cowper, have resigned theirs about the Princess. The Duke of Marlborough wrote to all concerned in the army, who had posts under the Prince, to resign them, or those in the army, and not to wait on the Prince. Mr. Cotterel notified to all the foreign ministers, either not to see the Prince, or not to come to Court.

News Letter

[1717, December 3.]—The difference between the King and the Prince is likely to make so great a noise in the world that you will probably be curious to know what can have been the cause of such an unfortunate event. I shall therefore endeavour to give you as full a relation of the whole matter as you can expect from a man who is at so great a distance from the Court as I am, and is informed of nothing but by third or fourth hand.

It seems the Prince and Princess in their familiar letters to the Duke of York and Queen of Prussia had formerly desired them to baptize the first child that the Princess should have after her coming to England, which they promised, and the Prince and Princess put them in mind of immediately after the young Prince was born. The King, knowing nothing of these engagements, which had been made without his privity, determined to stand himself, with the Duke of Newcastle and the Duchess of St. Albans. The Prince and Princess begged his Majesty to alter this resolution, but he refused, and the enemies of the Duke of Newcastle say that his Grace gave out he had carried his point against the Prince and Princess. The Prince being much out of humour with this proceeding, as soon as the christening was over, withdrew with the Duke of Newcastle into the corner of the room, and told him he was a rascal and a villain. The Duke complained to the King of this treatment, upon which the King sent the Dukes of Kent, Kingston and Roxburgh to the Prince to know whether he owned the words, which he did. On Friday the King called a Council, after which the Lord Chancellor was sent to the Prince with a writing of the King's own hand (not countersigned) requiring the Prince to remain confined in his apartment, under pain of his highest displeasure, and soon after the Vice Chamberlain brought another order that none but the Prince's own servants should be admitted to him; both these orders were obeyed.

On Saturday, the Prince writ a letter of submission to the King, and another on Sunday, both carried by Lord Lumley and both received. On Monday the Vice Chamberlain delivered to the Prince an order, written in the King's own hand, requiring him forthwith to leave St. James's, that the Princess might stay a few days longer if she pleased, that she should have leave from time to time to see her children upon application to the King, and that he would send them to see the Prince when he thought fit. Yesterday at nine o'clock at night the Prince and Princess retired to Lord Grantham's in Dover Street, in the utmost grief and disorder, the Prince cried for two hours, and the Princess swooned several times.

News Letter

[1717,] December 5, Thursday—The Lords yesterday received an appeal, and adjourned to Friday. The Commons sat last night till past eleven o'clock, and then the division concerning the words spoken by Mr. Shippen was 175 against 81. This day the Commons went into a Grand Committee on the supply, and resumed the adjourned debate about the reduction of the Army, and came to the following resolution, that the number of men of guards and garrisons for Great Britain, &c. be 16,347, including commission and non-commissioned officers; that £ 681,618 be granted for that service, and proceed to-morrow.

This night after nine o'clock, I sent by the post a letter to your Lordship with the King's relation of what has passed in the Royal Family, on the occasion of the baptism, which is a true copy of what the Secretaries are to send to the several Ministers in foreign Courts in their respective provinces. The Princess has been in great disorder since her coming from St. James's, and that which troubled her much seemed to be her being separated from the children, and to be deprived of Madame Gamin's, their gouvernante's assistance. Several physicians were called yesterday morning; after three o'clock in the afternoon she grew better, and rested indifferently well last night. They talk much of a speedy reconciliation, but some have the less expectation of success, because of the King's obstinacy and the Prince's proud temper, and of Baron Bernstorff's harsh inflexible humour, not proper for facilitating, but more inclined to exact severe conditions. Some say that they will insist for the Prince's entirely abandoning the Duke of Argyll, Earl Ilay, Viscount Townshend and Walpole, and that he take into his family only such as the King shall name or approve. They say the King did not visit the Princess since he came from Hampton Court last, nor saw her but at the Baptism, but that he visited often Madame Kilmanseck.

Yesterday, Mr. Walpole, as they say, began his speech thus: —That as he had formerly declared in the House he did now again that out and in place, he would still speak freely, let them call him Jacobite or what they pleased; and then insisted on several topics, that they might pay 16,000 men with £ 300,000 less than they do now; and having many papers in his hand said he was ready to demonstrate it, &c.: then spoke against a standing army, and proposed the number 12,000 as sufficient. Mr. Shippen spoke after, and said he was resolved to speak freely as his worthy friend had said, though they should call him a Jacobite or any thing else. He afterwards said that the King's speech was calculated more for the meridian of Germany than Great Britain, and that it was an infelicity the King was a stranger to their language and constitution. Mr. Lechmere, seconded by Sir David Dalrymple, moved for taking down his words. Then the dispute was about them. Mr. Methuen thought he said the King's speech seemed to be; Bromley and Hanmer spoke to the same purpose. Mr. Shippen, they say, allowed the words stranger to the language, but not constitution. However it was carried for these being the words, and voted that it was a reflection on the King's person and government, though some said the speech being the composition of the Ministers, it could not be construed a reflection on the King's person. General Lumley spoke for the number of 16,000 demanded by the Court, and gave his reasons. Sir Joseph Jekyll bestowed some eulogiums on him for it, and amongst other things said that Jacobitism was dwindling, and they say Mr. Shippen in answer said it was not, whereupon Sir Joseph said he was sorry for it, and that he knew that much better than he could pretend to do. Sir Joseph, Mr. Aislaby, Mr. Lechmere, and Mr. Smith were the chief speakers on the Court side. Mr. Walpole, and most if not all of his partisans voted for sending Shippen to the Tower, who supped last night with the Speaker, and was to dine with him this day, and in the ordinary time will go to the Tower. This is what is said without doors, and from second hands having not met with any of the members.

News Letter

1717, December 7. London—I sent you by last Tuesday's post a long account of the differences between the King and the Prince; I have since had an opportunity of reading the relation, which has been communicated to all the Foreign Ministers by the King's order, which is entirely to the same effect as that I sent you, only I could not but observe one passage in it which appeared to me unnecessary to the relation, yet at the same time of great consequence in itself, viz., that though the King was in the room where this outrage was committed upon the Duke of Newcastle, he was at so great a distance that he heard nothing of it, but the Duke of Newcastle thought it his duty to inform him.

Sir Clement Cottrel has by the King's order acquainted all the Foreign Ministers, that if they visit the Prince, they shall not be received at St. James's. Orders are sent to all persons who have employments both under the King and the Prince to quit one or the other. The Ladies whose husbands are in the King's service are likewise to quit the Princess's, but they are permitted to attend her during her present illness, which is very violent, and imputed wholly to her grief for this usage of the Prince and herself, and the separation from her children.

The Prince's party and Mr. Walpole's, making in all but twenty-eight, were against the standing army. There has been a discourse ever since Monday night that there was a treaty of an accommodation on foot, but the Prince told a friend of mine last night there was no such thing. The Prince is broke out in a rash.

Portland Papers, vol. V.

News Letter

[1717,] December 7. Saturday—The Lords on Wednesday received several petitions for appeals, and read a private bill, adjourned to Monday. The Prince of Wales has been feverish, kept his bed yesterday, has an inflammatory distemper, with bumps in his face, white on the head, and somewhat like a rash. The Princess continues still ill,

Portland Papers, vol. V.

has long swoons, frequent faintings, startings, and on Monday, Wednesday and Friday was violently attacked with pain and stoppage in her throat. She was cupped yesterday, and if these fits return more may be in great danger. Earl Grantham sent for Dr. Mead, Duchess St. Albans for Dr. Garth, and some sent for Sloane; the King's German physician and Sir David Hamilton are constantly with her. The Princess, they say, sent for Baron Bernstorff on Wednesday, who came there to her, he was again yesterday with her and the Prince, and was expected to be there again this day. The Princess Anne with her governess, Madam Gamine, has been with her.

There is a paragraph of Mr. Shippen's speech, handed about, which is as follows:—"I know these assertions interfere with what is laid down in the second paragraph of his Majesty's speech, but we are to consider that speech as the composition and advice of his Ministers, and are therefore at liberty to debate every proposition in it, especially those which seem rather calculated for the meridian of Germany than that of Great Britain. It is the only infelicity of his Majesty's reign that he is unacquainted with our language and constitution, and it is therefore the more incumbent on his British Ministers to inform him that our Government does not stand on the same foundation with his German dominions, which, by reason of their situation, and the nature of their constitution, are obliged to keep up standing armies in time of peace." Mr. Freeman made the motion for having Shippen's words printed. Mr. Aislaby seconded it, and said they were in the Pretender's declaration as some without doors say.

Edward Harley, junior, to Abigail Harley, at Eywood

1717–18, February 4.   Christ Church, Oxford— . . . .

To-morrow is to be the great struggle in the House of Commons, whether the army is to be under the military or the civil government; no other news stirring.

Portland Papers, vol. V.

Edward Harley, junior, to Abigail Harley, at Eywood

1717–18, February 6.   Christ Church, Oxford— . . . .

The Court were hard pushed on Tuesday, there were between four and five hundred members present, and they carried their point but by

Portland Papers, vol. V.

18. Walpole spoke very warmly against them, as did Mr. Jeffreys, for them Mr. Lechmere, Craggs, and Sir Humphrey Polesworth, the last noble Colonel, I fancy, has something more than half-pay. If the members can be persuaded to stay in town and keep together, it is thought the Court will not venture to bring in their terrible Bills this session. . . .

News Letter

[1718,] November 14, Friday— . . . .

The Lord Cowper was on Sunday with the King at Court, and on Monday with the Prince. Among other town tales, they say, the Lady Cowper being asked why her Lord left the Court, said that none could do business there with two madmen and a dragoon. In the House of Peers Sunderland managed for the Court with temper, and Stanhope with great warmth. Some say Bolingbroke is here, but many expect he will come soon. . . .

It is believed this session will be very short, and business despatched quickly. . . .

John Menzies to Lieut.-General Dillon

1718, Thursday, Nov. 13[24].— . . . .

The Parliament met on Tuesday, though many reports were spread to make it uncertain; enough to make the Tories delay their coming. . . .

Before they went further, Mr. Craggs by order laid before the House a good many treaties, but he had brought them in Latin and this created a warm and long debate. Mr. Hern said this was like the Roman Catholics saying their prayers in an unknown tongue, which we blamed so highly.

They went next to the main question, approving the measures and supporting the designs &c.

This debate lasted till 9 o'clock at night. Mr. Walpole opened the debate, and spoke long and pointedly against the Ministers, against the measures, against the action of Sir George Byng, against the war with Spain, &c. Mr. Shippen spoke often and well and with temper, having been convinced and better advised than last year. Sir William

Portland Papers, vol. V.

Historical Manuscripts Commission, *The Stuart Papers*, vol. VII (London, 1923).

Wyndham and several others of that side spoke well, and none better than General Ross. The three that bore the heat of the day for the Court were Craggs, Bladen, and Lechmere. The Court thought it fit to let the debate go on, because some considerable Whigs had joined that side, who could and would have made a terrible noise, such as Sir Joseph Jekyll, Lord Molesworth and others.

But at last the question being called for the Court carried it by 60 of majority, 215 to 155.

So now a war against Spain is certain, and it is said it will be proclaimed next week. We have this great advantage, that we knocked them down at first, and before they would imagine what would be the case. Those foreign Courts have strange short-sighted ways of thinking, and especially as to England.

The Jacobites universally are as glad in their hearts at this war as the Court is, and so for once these two agree.

In the House of Lords things went in the main much in the same manner, very long and very strenuous debates, but at last the Court carried it there also. Whilst they were in a Committee of the whole House, the majority was but 14. But when the House was resumed and what we call the full House, and where proxies take place, the Whigs had 20 proxies more than the other party, so that the majority was really 34.

The Tories are highly pleased with Mr. Walpole and his behaviour in the House, and they are brought to a better understanding than formerly by pains and good advice, but we are pretty long a seeing what is the prudentest part in this country too.

The Commons' address is just now come out, and here it is.

All, together, will give you a plain idea of our situation. Pray send all forward.

J. Menzies to the Duke of Mar

1718, Saturday, Nov. 15[26].—I trouble you with the two enclosed because I have no other way to send them and the persons concerned do not doubt of my care. From these you will have the [King's] Speech and, the Addresses and the remarks on Craggs' letter, which was the bottom and model of the Speech. I sent you some of those papers by way of Mr. Dillon with a brief and plain account of the beginning of this Parliament.

The Court has carried it in both Houses, both as to thanks or approbation for what is passed, and for support for the future.

Yet there was a great struggle, and many strong though not scurrilous speeches against the Ministry and the measures. The Court did not run into passion nor anything immoderate, but let the debates go on, both because their tail was really so deep in the well, and then several of their best Whig friends left them in this affair of a war with Spain and they were not willing totally to lose them. Such were in the House of Lords, Lord Cowper, Lord Orford, Lord Lonsdale, Lowther, &c., though this last named is a present Lord of the Bedchamber to the father, but not expected to be long so. In the House of Commons Sir Joseph Jekyll, and even the Lord Molesworth, though a most violent Republican Whig, &c.

Of the Tories a great number absent, as is usual and unaccountable, yet there is a pretty handsome number present. Of them several spoke very well against the management, against the Ministers, and against our being hurried into a war with Spain or indeed any war, when we are not able to stand upon our own legs. Some compared it to the delirious heat and strength of a poor man in a high fever, of which he is shortly to die.

But as to preventing this war into which the Court is running, they managed that point somewhat more tenderly, and struggled as having a mind to be ravished, and you would wonder to see the Jacobites as glad of this war as the Court is, which indeed they are heartily. So for once they and the Court agree.

Mr. Shippen spoke often and well to the nature of the thing but no personal reflections. In short has taken wise advice not to go to the Tower again.

Mr. Walpole spoke wonderfully home and well, no way extravagant neither, and he has got the esteem of the Tories for what is now past these two or three days, and there is like to be a good understanding as to what relates to the public good, which is all that is necessary, and in that there was never nor can there be any inconveniency. I told you how unacceptable such advices were last year, but *præstat sero* [better late than never].

The Court will carry their main design, which is war, by which the Emperor may be served and aggrandized, and many of themselves get more money. But there may be frequent disputes and struggles in Parliament as to the supplies and other material points, especially if more Tories come, and those that are here do stay, which no man on earth can answer for.

Hugh Thomas to the Duke of Mar

1718, Dec. 18 [29]. London.—Last Tuesday we had an express from the Regent [of France], who demands of us 10,000 men, on which an extraordinary Council was immediately called, where it was resolved to send them with all speed and to proclaim war against Spain the next day, which was accordingly done with all the usual solemnity. Whilst this was doing, a most violent debate arose in the House of Commons about addressing his Majesty to thank him for entering into this just war &c., which was opposed by Mr. Pulteney, the two Walpoles, Shippen, Hungerford and others with exceeding great heat. The debate lasted till near 7 p.m., but it was carried by 167 to 107, a vast majority. It was a little surprising that Sir Joseph Jekyll, who had formerly voted against the war, now voted and spoke for the Address. This makes the Tories all mad, and they call them courtiers, broken City merchants and officers but, before we have done with them, we shall make them yet more mad. To-day the bill for annulling the Acts against Occasional Conformity and against the growth of Schism was to be read a second time in the House of Lords, where the debates were so hot that the House was sitting at 7:30 p.m., so that how it went we know not, but doubtless for the bill by a great majority. This with the Declaration of War will make a total change of affairs. A Royal Visitation of both Universities is very much talked of and other great alterations in the Church.

WHIG PRINCIPLES ASSERTED

Chapter XIV
Church and State

After resuming the office of Secretary of State in the spring of 1718 Stanhope, though mainly concerned with foreign affairs, still took a leading part in measures designed to establish Whig principles in Church and State. The condition of the Church, bigoted and essentially Tory if not Jacobite at heart, gave cause for anxiety; the Universities, especially Oxford, were the homes of a very restricted learning and of a very abundant disloyalty; the Protestant Dissenters, as a body the

Stuart Papers, vol. VII.

Basil Williams, *Stanhope: A Study in Eighteenth-Century War and Diplomacy* (Oxford, 1932).

most devoted adherents of the new dispensation, were kept in a state of political impotence and restricted in their religious observances by intolerant laws; while the savage code against the Roman Catholics made them almost pariahs in the community and was little short of an incitement to rebellion. Here was ample scope for reform to a man of Stanhope's passionate sense of religious toleration. Hardly less important seemed to him reforms needed in the constitution. He had never forgotten or forgiven Oxford's abuse of the royal prerogative in 1711 when he created twelve peers at once to secure his control of the House of Lords; and was so impressed by the dangers of an early election that he seems to have meditated an indefinite prolongation of the Septennial Parliament. The two reforms he had specially at heart were, first the repeal of the special disabilities of Protestant Dissenters carried by the last Tory government, and second to make it impossible for such action as Oxford's to be repeated. The opportunity of dealing with these questions did not come till the 1718–20 sessions, when Bills were presented to restore privileges of which the Dissenters had been deprived and drastically to limit the King's right of creating peers. The first of these measures was passed, though in less tolerant form than Stanhope had designed; on the second he suffered his most serious defeat.

§ 1. *Dissenters' Privileges.* The Corporation, Uniformity and Test Acts of Charles II's reign were intended, among other things, to exclude all those not conforming with the Established Church of England from state or municipal offices and from the teaching profession. After the Revolution, which had been zealously supported by Protestant Dissenters, the Toleration Act of 1689 had modified in their favour certain provisions of these and other Acts, so far as the exercise of their religion and their license to teach was concerned. But the bar to state or municipal office still remained. The practice, however, had grown up among Protestant Dissenters of qualifying themselves for office by taking the Sacrament in church once before election, as the law required, and then relapsing to the services of their Dissenting chapels. In 1711 this form of evasion had been stopped by the Occasional Conformity Act, whereby office holders were forbidden to attend chapel services on penalty of a heavy fine and loss of office. Many of the leading Whigs had unfortunately compromised themselves by voting for this measure as a bribe to its chief advocate Nottingham to oppose the preliminaries of Utrecht. But Stanhope, who in 1711 was a prisoner in Spain, had no such backsliding on his conscience, and had given ample proof of his tolerant attitude in the debates on the Schism Act of 1714, which disabled Dissenters from teaching in schools. The Schism Act had never been anything but a dead letter, since the Tories had gone out before they could put it into operation and the Whigs had never enforced it: but it still remained on the statute book and might be revived, while the Occasional Conformity Act was a definite grievance. The Dissenters naturally felt that, in consideration of their loyal support of the Protestant Succession, the least the Whigs could do for them was to repeal these two obnoxious Acts. George I and his ministers were also anxious to retain their support and early in the reign had employed a certain J. Barrington Shute to conciliate the Nonconformists and even to induce them to take commissions on the Irish establishment in spite of the penalties they thereby incurred. As early as March 1717 Stanhope, Sunderland, the Lord Chancellor Cowper and Bernstorff had met to consider the repeal of the Occasional Conformity Act and also a Bill for the reform of the Universities, two measures upon which Stanhope and Sunderland declared the King had set his heart. All seem to have agreed on the repeal, but were not fully decided on the best time for moving in the matter; they also wished to sound the Archbishop as to the views of the Church. In the same month the Dissenters' grievances were referred to in the House of Commons, and a meeting of some 200 members of Parliament was held at the Rose Tavern, near Temple Bar, to discuss the repeal of the two Tory Acts. At this meeting Stanhope himself was present and pronounced in favour of early action, but found many of his supporters doubtful whether the time was opportune.

There were indeed difficulties, which no prudent government could overlook, in reviving ecclesiastical controversy in any new form. Only seven years before the Whigs had burned their fingers badly over the Sacheverell trial and were quite alive to the risks they ran in once more stirring up the ominous cry of 'the Church in danger'. Bolingbroke, then particularly anxious to ingratiate himself with the ministry, wrote to Stair in 1717,

> I am a little apprehensive of the effect which any measures in favour of the dissenters may have among the honestest of the Torys, those who [are not] Jacobites,

and in a later letter he declared that

> if the ministers are driven into the repeal of the Occasional Bill, they will raise a cursed storm. A multitude of Torys who are not for the Pretender, and who may be render'd as affectionate as any men in Brittain to the King's service, will be shock'd att it.

Recently, too, the religious unrest, chronic for nearly a century, had found new expression in the Bangorian controversy. This controversy was between Hoadly, the former Whig pamphleteer, now Bishop of Bangor, and his more orthodox opponents, who attacked his latitudinarian views on the authority of the Church and the rights of dissent as a direct blow, not only against the Church, but against revealed religion itself. In 1716 Hoadly inaugurated the controversy by his pamphlet with the provocative title, *A Preservative against the Principles of the Non-Jurors*. In March of the following year he expounded his views more fully in a sermon preached before the King and published by authority. This sermon in its day caused as much of a sensation as the *Essays and Reviews* of a later generation. During the spring and summer of 1717 nearly a hundred pamphlets poured from the press to support or refute the audacious bishop's views; and so heated became the controversy that for two days, it was said, no business could be done in the City. The Non-jurors, too, who refused to recognize bishops or clergy false to their oath of allegiance to the old dynasty, were a body still to be reckoned with. They had many sympathizers in the ranks of the established clergy, especially at Oxford, and even on the bench of bishops, which included the formidable Atterbury, the Jacobite Dean of Westminster and Bishop of Rochester. Thus all the elements were present for a revival of the cry of 'the Church in danger', so powerful an instrument in 1710 in the hands of the Tories against the Whigs and their allies the Dissenters.

One of the chief centres of disturbance in ecclesiastical affairs was Convocation. Since 1664 this body had lost its ancient right of voting its own subsidies to the King, and, for the next twenty-five years, though still formally summoned at the same time as Parliament, did not actually sit. In 1689 William III allowed it to discuss his scheme for a Comprehension of Protestant Dissenters, but was so much disgusted with its intolerance on that occasion that it was not again called together for business till 1700, as a result of the vehement Convocation controversy started by Atterbury in 1697. Since then it had again met regularly to discuss Church discipline and kindred matters, but had proved impracticable and highly troublesome. The upper house, composed of bishops, was fairly amenable to government influence, but the lower house, inspired by men like Atterbury to claim rights in the ecclesiastical sphere parallel with and independent of Parliament, was a constant source of disturbance. In the spring of 1717 it took upon itself to pass motions condemning Hoadly for his heretical opinions and was on the point of sending them up to the bishops for their assent, when, to avoid the scandal and end the en-venomed controversy, Convocation was prorogued till the following November. The Pretender took occasion to issue a manifesto protesting against the 'Elector's' unconstitutional action and asserting that lasting security for Church and State would never be obtained until he him-self was restored: but the manifesto somehow fell flat. Thereafter, though Convocation continued to be formally summoned at the same time as Parliament, letters of business empowering it to meet were issued only once for over a century. This drastic action was surpris-ingly successful in clearing the air. The bishops of course still had a voice in Parliament, where they could look after the interests of their flocks, if they were so minded: but the bishops of the eighteenth century, when the Whigs' supremacy had been well established, gave little trouble to the dominant power in the state, depending on it as they did for their elevation to the bench or translation to wealthier dioceses. On the other hand, the clergy of the lower house, many of whom were inclined to use Convocation purely for political purposes or for illiberal attacks on dissenting brethren and more enlightened bishops such as Burnet, Hoadly and Gibson, were deprived of one of their most dangerous weapons. However honest may have been this opposition, it was not to be supposed that a statesman of Stanhope's knowledge and breadth of view should suffer it to endanger the Protes-tant Succession or to cripple the Dissenters, who were among the most valuable and active of English citizens. When Convocation was again allowed to do business in the nineteenth century, the clergy returned to their proper function of considering the moral and spiritual duties of their order and their Church.

It was high time indeed that the leading Protestant state in Europe should make a demonstration in favour of religious toleration. Though more than half a century had passed since the treaties of Westphalia had brought to an end the last so-called religious war and purported to hold the scales even between Protestants and Catholics, religious toleration still played but a small part in European politics. In England there was growing alarm at the recrudescence of religious persecution on the Continent and the tendency of Protestant rulers to revert to Catholicism. Huguenots in France were still being sent to the galleys in spite of Louis XIV's assurances to Queen Anne, and even after the Triple Alliance only a few were grudgingly released on Stair's repre-sentations to the Regent. In Germany a new Catholic reaction ap-peared to have set in. In spite of England's protests the clauses of the Treaty of Ryswick which violated the *cujus regio ejus religio* principle of Westphalia had never been repudiated by either France or the Emperor. The Elector of Saxony, still officially the director of the Protestant states in the Diet, had embraced Catholicism as a means of retaining in his family the crown of Catholic Poland: in 1717 his son, the electoral prince, raised a flutter in the Protestant chanceries of Europe by making a pilgrimage to Rome, where, in spite of Sunderland's well-meant endeavours to waylay him with plausible Protestants, he also found salvation. In Poland five Protestant churches were destroyed by Roman Catholic mobs in 1718, and the Roman Catholic clergy were depriving Protestant congregations of their treaty privileges for the exercise of their worship and the education of their children. The Reformed sects were persecuted in the electorate of Mainz and the bishopric of Spires; while in the Palatinate, once a famous stronghold of Calvinism, the Elector's persecuting zeal became so outrageous and his language was so insulting in answer to the protests of the English agent Haldane that Haldane had to be recalled. Complaints were sent to the Emperor and even reprisals made by George as Elector and the King of Prussia against the Catholics in their dominions. In 1720 both Houses of Parliament sent up strong addresses, supported in the Lords by Stanhope, against such treatment of German Protestants. An edict from the Emperor himself in November of that year calling on the Elector Palatine to redress the grievances of his Protestant subjects did not finally dispose of the question. In England, it is true, the penal laws against Roman Catholics were still exceedingly drastic, but as Carteret said, defending the fines imposed on Roman Catholics after the discovery of the Jacobite plot in 1722, 'there is nothing so alien to the spirit of this nation than persecution for the sake of religion', and there was some excuse for this severity in the country's recent experience of James II, in the dependence of the Pretender on the Pope and Catholic Powers and in the large numbers of Jacobite recruits found in the Roman Catholic community. For the legal exclusion of Protestant Dissenters from official life there was no such excuse. Apart from any question of justice, the elementary motives of political security, as Stanhope wisely saw, made it expedient to remove all sense of grievance from the Protestant Dissenters and make them wholehearted allies of the existing system, especially at a time when Catholic activities on the Continent were causing alarm to all those of the Reformed religion who looked for help from England, the chief Protestant power.

Stanhope himself took charge of the measure for relieving Dissenters of their disabilities. Nursed as he had been on the pure milk of Locke's principles of toleration, he was manifestly well fitted to clear away

some of the worst abuses of the penal code; and in this task he had
the King for a staunch ally. George I was not usually much interested
in the purely internal affairs of his kingdom, but, having stout Lutheran
convictions and being deeply concerned in all questions affecting Protestantism, he had already promised the Dissenters that their grievances
should be remedied. Such support was all the more welcome, since
Stanhope could no longer count on the help of Walpole and his dissatis-
fied section of the Whigs even for a measure which seemed implicit in
the most fundamental Whig doctrines and was to be directed against a
policy that Walpole himself had opposed. In the King's speech of
November 1717 a promise had been made, in view of the alarming
attacks on Protestantism on the Continent, to 'strengthen the Protestant interest' at home, a promise naturally criticized by the Tory
Shippen, but almost as coldly received by Walpole in his new zeal for
Stanhope's Tory opponents. The bishops, too, were gathering their
forces against toleration to Nonconformists. There was indeed a small
minority among them, of whom Gibson of Lincoln, Hoadly of Bangor
and White Kennett of Peterborough were the most prominent, prepared for a genuine policy of toleration. But Wake, the Archbishop
of Canterbury, though he had originally voted against the Occasional
Conformity and Schism Acts, was now against their repeal; and
among the most vigorous opponents of a change were the fiery Bishop
Nicolson of Carlisle and Trelawney of Winchester, both in their
younger days counted among the more liberal Churchmen. Trelawney
boasted that of the twenty-six bishops on the bench twenty were
ready to oppose repeal and was convinced that "if the phanatigs can
get a bill to their minds, farewell to episcopacy. The corporations
must be kept as they are or the phanatigs by their own money and
the government's will have a parliament which will do our business
at once'; while Nicolson exercised all his considerable talents for
lobbying against what he called the 'Readmission of Occasional Hy-
pocrisy'. Manningham of Chichester went so far as to hope for the
failure of Stanhope's Mediterranean policy, as that would depress the
Whigs, 'then the poor Church may sleep a little longer with all its
Errors and Defects and Parents may be allowed to teach y^r children the
Catechism without usurping an authority over Xt.' Even the Chancellor
Cowper, though opposed to the Occasional Conformity Act, was luke-
warm on the question of admitting Dissenters to office. Nor would
Sunderland himself go so far as Stanhope, who was for doing away
with the genuine scandal of using the Sacrament simply as a form of
admission to office by boldly repealing the Test and Corporation Acts
in so far as they affected Protestant Dissenters. At any rate the pros-

pects of obtaining a majority for the measure in 1717 seemed so doubt-ful that it was postponed to the following year.

. . .

The measure he submitted went beyond Bolingbroke's worst appre-hensions, for it not only provided for the repeal of the Occasional Conformity Act as well as the Schism Act, but even proposed to re-lease Protestant Dissenters, in case the incumbent made a difficulty, from the obligation of taking the Sacrament at all in an Established Church on assuming office: in other words, without formally repealing them—a concession to Sunderland's scruples—the measure would have made a breach in the Test and Corporation Acts, then and for over a century longer regarded as the main bulwark of England's happy Establishment. This last provision illustrates Stanhope's practical and enlightened tolerance; it was also the best rejoinder to the Tories' strongest argument in favour of the Occasional Conformity Act, since it proposed to absolve Dissenters from the need of taking the Sacra-ment in an Established Church, a form meaningless to them and in-sulting to those who held the beliefs of the Church of England. In his opening speech Stanhope enlarged on the equity and advantage of restoring their natural rights to the Dissenters and of easing them from the stigmatizing and oppressive laws passed in more turbulent times and obtained by indirect methods: their zeal, as he said, for the Revolution and the Protestant Succession deserved no less. Then in a fine peroration he predicted that this relief would make for the union of all true Protestants and strengthen the Church of England itself, for the Church would still remain the head of all Protestant churches and the Archbishop of Canterbury be regarded as the patri-arch of the Protestant clergy throughout the world.

. . . The Bill passed a second reading by 86 to 68; but in committee Stanhope, in deference to Sunderland's fears that those clauses would not get through the Commons, did not insist on them against Cowper's amendment to expunge them. In the House of Commons Walpole, who, it was said, 'bore harder against the Court than any Tory durst attempt to do', once more opposed the relief to Dissenters on the flimsy ground that 'there were people enough to fill all offices without capacitating any more disqualified'. He even went so far in his party rage as to suggest that Stanhope's original clause, 'that would in a scandalous manner have evaded the Test Act', showed the ministry's sinister designs and would be a 'handle' to the disaffected who would inculcate into the minds of the people that many of the measures which occasioned an unfortunate prince's abdication were now renewed'. He laid himself open, however, to a telling attack from Lechmere for abandoning his former convictions, and did not even carry all his usual supporters with him into the lobby. Accordingly the Bill was passed by a majority of 41.

Stanhope, no doubt, could hardly do otherwise than yield to Sunderland's fears about the Test Act clauses, for the general feeling of the community was probably not misrepresented by Bolingbroke when he wrote to Stair:

> Should the test or the Act of Uniformity be medled with, I much apprehend the immediate consequence, and should any immediate disorder be prevented the certain seeds of future disorder will be sown.

Thus all the grace and statesmanlike liberality of his original proposal to give the Dissenters full civil rights were thrown away. For after Cowper's amendment had been carried, the Act for Strengthening the Protestant Interest merely left them in exactly the same position as they were before 1711, allowed to evade the spirit of the law if they had once taken the Sacrament before election.

A Tory Success?

[Note: The three letters of Edward Harley to Abagail Harley at Eywood are taken from the *Portland Papers*, vol. V—Ed.]

> 1718, December 25—The Church Bill was read a third time on Monday or Tuesday, I am not certain which; it was passed without a division. It consisted of three parts when presented by Lord Stanhope, the first repealed the obligation of taking the Sacrament upon entering into an office, the second takes away that clause of the Occasional Bill, which made it penal for one in station to appear at a conventicle, the third repeals the whole Schism Bill. Such warm opposition was made the second day that Lord Sunderland himself proposed the waiving the first part, and afterwards owned that it had never been part of the Bill, unless the Bishops of Gloucester, Lincoln, and Bangor had declared they would not appear for the Bill without it. I have here enclosed a list of those bishops who voted for and against the Bill.
>
> Upon the reading of the Bill a third time, Lord Nottingham offered a clause to be added to it to prevent the growth of Socinianism, that no one should be admitted into any place

without subscribing to the Articles of Faith, particularly that relating to the divinity of our Saviour, and to profess his belief of the Scriptures contained in the Old and New Testament. Lord Nottingham, Lord Oxford, Lord Anglesea, and the two Archbishops spoke for this, Lords Stanhope, Sunderland, Ilay against it. All the bishops that voted for the Church Bill voted against this clause, and to these came over Lichfield and Coventry, so that they threw it out. Well may they strip the Church and her members of her authority when they divest the head of both of His Divinity. Lord Nottingham read a letter from Exeter in the House which I have enclosed, and to which I refer you. I hope it will be published and spread over the kingdom, that people's eyes may be opened, and that no more poor souls may be deluded by these ignorant, fanatical infidels.

1718–19, January 8—Both Houses met yesterday. The Commons read the Church Bill a second time, upon which was a very warm and long debate. Hanmer, Jeffreys, Shippen, &c., spoke admirably well against it, as did several others. Upon a division the Bill was carried by 41 (an ominous number), 202 against it, 243 for it. The Prince was in the gallery. Several Whigs voted against it, among which was Wallop of the Treasury. The Court are very angry at the Speaker, they have something which is not yet known in agitation against him; it is thought they will endeavour to remove him from the chair by sending him to the house of Peers, or by some other way that is worse.

It is talked that Cadogan will be out, and Argyll put in. Bolingbroke's business is again revived. The Bishop of Rochester went to Court to compliment the Monarch on New Year's day. The meaning of several steps this prelate has lately taken are as yet a mystery, though people give shrewd guesses.

1718–19, January 11—I have no other news but a further account of the debate in the House of Commons upon the Church Bill, to send my dear aunt by this post. Sir Thomas Hanmer, Mr. Jeffreys, Mr. Shippen, Cousin Tom Palmer, Mr. Snell, and Mr. Strangeways with several others are allowed by everybody to have distinguished themselves very handsomely against the Bill, but Walpole bore harder upon the Court than any Tory durst attempt to do. He began with his reasons that made him against repealing the Bill, the passing of which he had formerly opposed. He said the Occasional Bill passed at a time when the Ministry seemed to intend some hardships to them, and that he thought that Act only a prelude to the abrogating their toleration, but that now this Bill had been brought into the other House by the chief of the Ministry with a clause in it that would in a scandalous manner have evaded the Test Act, which, though it was dropped, was a sufficient reason to discover their designs; that this would give a general alarm to the nation, and a great handle to the disaffected, who would inculcate into the minds of the people that many of the measures which occasioned an unfortunate prince's abdication were now renewed; that whereas the suspension of the penal laws and test was laid to that King's charge, he had mentioned before how the Test Act had been lately struck at; that whereas he was accused of seizing charters, there had been lately a debate in Westminster Hall for ten days together, the result of which might have laid most of the Corporations at their mercy; that the Ecclesiastical Commission had been declared illegal; that if fame might be credited there was a design of visiting the Universities. He desired them to remember that a noble Lord who presided in that King's councils, and was excepted out of an Act of Grace for it, was afterwards at the head of King William's affairs, and the reason assigned for this second station was, that he had persuaded his former master to those measures that ended in his ruin, but he hoped nobody set him as a pattern now. That he thought there were people enough to fill all offices without capacitating any more disqualified, and put the case, suppose a Secretary of State, either wearied with business or through restlessness of temper, desired to lay down, there was no occasion for sending abroad for one to succeed him, though he might be never so true a penitent, but that there might be found at home some man of abilities enough for that station (by which you will easily perceive he glanced at Bolingbroke, and does not favour his return). He concluded that to their comfort the heir of the crown could see the ill consequences of this, though the Ministry did not, and had openly protested against it.

When it was urged in the debate in relation to the Schism Bill that it was unnatural to deprive parents of the education of their children, Shippen said, since it was now the case of the greatest subject in England, he did not see why others should complain. The Tories made so brave a stand that it is thought the victory is of little use to the conquerors. The majority it was carried by I sent you in my last. Some of Walpole's party left him, though others not expected joined him, particularly Lords Castlecomer and Hinchinbroke, Mr. Wallop, Mr. Smith, Sir Robert Worseley, Sir John Cope, Governor Pitt and his eldest son, only four Scotch of the losing side. This account I send you from a letter I received from London on Friday.

§ 2. *The Universities.* Closely connected with the state of the Church and religion was that of the two English Universities. Cambridge was the more loyal of the two and, in spite of the Oxford gibe about the King finding it necessary to send books to Cambridge when he sent a squadron of horse to Oxford in 1715, seems to have maintained a somewhat higher standard of learning; but it was also suspect for High Church proclivities and distracted from its proper functions by the resounding quarrels of Bentley with his Fellows at Trinity and by the general want of discipline in other colleges. Oxford, however, was the real thorn to the government. Ormonde had been its Chancellor till he fled to France and was immediately replaced by his Tory brother, Arran. During the Rebellion it had needed a garrison to keep it quiet, and a college Fellow such as Thomas Hearne, who always spoke of George I as the Duke of Brunswick, was typical of its spirit. The King's birthday on 28 May and Restoration Day on the 29th were equally occasions for the riotous display of Jacobite sentiment. Dr. Ayliffe, a Fellow of New College, was deprived of his degrees and expelled for venturing to attack the Toryism and scandals of Oxford common-rooms. Nor is there any exaggeration in the following unvarnished description of University politics sent by one of the rare Oxford Whigs to the nephew of Wake's predecessor Tenison 'at Lamb-Hith'.

> Reverend Sir,*
> You cannot be ignorant of the deplorable condition of the University of Oxford, in which there is an entire opposition to His Majesty and his government, and that which is most to be lamented is, this being the nursery of above one half of the clergymen of this kingdom, the principles of rebellion are diffused from hence through the whole nation, and those which should watch over and cure others are infected themselves. If our light becomes darkness, how great is our darkness. Perhaps you may say as soon as once the rebellion is blown over, they will come to themselves, grow wiser, and return to their duty; but you are utterly mistaken, if these be your thoughts, for principles of opposition have taken deeper root than you or any other person else can imagine, that is not conversant here upon the spot.
>
> Rebellion is avowedly owned and encouraged, and he that does not run into the same excess is treated with all the contempt and scorn that they pour forth on him. Some tutors read lectures to their pupils on hereditary right, etc. And there

*Punctuation, etc., in this and the letter that follows revised by the editor.

Williams, *Stanhope.*

are several houses in which there's not so much as one (what they please to call) a Whig. There are but three houses, viz. Wadham, Jesus and Merton, whose heads are not violent Tories and Jacobites. Merton stands fairest for a cure, as having as yet several sound members left among them. But these will soon be overwhelmed with a great majority if there be not yet some care taken. Whether the government and His Grace your uncle ought not a little to look into this matter I leave you to judge. . . . [After setting out the chances for the election of Whig Fellows at Merton and stating that the Warden, though a Whig with two votes, is weak, and that, of the existing Fellows, five only are Whigs and the remaining eight Tories, one 'fierce' and another 'violent,' he proceeds:] There must be some persons who are clothed both with power and interest to bring this about. Sir, this is a matter of so much consequence that it should be worth the government's while to look after it. The peace of the kingdom does in a great measure depend upon amending the University for one of these things must lose his crown, or this University must be reformed. . . . Your humble servant

November 27th, 1715   J. R[ussell]

So great, indeed, was the scandal that some of the Universities' best friends felt that stringent measures must be taken.

. . . a Bill was actually drawn up in 1717, the effect of which would have been to deprive for a term of years the Universities and their component colleges of all rights of appointment and patronage; these rights during that period were to be vested in royal commissioners with very wide powers of enforcing their decisions; even the present Chancellors were to be removable at the King's pleasure and their successors appointed by the Crown. The reasons given in the preamble for these extreme measures were that it is

. . . notorious that many in those nurseries dedicated to religion, learning, loyalty and peace have been infected with principles of sedition. Riots and tumults have disturbed the peace of the universities and affronted the government; the offenders have been concealed or at least not detected and duly brought to punishment . . . and yet there can be no reasonable expectation of enjoying peace and tranquillity for any long time if the youth of the nobility and gentry, especially such as are designed for holy orders, are infected with false principles utterly inconsistent with our happy establishment in church and state.

The mere rumour of this drastic measure created a flutter in the Oxford and Cambridge dovecots and in Tory circles in London. . . .

This measure, if administered for a limited period by wise commissioners, might possibly have improved the low political and educational ideas of the Universities, but in the long run would have proved most pernicious. For, once in the grip of the State, the Universities would never have escaped from it and might have become mere forcing-grounds for supporters of the government. Stanhope himself appears to have taken no active part in drafting it, but he welcomed it and adopted it as part of his programme of reforms intended to establish the Protestant dynasty on a firmer basis. In 1719, when he had schemes in view affecting both Lords and Commons, his intention was to combine these schemes with this Bill to reform the Universities. But with the failure of the other schemes University reform also fell to the ground. For over a century the only innovations at Oxford and Cambridge, due chiefly to Gibson with the political support of Townshend, were the institution of twelve Whitehall Preachers from each University in 1723 and of the Regius Professorships in 1724. The preachers were to be chosen from among the Fellows for their scholarship and gifts of exposition and were to form a link between the administration and the Universities. Naturally good Whigs were at first picked out and from their ranks promotions to the Bench were often made. The main function of the Regius Professors of History at Oxford and Cambridge was intended to be the training of young men for the diplomatic or civil service, not only in history but in foreign languages. These measures may have done something to bring the Universities into closer touch with the public life of the country. The alarm created by the Universities Bill and the redoubled zeal of such Visitors as Trelawney in suppressing flagrant rebellion may also have had some temporary effect. But if so, it was evanescent. Thirty-five years later Pitt, taking up an allusion to Oxford as a broody hen, remarked:

> I know such a hen, I was bred under such an one, and will tell the House what she has been doing these twenty years;—raising a succession of treason—there never was such a seminary; and we must not be too sure that all she hatched would ever entirely forget what she had taught them.

GROWTH OF THE ENGLISH PEERAGE

When James I ascended the throne in 1603, the peerage numbered 59. The growth of the English peerage during his reign and those of his successors is as follows:

	CREATED	BECAME EXTINCT	NET GAIN
James I	62	17	45
Charles I	59	21	38
Charles II	64	53	11
James II	8	8	0
William III and Mary	30	21	9
Anne	30	24	6
George I	20	10	10
	273	154	119

Thus the English peerage in 1719 numbered 178.

Table adapted from Abel Boyer, ed., *The Political State of Great Britain, for the month of March 1719*, vol. XVII (London, 1719).

III
THE ISSUES

With the first introduction of the Peerage Bill into the House of Lords, the deep-rooted strife between the Whig factions came to a head. The controversy concerning the merits of that Bill we are able to follow on three levels: in Parliament, in the press, and, privately, in correspondence. As in the preceding section, we draw upon the labors of Coxe and the Historical Manuscript Commission; in addition, several letters are included from other sources, identified in the citations. An important exchange of letters between Stanhope and Newcastle, published in Williams's *Stanhope*, is reprinted in modernized form.

Clearly the flood of pamphlet literature which followed the introduction of the Peerage Bill played a considerable role in securing its ultimate defeat. Some of the ablest pens in England scribbled into the fray: Addison and Steele contended, with increasing rancor, over the likely results of restricting the size of the peerage. Each is represented with two pamphlets; the reader is referred to the collection of Addison's works for the final efforts, which, however, add little to what is printed here. Their debate is introduced by a selection from Dr. Johnson's *Life of Addison* depicting the circumstances of their quarrel. The other two pamphlets included here were widely circulated, in part because of the force of argumentation, but possibly also because they were ascribed to Robert Walpole himself. W. T. Laprade in his *Public*

Opinion and Politics in Eighteenth Century England (New York, 1936) contends, however, that the author was in fact John Trenchard, one of the most active of the Whig pamphleteers and the co-editor of a weekly periodical, *The Independent Whig*. Walpole's recent and authoritative biographer, J. H. Plumb, continues to ascribe to Walpole the two pamphlets, which he characterizes as probably the best of his career. Though the student can hardly settle this point, he will be better able to evaluate the issues involved if he reads carefully Betty Kemp's recent treatment of the financial relations between the king and Parliament.

Included to shed full light upon the parliamentary proceedings which sealed the fate of the Peerage Bill is the full text of the debates both in the House of Lords and the House of Commons, as they were reconstructed in the early nineteenth century from contemporary materials. In a long and active career in which he played many roles, William Cobbett (1762–1835), a radical journalist and some-time politician, assembled material bearing upon the proceedings of Parliament from its earliest times to 1803, when more regular practices of recording debates were established. His sources for the early eighteenth century are quite full, but one must not assume that he compiled a literal record of verbatim proceedings. Some speakers are given little or no attention, and Cobbett's order of speakers is not always reliable. Yet his achievement, like that of Coxe, was immense, and we stand in his debt for the records of parliamentary proceedings in those many centuries when Parliament desired no such records to be kept.

As is the case with any major ministerial defeat, a variety of explanations followed upon the Peerage Bill's demise. Some of these, both close to, and decades removed from, the events of 1719, are printed in the concluding pages of this book; they may be regarded as denouement. Finally a selection from a nineteenth-century historian, Viscount Mahon, is included, so that the student may compare his own views on the Peerage Bill with those of a scholar deeply interested in the constitutional implications of the

Bill, who was, incidentally, the great-great-grandson of the Bill's strenuous advocate, Earl Stanhope.

The student is cautioned against extrapolating Walpole's rise to power from these events; as J. H. Plumb has shown, that course was a difficult and complicated one in which accident and luck entered. Plumb holds as well that his emergence was a triumph of character; that character emerges clearly in the course of these documents.

PARLIAMENTARY DEBATE AND CORRESPONDENCE, FEBRUARY–APRIL 1719

Debate in the Lords on the State of the Peerage.] February 28. The Duke of Somerset rose, and represented, that the number of Peers being, of late years, very much increased, especially since the Union of the two kingdoms, it seemed absolutely necessary to fix the same, both to preserve the dignity of Peerage, and to prevent the inconveniencies that may attend the creation of a great number of Peers to serve a present purpose, of which they had a remarkable instance in the late reign: he therefore moved for the bringing in a Bill to settle and limit the Peerage, in such a manner, "That the number of English Peers should not be enlarged beyond six above the present number, which upon failure of male issue might be supplied by new creations: That instead of the Sixteen elective peers in Scotland, 25 be made hereditary on the part of that kingdom, whose number, upon failure of heirs male, should be supplied by some other Scotch peers."

The Duke of Argyle seconded this motion; which was also backed by the earls of Sunderland and Carlisle; but the last of these added, That this was a matter of so great importance, that it became the wisdom of that august assembly maturely to consider of it, before they came to any Resolution; and thereupon his lordship moved, "That a day may be appointed, for the House to be in a Committee, to take into consideration the present State of the Peerage of Great Britain."

The Earl of Oxford excepted against the duke of Somerset's proposal, and among other things, said, That as it tended to take away the brightest gem from the crown, it was matter of wonder to see it supported by those, who, by the great employments they enjoyed, seemed under the strictest obligation to take care of the royal prerogative; that therefore there must be a secret meaning in this motion; that for his own part, though he expected nothing from the crown, yet he would never give his vote for lopping off so valuable a branch of the prerogative, because this would put it out of the power of the crown to reward merit and virtuous actions. To this

The Earl of Sunderland answered, That though the number of peers were limited, yet the crown would still be the fountain of honour, and preserve its prerogative of creating new Peers, upon the extinction of old titles, for want of male issue, which happened frequently; and that those extinctions would give the prince on the throne sufficient op-

William Cobbett, ed., *The Parliamentary History of England from the Earliest Period to the Year 1803*, vol. VII (London, 1811).

portunities to bestow honours upon commoners of distinguished merit
and abilities. His lordship concluded with backing the earl of Carlisle's
motion, and no member opposing it, the debate was adjourned accordingly, till the second of March; for which day the Lords were
summoned.

The King's Message relating to the Peerage.] March 2. Earl Stanhope
delivered to the House the following Message from the King.

"G. R.

"His majesty being informed, that the House of Peers have under
consideration the state of the Peerage of Great Britain, is graciously
pleased to acquaint this House, that he has so much at heart the
settling the Peerage of the whole kingdom, upon such a foundation,
as may secure the freedom and constitution of parliament in all
future ages, that he is willing his prerogative stand not in the way of
so great and necessary a work."

Further Debate in the Lords on the State of the Peerage.] Then a
motion being made for an Address of Thanks for the said Message,
    The Earl of Nottingham excepted against it, saying, It was unusual
for the king to take notice of any thing depending in parliament, before the same was laid before his majesty in a parliamentary way.
    The Duke of Buckingham over-ruled this objection, and said, It
could not be supposed, that the king alone should be ignorant of what
every body else knew; and that since his majesty was pleased, for the
good of his subjects, to suffer his prerogative to be restrained, they
ought readily to accept, and thankfully to acknowledge so great and
so gracious a condescension.
    Hereupon it was agreed, without dividing, to present an Address of
Thanks to his majesty; but some words having passed between the
earls of Sunderland and Oxford about this extraordinary Message, the
House thought fit to interpose, and require from them, that the whole
affair should go no farther, and the intended debate was adjourned to
the next day.
    March 3. The Lords, in a committee of the whole House, of which
the earl of Clarendon was chairman, took into consideration the present State of the Peerage of Great Britain.
    The Earl of Sunderland ran over the several changes that have
happened in the Peerage since the reign of queen Elizabeth to this

time; urging the necessity of limiting the number of peers, and demonstrated the advantage of the scheme proposed by the duke of Somerset.

Earl Cowper endeavoured to shew, that what was intended to be done, with relation to the Scots peerage, was a manifest violation of the Treaty of Union, and the highest piece of injustice; for it was no less than to deprive persons of their right without being heard, and without any pretence of forfeiture upon their part, urging, That the Scots peers, who should be excluded from the number of the twenty five hereditary, would be in a worse condition than any other subjects, since they would neither be electing nor elected, neither representing nor represented, which could not fail of raising dangerous discontents amongst them; that, besides, it would be a breach of trust in those who represented the Scots peerage, wholly to divest their principals of a power, with which they had entrusted them only for a few years; and therefore his lordship was of opinion, that the Scots peers ought to have been consulted, before any steps were made in so nice and so important an affair.

These objections were replied to by the earls of Sunderland and Stanhope, Cholmondeley and Poulet, the dukes of Buckingham and Newcastle, the bishop of Gloucester, and some other English lords, who were supported by several Scots peers, particularly the dukes of Roxburgh and Montrose, the marquis of Annandale, and the earl of Ilay. In the first place, it was alledged, That the settling the peerage in the manner proposed, was rather a benefit than a disadvantage to the Scots peerage, whose representatives were thereby increased by nine, and all made hereditary; and as for those peers who for the present would be excluded, they would afterwards have a chance to come in, upon failure of any of the twenty-five: That this regulation could not be looked upon as a violation of the Union, two things only being made unalterable fundamentals of that contract, viz. religion, and the proportion of public taxes: to prove which, several Articles of the Act of Union were read: and that the consulting of the Scots peers in this affair, would be altogether improper and unparliamentary, and attended with great inconveniencies.

The Earl of Ilay, in particular, represented, That the bringing in a number of peers into that House by election, was certainly derogatory to the dignity of that august assembly, and of the highest tribunal in the united kingdom; and therefore he had long before wished to see this defect in the Union rectified, and the Scots peers freed from that ignominious mark of distinction, which made them be looked upon as dependent on the court and ministry, and not at liberty to vote, like the other members, for the good and interest of their country.

The Earl of Nottingham and the lord Townshend declared, That they were not against limiting the peerage, but only against the doing it in a manner, which, in their opinion, was unjust, and might be attended with dangerous consequences.

Resolutions of the Lords in relation to the Peerage.] But after a debate that lasted till near seven of the clock in the evening, by a majority of 83 votes against 30, their lordships came to the following Resolutions, viz.

"1. That in lieu of the 16 elective peers, to sit in this House on the part of Scotland, 25 peers to be declared by his majesty, shall have hereditary seats in parliament, and be the peers on the part of the peerage of Scotland.

"2. That such 25 peers shall be declared by his majesty, before the next session of parliament.

"3. That 9 of the said 25 shall be appointed by his majesty to have immediate right to such hereditary seats in parliament, subject to the qualifications requisite by the laws now in being.

"4. That none of the remaining 16 so to be declared by his majesty, or their heirs, shall become sitting peers of the parliament of Great Britain, until after the determination of this present parliament, except such are of the number of the 16 peers now sitting in parliament on the part of Scotland, and their heirs.

"5. That if any of the 25 peers so to be declared by his majesty, and their heirs shall fail, some one or other of the peers of Scotland shall be appointed by his majesty, his heirs and successors, to succeed to every such peer so failing; and every peer so appointed shall be one of the peers on the part of the peerage of Scotland, in the parliament of Great Britain, and so, *toties quoties* [repeatedly], as often as such failure shall happen.

"6. That the hereditary right of sitting in parliament, which shall accrue to the 25 peers of Scotland, to be declared by his majesty, shall be so limited as not to descend to females.

"7. That the number of peers of Great Britain, on the part of England, shall not be enlarged, without precedent right, beyond six above what they are at present; but as any of the said present peers, or such six new peers, in case they be created, shall fail, their numbers may be supplied by new creations of commoners of Great Britain, born within the kingdom of Great Britain or Ireland, or any of the dominions thereunto belonging, or born of British parents, and so, *toties quoties*, as often as such failure shall happen.

"8. That no person be at any time created by writ, nor any peerage granted by patent, for any longer estate than for the grantee, and the heirs male of his body.

"9. That there be not any restraint upon the crown, from creating any of the princes of the blood, peers of Great Britain, with right to sit in parliament.

"10. That whenever those Lords now sitting in parliament, whose sons have been called by writ, shall die; then it shall be lawful for his majesty, his heirs and successors, to create a peer to supply the number so lessened.

"11. That every creation of a peer hereafter to be made, contrary to these Resolutions, shall be null and void to all intents and purposes."

The Peerage Bill brought in.]
March 5. The Earl of Clarendon reported these Resolutions to the House, which being agreed to, the Judges were ordered to bring in a Bill there-upon; which they did accordingly on the 14th, when the said Bill was read the first, and ordered to be read a second time.

Edward Harley, junior, to Abigail Harley at Eywood

1718–19, March 1. [Christ Church, Oxford]– . . . .
There is not business enough before the Parliament to keep them sitting a week, but the Ministry themselves own the sessions will not end till Easter; everybody from hence concludes that some extra-ordinary business is upon the anvil, but of what nature I won't pretend to guess, since opinions upon it are so various.

There is much talk in London of a Bill being to be brought into the House of Lords to increase the number of Scotch Peers to twenty-five, and to make them hereditary instead of elective, and likewise to enact that the English peerage for the future shall not exceed the number of two hundred, exclusive of bishops, but that when any family is extinct, the king shall have the liberty of filling that vacancy. This is so great an alteration of the English Constitution and Scotch Union, that I believe the news of it will be as surprising to you as it is here, but the truth of it is not much disputed.

Lord Chancellor Middleton to Lord Montjoy

March 10, 1718–19. I am not at all a stranger to the probable consequences of men's speaking and acting according to their own sentiments in a certain affair: on the contrary, have had broad hints, nay plain indications what is determined to follow. I have put honour and integrity in one scale, and find it vastly to outweigh convenience; and am determined never to purchase the latter, by parting with the former: this is a fixed resolution now, when it is in my power to do the convenient thing, if I please.

Coxe, *Walpole*, vol. II.

Memorandum on the Peerage Bill

Endorsed in lord Middleton's handwriting, *"Conversation between lord Sunderland and me about the peerage bill."*

When the duke of Bolton first spoke to me about the matter, then under the consideration of the house of lords, for restraining the number of peers, I did not relish the scheme; but refrained expressing myself more against it at that time, being told the king was acquainted with it, and that the ministry thought it very good for the kingdom; besides, he either had not then, or did not show me the resolutions which were intended to be moved in the house of lords, so I was much in the dark. After the lords had passed their resolutions, I waited on him again, and continued of the same mind, but expressed myself determined not to debate or vote against a matter thought of such consequence; but could not be convinced of the reasonableness, of the thing.

On the 6th of March, lord Sunderland at Mr. Boscawen's, desired me to see him on the Sunday morning, that he might discourse me on this subject. At St. James's, he explained to me the motives and inducements the ministry had to push this matter; and I then showed my not comprehending the reason or necessity for bringing in the intended bill; but expressed myself resolved (considering my being in the king's service) not to speak or vote against the bill. His lordship seemed to think more would be expected from me; and used words of the king's being obliged to change hands, &c. but whether he meant, that he must be obliged to change the ministry, if the bill miscarried, or to remove those of his servants, who should not be for it, he did not expressly say; though from the nature of the discourse, and what

Coxe, *Walpole*, vol. II.

I was told by the duke of Bolton the first day, I am well convinced which he meant.

On 15th March, I discoursed this matter with my lord chancellor at St. James's, and expressed myself not convinced of the reasonableness of the intended bill: he was very warm for it, and seemed surprized at my being so uncomplying; but lord Coningsby coming in, broke off the conversation. The more I consider this matter, the more I am confirmed in my opinion, that the bill brought into the house of lords on 14th March, commonly called the peerage bill, is of that nature, that the commons ought not to pass it; and after having heard the arguments offered by the duke of Bolton, lord Sunderland, lord chancellor, and all that was offered in the house of lords, to induce them to come to the resolutions on which the bill is founded, without being convinced, I think I am not like to alter.

26th March, lord Sunderland, at my lodging, pressed coming into the bill—the king's desire, not the act of his ministry—resents it in foreigners and others, who represent it now a contest between the king and prince—the whig administration undone, if disappointed—the whig majority preserved the constitution in queen Anne's time—this is a way to settle it—ridiculous not to say mad things will be done hereafter, when a certain event happens—must advise the king to change hands, though he will. . . . [some words illegible] lords will consent to part with scand. magnat. [an abbreviation for *Scandalum Magnatum*, the use of language derogatory to a peer or a great officer of the realm, which had been made a special offence in 1275; often scan. mag.—Ed.]—that commons may administer an oath on elections—the king will consent, crown shall not pardon before or after judgement, on impeachment—if other things can be thought of, thinks will be come into; else the bill will drop without prejudice—professed regards for me—would have me communicate it to my brother. I said I would, to him and others—desired leave to go for Ireland, and to be absent, else would be in the house, and vote with my judgement—He told me, the king would tell me his own thoughts; I offered to wait on the king, if he commanded it, after his lordship had told him, what my thoughts were, and would repeat them to him—said the prince had launched out £ 40,000—A lord offered to be bribed; poor, ill used by his father.—28th March, lord Sunderland came to me, told me he had spoken to the king, who was uneasy at my not, &c. but being urged, consented to my going to Ireland—urged it might be sometime the coming week—that I should not say on what occasion, but on my own—that I was wanted, &c.—and desired my brother would not be warm; I said I would go out of town for a few days, then return; kiss the king's hand, and go away—he desired some time this week—I promised.—Lord Coningsby, 29th March, meeting me at court, asked me, when I went for Ireland—probably, he knew it was concerted at St. James's, to have leave.

Mr. Secretary Craggs to the Earl of Stair

Cockpit, March 10, 1719

. . . You will have heard with what a swing the Peerage Bill is like to be carried in the House of Lords, but I assure you it will periclitate in ours. . . . You cannot imagine what a prejudice was raised in the minds of our party. The Germans, all but Bernstorff and the Duchess of Munster, go about talking against it. They are extremely concerned for the king's prerogative, and, I fancy, do not despair some time or other to be peers. The young family [Prince of Wales's party] set all their weight against this bill. 'Tis a pretty figure they make, now we apprehend an invasion. You must know that, by what I meet hitherto, they and their vassals and creatures take the turn of despising this news and calling it a job of the ministry, and say that if it is true we may thank the Quadruple Alliance. . . .

John Murray Graham, *Annals and Correspondence of the Viscount and the First and Second Earls of Stair* (Edinburgh & London, 1875), vol. II

John Cochrane to the Earl of Dundonald, Soho Square

1718–19, March 12. Edinburgh—I delivered your letter to Lord Balmerino; he was very willing to sign it, but not forward to take much trouble about it. All that I could push with him and Lord Blantyre was to have a general meeting of the Peers that are here to-morrow. They think it impracticable to get it signed by any but those near the town, because of the time limited by you for the return; but they propose that circular letters to you from all the Peers shall be procured, declaring their dissent, in the hope that they may come in time.

Portland Papers, vol. V.

The Earl of Ruglen to [the Earl of Dundonald]

1719, March 12. Edinburgh—Your Lordship's of the 7th by Mr. Cochran came safe this evening, for which I return you many thanks, as my Lord Cassillis does likewise, for we are both of your opinion,

Portland Papers, vol. V.

and I assure you that all the nobility here we meet with are in the utmost consternation and anger at the surprising doings against us, and at the same time have the highest esteem for those worthy English Peers, that have spoke so well upon our subject, but an abhorrence to any of our sixteen that have gone into this destructive Bill, which we hope will not pass, and for that end all imaginable pains will be taken to get the petition well subscribed. Your Lordship will be pleased to let all our friends know this, that they may be active to preserve our peerage, which you espouse so generously.

Postscript.—March 14—This letter that I had written should have gone by last post, but an accident stopped it. Yesterday the Peers did sign the petitions in my lodgings, except three or four. Considering how many have gone out of town to their country seats, it is very much that so many have signed in so short a time, which I assure your Lordship was very unanimous. It is not to be expressed how much all sorts of people talk against this; and the Peers at a greater distance will be sending up petitions with all expedition, but pray let not this which the bearer brings be delayed, for the Lords here thought it absolutely necessary to dispatch this one instantly, that it might be known above how disagreeable such a Bill as we are told of will be to so great a number of the nobility. I hope the petition will have good success, and that all our friends that are concerned will concur; the Lords here are all extremely sensible of the honourable part your Lordship acts, and nobody more than myself.

Lord Balmerino to [the Earl of Oxford]

1718–19, March 13. Leith—This day all the Lords who were in Edinburgh met at the Earl of Ruglen's lodgings, and very heartily signed both addresses. Though the number is not great, I did not expect to have found half the number, this being the vacation time, when everybody is gone to the country. Your Lordship cannot doubt but every Peer here has the present design in detestation, except such as expect to be of the twenty-five. As for me, I always expressed my abhorrence of it, when I might have expected to be of the number; yet it is fully owing to your Lordship that we have taken the pains to address, for many thought all opposition to this gross oppression vain, and that it would be done so suddenly that addresses would come too late. As for me, I have given over the world; I neither meddle with public nor private affairs, yet I see your Lordship has power to draw me back a little. Whatever come of this, above an hundred Peers in Scotland owe your Lordship humble thanks, but we who were in town did not think it fit to detain Mr. Cochran for procuring hands from the country (which would have been very easy), but it would have made him return too late.

The Earl of Glencairne to [the Earl of Dundonald]

1718–19, March 16. Finlass—Last night I had the honour of your letter anent our peers. I am heartily sorry I was not so lucky as to be at Edinburgh when Mr. Cochrane was there, that I might have signed that petition to the House of Commons and shown my dissent to this new creation of twenty-five Peers, which must infallibly ruin us and our posterity to all intents and purposes. I assure you I would go to the world's end to prevent it, for sure I am never such another barefaced thing was ever thought of.

I hope in God it sha'nt pass the Commons, and, if it don't, if we forget our duty we're to blame. I am sure if we Peers had been advertised sooner, our meeting had been very full. It came so suddenly nobody could be aware of it.

Let me know how it is like to go in the House of Commons, and if they do assist us they shall never want my prayers; but I am so full of fears I know not what I am doing.

Postscript.—Pray send me a good Smithfield whip.

Portland Papers, vol. V.

The Earl of Eglinton to [the Same?]

1718–19, March 19. Eglinton—I had the honour of your Lordship's and at the same time two addresses sent me from Edinburgh against this Bill, which is to take away the power of election from the Peers of Scotland and in place thereof the King is to make twenty-five of the Peers hereditary. I would gladly know the advantage that accrues to those who are not of the twenty-five; by this method, for my part, I . . . [wonder] how any man of common ingenuity can agree to an act of such injustice.

All the Peers of Scotland are much obliged to your Lordship for the care and concern you have expressed in this matter, but I am

Portland Papers, vol. V.

afraid all will not hinder the Bill from carrying, for the Ministry never have hitherto been disappointed of anything they attempted. It is true this Bill touches the Commons, for, except six as I think, there shall hardly ever another Commoner be made a Peer, and perhaps forty will get the promise to be one of the six that they may vote for the Bill; this may ensnare some, but others will not be so easily caught. I truly believe Mr. Walpole and Sir Thomas Hanmer and Mr. Compton think they deserve the honour of Peerage as well as "Stenop" [Stanhope?] or Cadogan, how far these gentlemen may have power to disappoint the Bill I know not.

I acknowledge I almost despair, for I think God will permit violence and oppression to take place, until He fill up the measure of our iniquities. However, all ought to be done that is possible against this Bill, and therefore I have signed the address against it, and sent it to my Lord Cathcart, and others in this country, but I am afraid it will hardly come to London in time. If the Bill pass, I hear most if not all of our present representatives are to be of twenty-five; there are three of them have not one foot of inheritance in Scotland, and I can name four or five more that all their estates together are not so considerate [*sic*] as either your Lordship's or mine. If this be justice, let God and the world judge.

The Earl of Ruglen to the [Earl of Dundonald]

1719, March 21. Edinburgh—The two enclosed petitions came hither this afternoon; it was thought fit to send them to your Lordship by this night's post without loss of time, and when the others come, they will be sent up with all expedition. I hope Mr. Cochran arrived safe; pray write what will be the fate of that Bill concerning the Peers here, the more it is talked of, the aversion grows the greater with all sorts of people.

I beg your Lordship to acknowledge the receipt of this with the first post, for I should be very uneasy if it should mis-carry.

Portland Papers, vol. V.

The Same to the Same

1719, March 24. Edinburgh—The two enclosed petitions came hither this evening from the noblemen of the shire of Aberdeen, which

Portland Papers, vol. V.

I send you by this night's post. It was expected by yesternight's London packet that we should have heard from your Lordship, and of the arrival of Mr. Cochran, but I hope the next post will bring us that account, and that our petitions shall meet with success.

Lord Kellie to [the Earl of Dundonald]

1719, March 30. Kellie—Would have signed the petitions against the Peerage Bill if they had come to his hand, but the short time they were to be returned in, made it not possible that they could come to the distance he lived at from Edinburgh, so signifies his opinion by letter.

Portland Papers, vol. V.

Lord Blantyre to [the Earl of Dundonald]

1719, March 31. Lenoxlove—I return you my hearty thanks for the care you took in putting it in my power to show the dislike I had to the hereditary peers being made. I hope the petition we have signed to the Commons will meet with a better treatment than it had in the House of Lords; and I think the objections Lord Sunderland made of minors and Lords' eldest sons signing it were not worthy so great a man. The reason that so few sign should be made known to the Commons, as it proceeds from the distance we are from each other, and having no occasion to meet all at Edinburgh.

Portland Papers, vol. V.

Mr. Secretary Craggs to the Earl of Stair

Cockpit, March 31, 1719

. . . Our Peerage Bill here has met with many mines, and we have countermined them as well as we can; but as I am far from answering for the success in the House of Commons, so am I not yet willing to despair, for I think matters are rather mended since I wrote you last. But we have really upon this and all occasions too many knaves and fools to deal with; besides, the young Court put their whole strength openly upon it, and for the first time do not, as I understand, spare money, which, I promise you, comes very hard from that quarter. . . .

Graham, *Stair Annals*, vol. II.

I'll tell you a story will make you laugh, in return to those in your private letter. Lord Sunderland and Stanhope and myself go into the [king's] closet together, and if one comes after the others are gone in, he follows without asking. Cadogan asked Sunderland two days ago if he had spoke to the king about the transports: says Sunderland, 'We shall immediately;' whereupon Cadogan, seeing the closet door open, said, 'Then I will go in with you;' and so bounced in with us. You may imagine we did not stay long; but as we came out he pretended to have forgot somewhat, which I who went out last heard him mention, of Egerton's regiment; and so stayed behind half an hour, as if there was some secret only for his own use. He swears and damns himself that he has done his best for this bill [the Peerage Bill], but too many circumstances attest the contrary.*

*A more suitable field than at home was soon after this found for Lord Cadogan's energy by his being appointed ambassador at the Hague.

The Peerage Bill Postponed

The Peerage Bill dropped. March 16. The Lords having read this Bill the second time, three Scotch lords petitioned to be heard by their counsel against the said Bill; but it being represented by some English peers, that the Lords being sole judges of what relates to the Peerage, they could not allow their rights and privileges to be questioned and canvassed by lawyers; and having to that purpose cited a precedent, viz. the case of the late duke Hamilton, when he claimed a seat in that house as duke of Brandon, the said petition of the three Scotch Lords was rejected without dividing. March 18, the Lords, in a grand committee, took the said bill again into consideration, but adjourned it to the 20th.

April 2. It being moved in the House of Lords to receive the report from the committee of the whole House upon the Bill for settling the Peerage of Great Britain, the same was put off to the 6th, when the Amendments made to the said Bill were agreed to, and the Bill ordered to be engrossed. But on the 14th, the day appointed for the third reading, lord Stanhope observed, That this Bill had made a great noise, and raised strange apprehensions; and since the design of it had been so misrepresented, and so misunderstood, that it was like to meet with great opposition in the other House, he thought it advisable to let that matter lie still, till a more proper opportunity: And thereupon the third reading of the said Bill was put off to the 28th of that month: by which Resolution the said Bill was dropped for the present session.

The Marquess of Granby to his father the Duke of Rutland

1719, April 12. London.—On family affairs. I do not know when I shall be able to leave town. If it is true, as reported, that the Ministry have laid aside the thoughts of bringing the [Peerage] Bill into our House, and intend to prorogue the Parliament, I hope to set out on Thursday. But I am informed, on the other hand, that at a private meeting of the chief Ministers last night it was resolved to send it down to us to take its fate. The House is extremely angry with it, and undoubtedly will throw it out the first day. "I am told several members have talked of bringing a pan of charcoals into the House to burn it, others sending for pair of shears to cut it, and 'tis certain there are precedents of both being done." I congratulate you on your success at Newmarket.

Historical Manuscripts Commission, *The Rutland Papers*, vol. II (London, 1889).

Lord Colvile to [the Earl of Dundonald]

1719, April 4. Craigflower—It was signified to me this afternoon by the Earl of Ruglen that if I would write a letter to you declaring my concurrence with the rest of the Lords in their petition against the Peerage Bill, it would come in time enough to be presented to the Commons. I hope this extraordinary occasion will excuse the trouble I give you to assure you that I do concur with them.

Portland Papers, vol. V.

The Earl of Ruglen to [the Earl of Dundonald]

1719, April 4. Edinburgh—Nothing has been omitted by me to do all that was possible in the affair of our great concern, and truly the Lords that were here signing have done their part. All are extremely sensible of your zeal for the peerage and your country.

Portland Papers, vol. V.

The Earl of Ruglen to [the Earl of Dundonald]

1719, April 23. Barnton—The good news your letter brought of the Peerage Bill being dropped was extremely agreeable, and I hope such an attempt again will never be made. . . .

Portland Papers, vol. V.

The King's Speech

The King's Speech at the Close of the Session. April 18. The King came to the House of Peers, and, after passing several Bills, put an end to the session, with the following speech which the Lord Chancellor read to both Houses.

"My Lords and Gentlemen:

"I am now come to put an end to this session, in which you have shown many great and seasonable proofs of your duty and affection to my person and government, and of your care for the safety and welfare of your fellow subjects.

"By the blessing of God on our endeavours, we have hitherto disappointed the ill designs of our enemies, who flattered themselves with success from our unhappy divisions.

"We perceive, by the rash and wicked councils which have lately prevailed in the court of Spain, that the desperate and extravagant projects of one ambitious man, though not capable of giving fears to their neighbours, may occasion to them some expence and trouble.

"That court, being influenced by counsels odious and destructive to the Spaniards, who find themselves neglected and oppressed, after having endeavoured to foment conspiracies and seditions, both here and in France, and stooped to practices unusual, accompanied by manifestoes of a style unheard of among great princes, has at last proceeded to acknowledge the Pretender.

"As this news has given great surprise to all Europe, I question not but it will be received by every good Briton with indignation and contempt.

"It is our happiness at this juncture, to find ourselves assisted by the greatest powers of Europe against an enemy that has no allies, but those who would betray the governments under which they live and are protected.

"Gentlemen of the House of Commons;

"I thank you very heartily for the supplies you have granted me this year; The manner in which you have raised them, without any new burden to my people, the great addition you have made to the fund for sinking the debts of the nation, the discharge of the Exchequer Bills, and the provision you have made to pay whatever remains justly due to foreign states and princes, are the strongest proofs of your wisdom, as well as of your zeal for my service, and the good of your country. You may observe, I have hitherto been very cautious of making use of the power you have given me, to increase our forces by sea and land. If our enemies should oblige me to a greater expence, it shall be employed for your service. This is what the trust you repose in me requires at my hands, and what I owe to so dutiful and affectionate a House of Commons.

"My Lords and Gentlemen;

"There being nothing more desirable, at all times, than a firm union between Protestants; I reflect with satisfaction upon the law you have passed this session, which will, I hope, prove effectual to that purpose. As it is a signal instance of moderation and indulgence in our Established Church; so I hope it will beget such a return of gratitude from all dissenting Protestants, as will greatly tend to her honour and security; both which I shall ever have near at heart.

"I have always looked upon the glory of a sovereign, and the liberty of the subject, as inseparable; and think it is the peculiar happiness of a British king to reign over a free people. As the civil rights therefore, and privileges of all my subjects, and especially of my two Houses of Parliament, do justly claim my most tender concern; if any provision, designed to perpetuate these blessings to your posterity, remains imperfect, for want of time during this session, maturely to discuss and settle matters of so great importance, I promise myself, you will take the first opportunity to render my wishes for your happiness complete and effectual, and to strengthen the union, which is of so much consequence to the welfare of this kingdom.

"If the circumstances of my affairs shall allow of my going abroad this summer, I shall take the same care of your interest as if I remained here. The many negotiations which will be on foot to restore the peace of the North, in which the trade and tranquillity of this kingdom may be very much concerned, will make my presence there of great use to these my dominions; And, as in that case I design, by the blessing of God, to meet you early next winter; I will only recommend to you most earnestly, that, laying aside all animosities, you would, in your several countries and stations, use your utmost endeavours to preserve the public peace, and see a due execution of the laws."

Then the Lord Chancellor prorogued the parliament to the 19th of May following; and it was afterwards, by several prorogations, farther prorogued to the 23d of November.

FINANCIAL ISSUES

The King's Revenue

The third element in the framework of eighteenth-century government, the King's revenue, is associated not with the degree of the Commons' independence of the King, as are the first and second elements, but with the degree of the King's independence of the Commons. In the period 1689–1716 steps were taken to relate the King's revenue more accurately to his commitments. This improvement in the King's financial position, however, made him more and not less dependent on parliament, for it was accompanied not only by the establishment of parliamentary control over the spending of the revenue granted to him by parliament, but also by an increase in the proportion of revenue which he obtained from parliament. At the same time, parliamentary control was extended both over the raising of money by borrowing and over the spending of money so raised. The extended control over the raising of the King's revenue, and the new control over its expenditure, affected the King's prerogative of summoning and dissolving parliament, for it ensured that parliament should meet every year and it ended the possibility of long intervals between parliaments. So, in the sense that financial developments brought annual sessions and ensured that the summoning of a parliament should not be long delayed after the dissolution of its predecessor, this third element in the framework of eighteenth-century government is closely connected with the first, the life of the Commons. It is also connected with the second element, the composition of the Commons. For the tighter control was exercised not by parliament as a whole but primarily by the Commons, and this increased the strength and independence of the Commons both in relation to the King and in relation to the House of Lords. Again, the Commons' financial control is linked with the ascendancy of the First Lord of the Treasury, and with his management of the Commons by the distribution of the King's patronage to members of parliament.

The financial developments of the period 1689–1716 are not connected only indirectly with the achievement of a balance between King and Commons. They contributed directly to this balance by establishing a position of financial equilibrium, in which the King's income was not only fixed by parliament but guaranteed to him by parliament, and in which public expenditure was controlled partly by parliament and

Betty Kemp, *King and Commons, 1660–1832* (London, 1957). Reprinted by permission of Macmillan & Co., London, The Macmillan Company of Canada, and St. Martin's Press, Inc.

partly by the King, while the King's private expenditure remained wholly outside parliament's control. This financial balance between King and Commons was based, as was the constitutional balance between them, partly on statute and partly on convention, but it owed more to statute. The financial balance, shaken in 1782 and again in the early nineteenth century, was not finally destroyed until 1830. Its destruction, compared with the destruction of the constitutional balance, was simple: the Commons gained what the King lost.

The first step towards the achievement of the financial balance between King and Commons was based not on statute but on the vindication of claims made by the Commons. Since 1625 money Bills had been phrased in the form of a grant to the King, not from parliament, but from the Commons, with the advice and consent of the Lords. In the 1660s the Commons insisted that money Bills must always be introduced into the House of Commons, and in the 1670s the Commons further claimed that money Bills could not be amended in the House of Lords. The Lords' protests were unsuccessful, and in 1678 the Commons incorporated both claims in a Resolution. This claim that parliament's control of the King's revenue, like parliament's life and parliament's composition, was peculiarly the concern of the Commons, was never in the period 1660–1832 incorporated in statute; but it was, in practice, conceded by the Lords before 1689, and they were not able seriously to challenge it again before 1832. Parliament's statutory gains in financial control between 1689 and 1832 were therefore in effect the Commons' gains.

In 1660 the public revenue was, as it always had been, entirely the same as the King's revenue, and this position was not changed before 1689. Between 1660 and 1689 the King was dependent on parliament for only a part of his revenue, and he was not accountable to parliament for the spending of any of it. In time of peace the King was expected to defray the expenses of government out of his ordinary revenue, and he was not expected to ask for extraordinary revenue except in time of war or preparations for war. Over borrowing, by means of which the King was free to supplement his ordinary and extraordinary revenue, parliament had no control. Indeed, parliament's control over extraordinary revenue was limited to the authorization of its collection: the proceeds of taxes so authorized were spent without any reference to parliament.

Before 1689 the Commons had made occasional attempts to ensure that money granted for extraordinary purposes, and raised by taxes, was spent for the purpose for which it had been asked. In William's reign, however, the Commons regularly began to state, either in the

Bill granting a tax or in a separate appropriation Bill, the specific purpose for which the money collected was to be used, and made some
attempt to ensure that it was so used. This was of fundamental constitutional importance, for it was the first step towards parliamentary
control of public expenditure. The position then achieved lasted until
1787, when, with the establishment of the Consolidated Fund, the
system of appropriating each tax was superseded by the simpler system
of appropriating a specific sum for each object of expenditure. Control
was made more effective by the system, which began in William's reign
and became regular in the early eighteenth century, of presenting to
the House of Commons each year estimates showing how it was
proposed to spend the money asked for the services which parliament
supplied. These estimates, prepared by the government department
concerned, were discussed, and often reduced, in Committee of Supply.
On the other hand, attempts made in William III's reign and in Anne's
reign to superimpose upon the Exchequer system of audit a parliamentary audit, conducted by Commissions of Public Accounts composed
of members of parliament, were not effective and no similar attempt
was made in George I's reign.

Although the King's ordinary revenue continued after 1689 to be
spent without reference to parliament, the extent of parliamentary
control over public expenditure was further increased by the fact that
the inadequacy of the ordinary revenue led parliament not to add to
it but to reduce the King's commitments. After the Peace of Ryswick
William III did not provide for military and naval expenditure out of
his ordinary revenue: this responsibility was assumed by parliament
and provided for by money voted each year by parliament, and the
spending of the money so voted was subject to parliamentary control.

This large increase in the field of expenditure controlled by parliament, which was also the first real step towards the separation of the
King's private expenditure from public government expenditure, inaugurated a period of balance between King and Commons, in which
public expenditure was controlled partly by the King and partly by
the Commons. . . . The achievement, at the end of the seventeenth
century, of a balance between King and Commons in the control of
public expenditure was accompanied by the achievement of a position
in which parliament guaranteed to the King a fixed annual income.
The size of the income required by the King was estimated by parliament in 1660 and on several occasions during the succeeding reigns.
Not until 1715, however, did parliament guarantee to the King the
amount estimated, by undertaking to supplement, if necessary, the
amount actually collected. The rule that if the amount collected

exceeded the estimate the surplus should be surrendered was abandoned under George II, but the benefits of this relaxation, which were considerable, lasted only for his reign. . . .

Only in George II's reign, therefore, had it been in theory possible for the King to disturb the financial balance between King and Commons, that is, to increase his revenue by saving or by making the sources of his hereditary revenues more productive. In practice, it was never possible: even George II's frugality did not succeed in doing more than achieve, towards the end of his reign, a small surplus on the Civil List, and the great increase in the value of the crown lands in the early nineteenth century came too late to increase the King's income. Moreover, the only loophole through which the King could, at any time after 1660, increase his revenues to any appreciable extent without recourse to parliament—borrowing—was not open to any of the Hanoverians. This loophole was closed in William III's reign: the establishment of the system authorizing the King to borrow up to fixed amounts on the security of taxes granted by parliament, the foundation of the Bank of England, which was forbidden to lend to the King without parliamentary sanction, and the beginning of the National Debt, subjected the King's borrowing to parliamentary control, and, by way of compensation for the loss of freedom involved, made it easier for him to borrow by providing a parliamentary guarantee for his loans.

PAMPHLET WARFARE

The Thoughts of a Member of the Lower House, in Relation to a Project for Restraining and Limiting the Power of the Crown in the Future Creation of Peers

> Better to reign in Hell, than serve in Heaven.
> Devil's speech, *Paradise Lost*.

As I have not the honor to be a member of the Upper House of Parliament, so I do not presume to know what is doing there; but claim the privilege of a freeborn Englishman to speak or write my mind impartially and openly, upon any proposition in which I conceive my own or my country's liberties are concerned, whilst there is no law to forbid me: and much more so, when what I have to say is in vindication of the laws and the constitution in being.

The common subject of popular discourse is concerning a project said to be in agitation, which is to give the king power to create twenty-five *Scotch* peers to sit in their own right in Parliament, in lieu of the sixteen who are to be elected by the peerage there; and after the creation of six more for *Great Britain*, the prerogative of making any further creations is to be taken from the crown, unless upon the extinction of the families in possession of the peerage.

Now I am free to own that I think such a law would be fatal to the monarchy, and the liberties of the people, and make our government aristocratic, without the outward appearances of it, or the regulations which are peculiar and essential to that sort of dominion; and consequently it will reduce us to the worse part of oligarchy.

Our present constitution consists of the king, the peers who act in their own right, and the representatives of the people. In the union and agreement of these constituent parts consists our government. If they differ irreconcilably, there is an actual dissolution of it without any remedy but the last. And since it's impossible, in the nature of human things, that men's opinions and interests will not often clash, therefore the institutors of this species of monarchy have contrived so proper a balance of power between the several parts of it, that each state can give some check to both the other; and two concurring, have always the means in their power to bring the third to reason without recurring to force, which dissolves the government.

If the king has the prerogative of raising money, and could protect the instruments of unlawful power, it's evident the monarchy would be absolute; but that privilege remaining in the people, the crown must often recur to their assistance, and then they always have it in their power to do themselves right: this keeps the ministry in perpetual dependance and apprehension.

On the other side, if the House of Commons was fixed and indissolvable, the government would soon devolve into an ill-contrived democracy, and the crown would have no remedy but acquiescence or force. Such a body of men would soon find and feel their own strength, and always think it laudable to increase it: and there are so many emergencies which happen in all states, that there can never be wanting favorable opportunities to do it; when the ambition of some, the resentment of others, and the appearance of public good, spur them on, till at last by insensible and unobserved degrees, even to themselves, they would engross and possess the whole power of the state. There has been but one instance since the institution of this monarchy, when the Commons have been trusted with such a power; and if a noble historian is to be believed, that house consisted of men as uncorrupt, of as much wisdom and public virtue, as ever sat within those walls: yet the lust of dominion soon got the better of all their virtues, and they first garbled their own house, by expelling their refactory members; then deposed the king, and at last the House of Lords; and assumed a greater tyranny to themselves, than they opposed in the crown.

The effectual remedy our constitution has provided against this evil, is a dissolution, which breaks all cabals and conspiracies, and gives the people (who can never have an interest in public disturbances) an opportunity to choose others in their place, more calm, of less violent dispositions, and not engaged in such attempts; this power, hanging over their heads always, must be a constant restraint upon their actions.

But the circumstances of public affairs often do not admit of this remedy without the most extreme necessity: the Lords are always at hand to screen the crown, whose honors and dignities flow from it and are protected by it. Whilst kept in a proper dependence, the Lords must ever support that power which supports themselves: yet they never can have an interest to make it arbitrary, which would render themselves useless to it, and level themselves again with the people.

There is not a more certain maxim in politics, than that a monarchy must subsist by an army or a nobility; the first makes it a despotic, and the latter a free government. I presume none of those noble personages themselves, who have the honor to make up that illustrious body, do believe they are so distinguished and advanced above their fellow-subjects for their own sakes. They know well that they are intended to be the guardians as well as the ornaments of the monarchy, an essential prerogative of which it must be to add to, and augment their number in such proportion, as to render them a proper balance against the democratic part of our constitution, without being formidable to the monarchy itself, the support of which is the reason of their institution.

Without this power in the crown they must be dangerous to it and be able to impose whatever conditions of government they please. It is the only resource the king and people have against any exorbitances and combinations of their body. Whilst such a prerogative remains in the crown, there can seldom or never be an occasion to make use of it. Their lordships are too much concerned in the preservation of their own dignities, to provoke the crown to a remedy which is always at hand; and the crown cannot debase the nobility, and make it cheap, without lessening its own splendor and power. And this seems to be the only limitation the nature of the thing will admit of, without dissolving the species of government.

If this prerogative is taken away, the House of Lords will be a fixed, independent body, not to be called to account like a ministry, nor to be dissolved or changed like the House of Commons. The same men will meet again with the same resolutions, probably heightened by disappointment, and nothing can stand before them. If their lordships should take it into their thoughts to dislike the ministry, and commit them to prison, I would willingly know who shall fetch them out. Or, if the House of Commons should be so unwary as to give them offence, and their lordships think fit to declare that they could no longer act in concert with a body of men who had used them ill, it's evident the crown must choose another more to their lordships' fancy, and afterwards use its utmost efforts to keep them in a becoming complaisance to their betters. If they should resolve to have all the great employments of *England* in themselves and families; or if they should take a conceit to be like the nobles of some other countries, to pay no taxes themselves, and yet receive the greatest part of what is paid by others in salaries and pensions; then I would ask the advocates for such a law, what recourse the crown and people have? And I shrewdly suspect they will propose no other than what the Commons of *Denmark* made use of on the very same occasion.

The Lords have already all the property of *Great Britain* under their jurisdiction; and I think that no one will say that there is any difference in nature between the last appeal without being accountable, and a power of legislation but what consists in the moderation of the judges. And if this exceedingly great power must irrevocably be vested in the very same persons, I see nothing the Commons have left to desire, but to entitle themselves to their favor and protection, by wearing their badges as formerly.

But as their lordships are too wise and virtuous to attempt any such actions of knight-errantry as are above mentioned, so they will be under no necessity to do it; for there is an easier and gentler way of attaining the same ends. There are so many emergencies, difficulties and factions that arise in all states, the crown will often be so necessitous, and the Commons divided, that a fixed and powerful body, always determined to their own advantage, by a dextrous management of such events, must soon possess themselves of all they desire; and it will be in vain to oppose with one view what will often be given them with another.

I will not presume to judge whether their lordships' judicature was always what it is now; but every day's experience shows in lesser instances what a body of men, united in the same interest, are capable of doing. We have more often than not seen a number of incorporated merchants prove a match for the whole kingdom, and I fear shall too often see it again. History tells us how the priesthood, by being a united and regular body, always lying upon the catch, and acting with the same views, from living upon the charity and benevolence of their hearers, became in a few ages the lords and masters of mankind, in defiance of that religion they professed to teach.

It is true, this prerogative of the crown is liable to be abused and has been so in a late glaring instance; but if there is a sufficient reason to take it away, I doubt there will be few remain. The king neither has nor can have any prerogative but what the people are interested in: it is a trust for the public good and in its very nature it is capable of being betrayed; but the proper remedy is to punish the authors and advisers of the abuse, and not destroy the whole constitution for an enormity of one part of it.

It is a proper object of the legislative power to consider whether any men ought to enjoy the highest privileges and honors in a common-wealth as a reward for their endeavoring to destroy it; but with all the clamor this grievance has justly produced, has there been anything like this attempted? No, on the contrary, the grand criminal [Oxford] sits triumphant, glories in his wickedness, and carries off the price of it; and his rival [Bolingbroke] in guilt and power, even now presumes to expect an act of the legislature to indemnify him, and sanctify his villainy, and I doubt not that both expect once more to give laws to the kingdom.

It is urged that it is safer to trust this power with the Lords than an unlimited one with the crown, to make what creations it pleases, though to serve the vilest purposes. But the nature of the power is very little understood by those who hold this opinion, which can never be truly dreadful except when it is unaccountable and irretrievable. The crown must often apply to the people for their assistance, and the people as often have the opportunity to represent their grievances, and punish the authors of them, which must necessarily keep the ministry within some bounds; but there can be no limitation to the House of Peers, if such an act passes, but what flows from their lordships' justice, moderation and satiety of power.

Even that daring minister hardly ventured upon such an act, if he had not had a House of Commons to support him, and hoped to cover all his crimes in a revolution. I am persuaded he never once dreamed under a just government to find the impunity and indulgence he has since been favored with, even from the very persons who make those crimes the pretence for such an attempt. If nothing else was intended by it, except to prevent the like grievance, there is an easy and ready way to do it, by providing that no peer shall give his vote within a limited time after his creation, without the consent of the House. To obtain this, there would be no need of court intrigues, solicitations, or keeping the secret till the latter end of the sessions, when the country members are at their seats and the lawyers in their circuits.

Having, as I conceive, amply shown that a law of this kind would totally overturn our constitution, and change it into an oligarchy, I should think it frivolous to descend to lower considerations, did we not too often see men affected with arguments which regard themselves and families, whilst they are insensible of what they suffer in common with the whole nation. Therefore I shall offer some of the lesser objections to it.

It is a most violent and outrageous breach of the Union and dispossesses one of the estates of *Scotland* of the most valuable part of their peerage, and of that right which they expressly stipulated to be reserved to them when they consented to part with the rest, by which means they will be in a worse condition than the meanest subjects in the kingdom. They will neither be capable of sitting in the House of Lords or of Commons, or of giving their votes for either; in consequence they will be the only subjects in *Great Britain*, not represented, or capable of being represented in Parliament: this disability and severe punishment is inflicted upon them without any crime done, or pretended to be done by them, and even without any pretence of public necessity; on the contrary there is a visible danger in doing it, and I doubt not that in proper time it will be made a pregnant argument for keeping up standing troops to oblige their submission to it.

It is giving a power, without reproach or clamor, to add such a number to the upper house, as must, without uncommon virtue in their lordships, lay all things waste, and at the mercy of the ministry, without the possibility of their being called to an account. If the making of but twelve peers at once, to serve a court purpose, was such a blow upon our liberties, what are we not to fear from the creating of thirty-one, done by the countenance, if not direction, of an Act of Parliament, which takes off all that odium and load of scandal which the former abuse justly occasioned?

If it may be lawful to suppose so unlikely a thing, as that the ministry are capable of acting against the public good; or if, for our sins, the nation was punished with the loss of the present set, and Tories could work themselves into their places and form a scheme for their own security which may entail a civil war for the nation; what may not be apprehended from such a power entrusted to them?

It takes away from the king the brightest jewel of his crown, which is the distribution of honors, and in effect of offices too, which must then be at the mercy of that House. It deprives the Commons of *England* of attaining those honors which ought to be the rewards of virtuous actions, and the motives of doing them. I presume no one will suggest that all merit is exhausted by their present lordships; and therefore what imaginary reason can be given, why any number of men, who enjoy themselves the highest dignities and privileges in a commonwealth, should shut the doors upon all others who may have equal birth, desert, and fortunes?

As it makes the king and ministry entirely at the mercy of the Lords, so it makes the Commons more dependent upon the crown; for when the advantages of the nobility are so great, and the means of attaining them so difficult, what applications and solicitations must be made to the ministry upon the least appearance of a vacancy? This will keep the most considerable members of the lower house in a perpetual dependence and give the ministry much more trouble than they affect to avoid.

But amidst all the numerous objections to this worthy scheme, I am free to own that there is one thing in it which deserves commendation: it has produced a never-before-known unanimity amongst our great men. It has yoked the lion with the lamb, the Whigs with the Tories, men in power with those they have turned out of it: ministers of state are become patriots, complain of their own power, and join with their professed enemies in lessening that prerogative they have so often occasion for.

I confess that such phenomena and uncommon appearances, like comets or eclipses, are apt to fright ignorant people and make them expect some great event at hand. As those who are more familiar with the stars know the latter are only the common and regular productions of nature, so such who have more narrowly observed the virtues of our great men, especially during the last session of Parliament, are well assured they intend nothing but to serve their country. However, I think they will both judge right, upon such great occasions, to scatter their lesser conjurors abroad and disperse the malign influence such constellations and unusual conjunctions may have upon weak minds.

Dr. Johnson: The Instability of Friendship

It so happened that (1718–1719) a controversy was agitated, with great vehemence, between those friends of long continuance, Addison

Samuel Johnson, *Lives of the English Poets*, first published in 1779 and 1781 (2 vols., London, 1906).

and Steele. It may be asked, in the language of Homer, what power or what cause could set them at variance? The subject of their dispute was of great importance. The Earl of Sunderland proposed an act called the Peerage Bill, by which the number of peers should be fixed, and the king restrained from any new creation of nobility, unless when an old family should be extinct. To this the Lords would naturally agree; and the king, who was yet little acquainted with his own prerogative, and, as is now well known, almost indifferent to the possessions of the crown, had been persuaded to consent. The only difficulty was found among the Commons, who were not likely to approve the perpetual exclusion of themselves and their posterity. The Bill therefore was eagerly opposed, and among others by Sir Robert Walpole, whose speech was published.

The Lords might think their dignity diminished by improper advancements, and particularly by the introduction of twelve new peers at once, to produce a majority of Tories in the last reign; an act of authority violent enough, yet certainly legal, and by no means to be compared with that contempt of national right, with which some time afterwards, by the instigation of Whiggism, the Commons, chosen by the people for three years, chose themselves for seven. But, whatever might be the disposition of the Lords, the people had no wish to increase their power. The tendency of the Bill, as Steele observed in a letter to the Earl of Oxford, was to introduce an aristocracy; for a majority in the House of Lords, so limited, would have been despotic and irresistible.

To prevent this subversion of the ancient establishment, Steele, whose pen readily seconded his political passions, endeavored to alarm the nation by a pamphlet called *The Plebeian*; to this an answer was published by Addison, under the title of *The Old Whig*, in which it is not discovered that Steele was then known to be the advocate for the Commons. Steele replied by a second *Plebeian*; and, whether by ignorance or by courtesy, confined himself to his question, without any personal notice of his opponent. Nothing hitherto was committed against the laws of friendship, or proprieties of decency; but controversialists cannot long retain their kindness for each other. *The Old Whig* answered *The Plebeian*, and could not forbear some contempt of 'little Dicky, whose trade it was to write pamphlets.' Dicky however did not lose his settled veneration for his friend; but contented himself with quoting some lines of Cato, which were at once detection and reproof. The Bill was laid aside during that session, and Addison died before the next. . . .

Every reader surely must regret that these two illustrious friends, after so many years passed in confidence and endearment, in unity of interest, conformity of opinion, and fellowship of study, should finally part in acrimonious opposition. Such a controversy was *Bellum plusquam civile* [a war worse than civil] as Lucan expresses it. Why could not faction find other advocates? But, among the uncertainties of the human state, we are doomed to number the instability of friendship.

The Plebeian and *The Old Whig*

THE PLEBEIAN
BY A MEMBER OF THE HOUSE OF COMMONS
No. 1. Saturday, March 14, 1718–19
CONSIDERATIONS UPON THE REPORTS RELATING TO THE PEERAGE

> "—Hoc miserae Plebi—commune Sepulchrum."
> Hor. I. Sat. viii. 10.

> —In this detested ground
> A common tomb the vulgar found.
> FRANCIS.

All men in high stations have their enemies, who are ready to suggest on every occasion whatever may tend to lessen their credit, and make them odious to the public. The persons at present in great authority have been pursued by this Evil Spirit; but it would be unjust to give too easy belief to the insinuations of malicious people. At the beginning of this session it was reported, with much assurance, that a wonderful discovery was made, that all the charters of England were forfeited into the hands of the Crown; and this happy incident, as they called it, was to afford an opportunity of introducing a law much for the public service. But this was so far from being true, that the bill which came down from the House of Peers was a confirmation of the charters, without so much as a declaration of any forfeiture. Perhaps it might have been true, that some little lawyer had found out some mean chicane in law, worthy enough of the pursuit of such a person, in a private corporation-squabble; but such a project in order to a universal forfeiture, could never have weight with any judicious man whatever.

The Works of Joseph Addison, edited by Richard Hurd, vol. V (London, 1856). Hurd includes in his edition the four issues of Steele's *Plebeian*, two of which appear below, as well as the two numbers of *The Old Whig*.—Ed.

Nobody could be so very a novice in business, or so extravagant in politics, as to put his Majesty upon an undertaking, which contributed more towards the ruin of King James, than any one thing, or perhaps than everything else besides. When this report was blown over, the next thing insinuated to the public was a design of making a jest of what justice has been accidentally done to the nation, by repealing the attainder of one of the greatest offenders of the late reign. It is very certain no such attempt will be now made. There has been a just indignation shown already at the bare mention of it, and it is unfair to charge any particular person with having had any such intention; much less should a scandalous discourse gain credit, that any great officer belonging to his Majesty would correspond abroad with an attainted fugitive, intercede for him at home, and even prostitute the character of an ambassador so low, as to become the messenger of a traitor. These two unjust accusations were laid at the door of some great people at the beginning and towards the middle of this session; and now at the end of it, the public is alarmed at the report of another design of a more dangerous nature than either of those already mentioned. But as those former reports have not proved true, so I doubt not but this will likewise vanish in the same manner. However, as I was ready to have appeared in public on either of the former occasions, if there had been a necessity for it; so, if I am a little more forward in the present affair, I hope the importance of it will justify me: and if I should lose my labour, I shall however show that good intention for the service of my sovereign and fellow-subjects, with which I have always exposed myself at a dangerous crisis.

It is affirmed by some people, that a bill will be offered to the House of Commons, in which the present sixteen Peers of Scotland are to be made hereditary, to the exclusion of their electors, and nine more added upon the same foot; and six more are to be added to the number of English Peers; and then the Crown is to be restrained from making any new Lords but upon the extinction of families.

At first sight, this proposal must appear very shocking; it carries with it so great an alteration of the constitution; it implies so direct a breach of the Union, and of natural justice; and encroaches so much upon the natural prerogative of the Crown.

As to what relates to the Scottish Peerage, I must confess I am at a loss to say anything to it. If the most solemn contract betwixt two nations is to be violated; if persons are to be deprived of their right without being heard, and without any pretence of forfeiture; if those who have a power intrusted to them by their principals only for a few years, can size it to themselves and their posterity for ever; what use will be made of power so acquired, I leave every one to judge.

The shutting up the door of the House of Lords, in the manner talked of, cannot but prove a great discouragement to virtuous actions, to learning and industry, and very detrimental to the House of Peers itself, by preventing such frequent supplies from going into it as the nature of such a body requires; for want of which, it may in time become corrupt and offensive, like a stagnated pool, which hitherto has been preserved wholesome and pure by the fresh streams that pass continually into it.

I am not unaware that it will be said, *That the frequent extinctions of families will salve this inconvenience, and make room for the rewarding of merit*. But this expedient, I fear, is not much to be depended on; for the uncertainty of the time when the Crown will have any such power, will make it much the same as if it was never to have it at all. Besides, it is to be considered, that the patrons of this proposal argue vehemently for it, *on account, that this will be a means to ease the Crown from the great importunity of Pretenders to Peerage*. If so, it is certain in what manner they will proceed in all vacancies, which will be by filling them up instantly; or else the inconvenience would be increased as to importunity, and not diminished. This being the case, it is very evident by what sort of people those vacancies will be supplied; undoubtedly by the creatures and relations of those Peers who have at that time the greatest influence in the House, and whose requests to the Throne will very much resemble *demands*; and this honour, in all probability, will only be thought proper for their own families. An instance of this we have in the distinction of the Garter. At the first institution of that order, and till of late years, several Commoners had the honour (as the reward of merit) to be of that noble body; but at present it would be looked upon as a high presumption in any Commoner to pretend to it, let his services be never so great.

But another consequence, of a much higher nature, attending the limitation of the number of Peers, is the danger there will be of changing the Constitution by this means into an Aristocracy; and this may at any time in such case be effected by the confederacy of two or three great families, which would form such a body amongst the Lords as the Crown would not be able to control. That this kind of government is one of the worst sorts of slavery, is too well known to be disputed. In a Democracy a great many different persons may come to have a share of power by several incidents; but in the other state it is birth only that entitles to superiority; and the milk such nobles are nursed up with, is hatred and contempt for every human creature but those of their own imaginary dignity.

These being some of the inconveniences and hazards which naturally occur upon this proposal, let us see what are the advantages which, on the other hand, it is said, will flow from it.

First, "That this will be a bar upon the Crown, and prevent the King upon the throne from flinging in a great number of Lords on a sudden, only to answer a present purpose, as the late Queen once did."

Secondly, "That it will be a means to keep property or great estates in the House of Commons, from whence they are generally drawn out into the House of Peers."

These are said to be such plain Whig-points, as no Whig can oppose.

Whiggism, if I understand it aright, is a desire of liberty, and a spirit of opposition to all exorbitant power in any part of the constitution. Formerly the danger on this account was from the Crown; but since the Habeas Corpus Act, and the many restraints laid upon the Crown in King William's time, and the great and numerous limitations of the Succession Acts, the prerogative of the Crown is reduced so low, that it is not at all dangerous to the Commons. Besides, the Crown has frequent occasions for the assistance of the Commons; but the Lords never. The Lords are judges of the property of the Commons in the last resort; and, even in cases where they themselves are concerned, they have their actions *de Scandalis Magnatum,* and exercise a power of imprisoning, not confined within any very certain boundaries. And therefore the chief circumspection of the Commons ought to be employed at present, that those who have so much power already do not get more than the Commons will be able to withstand in any manner. I confess the making a great number of Lords on a sudden has one inconvenience: it may prevent some good to the public, but cannot do any great hurt, and is more grievous in its consequences to the Crown than to the people. The increasing the number of Peers is always to be wished for by the Commons, because the greater their number, the less considerable they become, and the less within the influence of court favours; by which means alone ministers are kept in awe, and remain in a situation of being called to account for their actions. Were it otherwise, they would be out of the reach of any accusation. They would know exactly by whom they were to be tried, and their judges might be their accomplices. And should this once come to be the case, what might they not attempt with impunity?

On the other hand, if their Lordships complain of the great number of Peers as a grievance to themselves, why are they desirous any more should be made? If twelve at once was so bad a precedent, what is fifteen, taking it in one light? what is thirty-one, if you take it in another?

If, at the Union, sixteen Scottish noblemen were found to be a just proportion to represent their whole nobility, what has happened since, to give reason to increase their number to twenty-five? Why may they not as well a few years hence, especially if the head of a clan is to be taken in, who may not like the set of nobles at that time, demand to be made fifty, to give his followers the majority; and so from time to time continue to play the game into each other's hands, as long as there is one nobleman left in Scotland, or any Civil List in England? If the Commoners of England are to be excluded from the House of Lords, why are they not excluded forthwith? It cannot be supposed that titles *in petto* [in secret] are kept on purpose to bribe persons of consequence in the House of Commons, to drive such a bill through that part of the legislature.

Upon the foot the Constitution has subsisted many years, the Crown, in all great emergencies relating immediately to itself, has been able to fence against the Lords by adding to their number, and against the Commons by dissolutions; and in like manner in cases of difference betwixt the two Houses. But if such a law as is mentioned above should be made, and any difference happen hereafter betwixt the Crown and the House of Peers, or betwixt the two Houses of Parliament, the Crown may not have it in its power to influence the Lords in relation to the Commons. And therefore it must be the inevitable consequence of such a misfortune, that both the Crown and the Commons must submit to the Lords. In former times, the greatest art and care of the Crown and ministers used to be the preventing of jealousies and differences betwixt the two Houses. This proposal, I fear, would be raising an implacable animosity and hatred, scarce ever to be reconciled.

The great advantage that the number of their body cannot be increased, is at present the most valuable privilege of the Commons, and the only thing that makes them considerable. The Lords are possessed of many great privileges that they will not permit the Commons to share with them; and therefore the Commons would be highly wanting to themselves, if they should add this advantage likewise to the Lords, which is the only one that they enjoy distinct from them.

It has been used as an argument, by some people, for the increasing the number of the Lords, "That the Crown formerly increased the

number of the Commons, in particular in Queen Elizabeth's reign."
But I desire it may be understood, that the sending members to parliament at that time was not desired as a favour, but imposed as a burden.
Queen Elizabeth erected several new corporations; but then the reason
for it was, she relieved several ancient and decayed ones from sending
any members at all. And how little this resembles the present case is
easily perceived.

The other advantage, which it is said will accrue from this proposal
is, "That it will be a means to keep property amongst the Commons."

I cannot see that there is occasion for so extraordinary a step as
this, and accompanied with so many evils, to procure us this assurance.
Property or wealth in every age flows faster back to the Commons by
the extinction of families, but much more by the want of economy in
the Peers, than it is drawn from them by the promotions of the
Crown. Besides, we see estates are often extinct before families; and
property is very rarely increased in the House of Peers. Indeed, if a
restraining bill should pass, I do not doubt but it would soon be
followed with a bill to prevent Lords from alienating their estates, for
which many plausible reasons are to be produced; and then, without all
dispute, the balance of property would be soon turned on the side of
their Lordships.

These are all the arguments I have heard for this supposed bill;
which is neither a Whig nor a Tory point, but would be a scheme
that might hereafter set up some nobles above the Crown and the
Commons both. For as to what is commonly said, That the Lords
would get nothing, no new power would be added to them by this
means; I beg leave to state this matter in a proper light. Suppose the
balance to be now *even* betwixt the Lords and the Crown, as it
certainly is, or else the Constitution would not subsist in quiet; is it
not plain to the most common capacity, that when two scales are
upon an equal poise, if you take any weight out of one of them, you
give the advantage to the other, without putting anything into it?

How dangerous it may prove to vary the balance of power in a
limited monarchy, we may learn from the ruin of one of the best-
founded governments among the ancients. [Steele then goes on to
discuss the consequences of vesting great power in the hands of the
Ephori, noblemen of the Greek state, Lacedaemonia] . . . But, begging
pardon for this digression, which is only intended for the curious, and
to return to my subject: There are other and more modern instances,
and living historians of our own, who can satisfy us, that too great a
power in the hands of the nobility has brought on the ruin of many

free nations. This was the case of Sweden a few years ago, as appears plainly from the very ingenious labours of a venerable prelate of the present House of Peers. This was the case of Denmark, of which a very accurate account has been given by a noble lord of a neighbouring kingdom, a member of the House of Commons. Nothing can be better writ, or more instructive to any one that values liberty, than the narrative of that tragedy in that excellent treatise. I wish gentlemen would see there, how Commoners were treated by the nobility when they had the power over them. This noble lord will inform them, that "they laid heavy impositions on the Commons at pleasure; which weight they themselves would not touch with one of their fingers." And when the Commons presumed to complain, though they were just come "from saving from a foreign yoke, not only the capital city of their country, but the whole kingdom, the royal family, nay, those very nobles that dealt so hardly by them:" I say, when the Commons ventured to complain, let any Englishman but hear the answer that was given them: "A principal senator," says his Lordship, "stood up, and in great anger told the president of the city, that the Commons neither understood nor considered the privileges of the nobility, nor the true condition of themselves, who were no other than slaves." The Commons, fired with indignation at this treatment, and resolving, if they were to be slaves, to be slaves to their prince rather than slaves to their fellow-subjects, instantly surrendered all their liberties to their King; and the Lords were forced to follow their example with so much haste, that "in four days time that kingdom was changed," says my noble and honest author, "to as absolute a monarchy as any in the whole world."

In short, it has been for our ancient Constitution that we have struggled with so much vigour for many years together: it is for that we have poured out a river of English blood, and a treasure unheard of in any former age. This Constitution may have its imperfections; but, faulty as it is, our ancestors have conveyed down liberty to us through that channel; and we ought to continue it on, as well as we can, to our posterity, and not give way to the new-modelling schemes of every extraordinary genius. It would certainly be new-modelling the Constitution in a great measure, to take a considerable part of what power is left to the Crown from the Crown, and by that means add very much to the power of the Lords.

Besides, it is to be remembered, that the evil, which may be brought upon the Commons by this means, will be irretrievable. Those persons deceive themselves, who think, that if such a law should prove destructive, it may be annulled, nothing being more usual than for one parliament to repeal the acts of another. This is true in common cases, because almost all laws relate to every part of the legislature, and any inconvenience is felt in some measure by each of them; but this will be a law which will relate chiefly, nay solely, to the Lords; and, whatever injury the Crown or the Commons may receive by it, their Lordships will be very sensible of the advantages of it to themselves: and nothing can be more vain, than to imagine that the Commons will be ever able to shake off any exorbitant power that the Lords shall be once possessed of, unless it be by an universal destruction, like those just mentioned, which will swallow Lords and Commons and all estates together. For which reasons, this project, if it should ever be offered to the Commons, is not only to be opposed with all the zeal imaginable, but every step, every attempt towards it, is to be detested. He that gives the power of blood, is a murderer; and he that gives the power of tyranny, is a tyrant. I shall add but one word more: The greatest traitor to civil society that ever yet appeared, will be the man, if such a one can be found, who shall contend for such a bill, should it be proposed amongst the Commons, with the assurance in his pocket of being a Peer as soon as the bill passes: and should he succeed, (which God forbid!) that honour, which is to be the reward of so base a treachery, will be a lasting mark of infamy to the family that bears it, whilst any notion of honesty remains amongst mankind.

THE OLD WHIG
No. 1. Thursday, March 19, 1718–19
ON THE STATE OF THE PEERAGE
WITH REMARKS UPON THE PLEBEIAN

> What none of all the gods could grant thy vows,
> That, Turnus, this auspicious day bestows.
> DRYDEN

I find that men, who have turned their thoughts to what is now the great subject, not only of our parliamentary debates, but of our private conversation, are apt to complain, it is a matter of such a perplext nature, and admits of so many arguments on either side, that they are rather bewildered than instructed, by what they have heard in discourse, or seen in print, upon this occasion. But, as I think this perplexity does not arise in men's minds from the nature of the thing itself, so much as from the way of handling it, I shall endeavour to draw out the whole state of this affair with such brevity and method, as may neither tire nor puzzle the reader; but carry his thoughts through a series of observations and arguments, that will regularly grow out of one another, and set this matter in its full light.

1. Those who are thought the best writers upon government, both ancients and moderns, have unanimously agreed in opinion, that the most perfect and reasonable form is a mixt government, in opposition to that of any single person, or any single order of men. For whether the supreme, that is, the legislative power, be lodged entirely in a prince, or in an aristocracy, or in a democracy, it is still looked upon as tyrannical, and not properly calculated for the happiness of the whole community.

2. It is also established as a maxim among political writers, that the division of the supreme or legislative power is most perfect, when it is distributed into three branches. If it all centres in one man, or in a body of men of the same quality, it is that form of government which is called tyrannical. If it be thrown into two branches, it wants a casting power, and is under such a divided authority as would often draw two different ways, and produce some time or other such a discord as would expose the weaker to that which had most strength in it, and by degrees end in a single authority. If it consist of four branches, it wants likewise a casting power, and is liable to the same inconveniences as when it is composed of two. And if it be divided into five or more parts, it necessarily runs into confusion, and will not long retain either the form or the name of government. For this reason, three branches in a legislature have been always fixed upon as the proper number; because it affords a casting power, and may moderate any heats in any two contending branches, and overpower the third in case it should prove unreasonable, or refuse to come into measures apparently necessary for the good and preservation of the community.

3. The most natural and equitable division of these three branches of the legislature is, the regal, the noble, and the plebeian; because the whole community is cast under these several heads, and has not in it a single member who is without his representative in the legislature of such a constitution.

4. In the next place, it is necessary that these three branches should be entirely separate and distinct from each other, so that no one of them may lie too much under the influence and control of either of the collateral branches. For if one part of the legislature may any ways be invested with a power to force either of the other two to concur with it, the legislative power is in reality, whatever it may pretend to, divided into no more than two branches.

5. It is the usual boast of Englishmen, that our government is fixed upon this triple basis, which has been allowed even in speculation, and that by persons who could have no eye to our Constitution, a form the most accommodated to the happiness of a community, and the most likely to stand secure in its own strength. But if upon examination one branch of its legislature is liable on any occasion to be entirely mastered and controlled by one of the other, it is certain that nothing can be more desirable than such an improvement in our constitution as may remove out of it this visible imperfection. If a king has power, when he pleases, to add what number he shall think fit to a body of nobles who have a vote in the legislature, it is plain he may secure his point in that branch of the legislature, and by that means command two votes out of three. This has made many assert, and I wish I could hear a satisfactory answer to it, that there are not probably more than two branches in our legislature, notwithstanding we flatter ourselves that they are three.

6. In this case, a precarious power of nobles, so far subject to the regal power in their legislative capacity, might sometimes be more pernicious to the public than if the power of both the branches were confessedly united in the sovereign; because we might well suppose a bad king would scarce venture upon some things, were the whole odium of them to turn upon himself; whereas a body of Peerage, should they only be created in an emergency to carry any unjustifiable design, would serve to divert or silence the murmurs of the public.

7. It is a known saying of the late British king, "That if his friends could gain him a House of Commons, he would throw his troop of guards into the House of Lords, rather than miscarry in his measures." And whether it is possible for a court to gain a House of Commons of what complexion they please, and what would be the consequences at some time or other of their success in such an attempt, whilst the Crown is possest of a certain means, by virtue of its prerogative, of filling the House of Lords with its own creatures, are points too evident in themselves to be insisted upon.

8. The foregoing reflections are like first principles that have scarce been ever called into dispute, and have not only been the avowed maxims of those who have been distinguished by the name of Whigs, but have furnished matter of complaint to every party in its turn. This power of the prerogative has always occasioned murmurs, when either side has found it exerted to their prejudice. We have often wished for a redress of it, and have now an opportunity of coming at it, which, if

we do not lay hold of, is not likely to offer itself again so long as we are a people.

9. It is proposed, to prevent those many inconveniences which may arise from an arbitrary creation of Peers, in what proportion and at what time the sovereign shall please, to restrain the Peers to a certain number. It is evident that such a law would remedy those many evils that may proceed from such sudden and numerous additions which have been made to the House of Lords in the most critical conjunctures. But I find there are objections made to this expedient, from the consequences it would have upon the Crown.

10. It is represented, that it will be the cutting off a branch from the prerogative. But if this be only the cutting off a branch which is pernicious to the public, it is certainly a very good argument for doing it, when we can; and that this power is of such a nature, can scarce admit of a dispute. Besides, that the Crown, far from being lessened by it, will receive a greater lustre, by parting with a prerogative that has so often given offence, and may some time turn to the destruction of the subject.

11. The Crown, as a branch of the legislature, cannot desire a greater prerogative than that of a negative in the passing of a law; and as it ought not to influence either House in their debates, what can a good king desire more than the power of approving or rejecting any such bill as cannot pass into a law without the royal assent?

12. The Crown will have still all the power in it of doing good to the people, in which the prerogative of our British kings will be still unlimited. In short, it neither touches the executive nor the legislative power of the Crown, nor takes away the prerogative of creating Peers, but only of doing it in such a manner as seems repugnant to reason and justice. The British king will still be the source of nobility, and hold in himself the principle of Peerage, though it is not to be lavished away on multitudes, or given occasionally to the detriment of the public.

13. Besides, what does the Crown do more in parting with a branch of its prerogative, than what the two other parts of the legislature have frequently done, with regard to their respective bodies, when they have found any of their rights or privileges prejudicial to the community? All such self-denying acts are of a popular nature, and have been passed with the good-liking and applause of their fellow-subjects. Nay, the Crown has never more recommended itself to the affection of the people, than when it has retrenched itself in any exorbitance of power

that did not seem consistent with their liberty; as in passing the bill of Habeas Corpus, and that for establishing Triennial Parliaments.

14. Indeed, were this a point extorted from the Crown in its necessities, it might be generous at such a juncture to appear in the defence of the prerogative; but this is not our case: we are only disputing whether we shall accept of a voluntary concession made by the sovereign himself, who out of his unparalleled goodness has shown, by this instance, that he places the true dignity of the British monarch, where it always ought to be placed, in the liberty of his people.

15. Having considered this alteration proposed to be made in our Constitution with relation to the Crown, let us now consider it with regard, first, to the House of Commons, and, in the next place, to the whole body of the English commonalty; and if we find that it will prove advantageous in its consequences under both these views, it is undoubtedly an alteration very much to be wished for.

16. The number of Peers is in a few reigns increased from fifty-nine to near two hundred and twenty; and there is no question but that in as few succeeding reigns their present number will be doubled; nor will posterity be able to see an end of them, unless it be timely prevented. Nay, we have all the reason in the world to apprehend that their number will hereafter swell in greater proportions than it has done hitherto. It is a general remark, that since the act has passed for triennial elections, Commoners of great estates are more desirous than ever of gaining a place in the Upper House, which will exempt them from such a constant dependence on their electors, and the frequent returns of trouble and expense in their elections. At least, it is natural to suppose that every king will make such additions as will give his friends a majority; nay, if we may conclude from experience, every minister who differs in his politics from his predecessor, will bring to his assistance a sufficient number to turn the balance in his favour. And it is obvious to every one how quick is the succession of ministers in this country.

17. The first good consequence, therefore, of the proposed alteration to the House of Commons will be this, That it will fill that House with men of the largest fortunes and the greatest abilities; for we may well suppose that such men will set themselves forward to be elected into such a seat, when it is the highest honour they can have immediately in view. By this means, those will be the representatives of the people, who have the greatest stake among them. Those will have the giving of money in their power, who have the most of it in their possession. But, above all, the influence of the House of Commons, and con-

sequently of all the Commons of England, will preserve itself in its due strength; for, of all maxims, none is more uncontested than that power follows property. But what additional strength would this give the House of Lords, if the richest members of the House of Commons may be draughted out of it in such numbers as the present frame of our Constitution permits? Nor would the inconvenience be less with respect to men of great parliamentary abilities, if, instead of continuing to add weight and authority to the Lower House, they may be called up at any time to the employ the same abilities in aggrandizing the figure of another House.

18. And as the proposed alteration will be a proper means to give a figure to the House of Commons, so will it likewise be an expedient to preserve their integrity, as it will take off one method, and indeed the most effectual method, of bribing men of over-grown fortunes. When a Peerage dangles before the eyes of the most wealthy Commoner, it may have charms in it to one, who would have a contempt for any offers of another kind. A man's ambition is as susceptible of bribes as his avarice, and it should be the care of a legislature to cut off all temptations to corruption in the one as well as the other. It is true, the alteration proposed would not utterly remove the influence of such a motive; but it would certainly very much weaken it, and render it infinitely more ineffectual than what it is at present.

19. If this method restrains men of the greatest figure of the Lower House from making their way so easily to the Upper, it will evidently tend to the bringing a greater number of places of the highest trust, honour, or profit, into the hands of the most able and wealthy Commoners. Men so accomplished will have a diffusive influence both in their own House and in their respective counties; and it will be necessary for all governments to find out proper rewards and gratifications for such men; and gratifications of this kind no Commoner will envy them, since they enable them to be beneficial to the body of people whom they represent, and do not in their nature deprive us of their strength and assistance in that branch of the legislature to which we belong.

20. However, the proposed restraint on the number of Peers is far from being an exclusion of such Commoners who are recommended by their fortunes, or their abilities. According to the calculation generally received, there may happen two extinctions or vacancies, taking one year with another, in the body of Peers, as fixed and ascertained by the new scheme, in case it should obtain. And surely the Commons of England will think it sufficient to lose annually two of their most

considerable members, whatever may be the opinion of particular persons, who are in haste to leave their company.

21. A restraint upon the number of the Lords will necessarily restrain the influence of that body in the election of members to serve in the Lower House. It is very well known, that few members of the House of Commons are advanced to Peerage, who have not one or more corporations under their direction; nay, that very often this is one reason for their promotion. If, therefore, this´perpetually increasing body of Lords continues on the foot it is now, in proportion as their number is augmented, their influence in elections will grow more general, till at length, as the Upper House are the creature of the Crown, the Lower House may be in a great measure the creature of the Lords. And it is worth while to consider whether in process of time, unless seasonably prevented, the House of Commons may not be filled with the stewards and bailiffs of our Peers.

22. In the next place, let us see what would be the consequences from such an alteration upon the whole bulk of the English commonalty, which should always find the first place in the thoughts of their representatives. If they should gain only this single advantage, I think it is a very considerable one, that it will hinder the nation from being overrun with Lords. We know that, in the sale of an estate, it is no small recommendation to the buyer, that there is no Lord within so many miles of it, and the distance of such a borderer is often looked upon as an equivalent to a year's purchase. But who can be secure from such a neighbour, whilst the species is so apt to increase and multiply? I shall not insist upon paying of debts, which is looked upon as a moral duty among Commoners, who cannot but be sorry to see any additions to an order of men that are sheltered by privileges from the demands of their honest and industrious creditors. To which many considerations of the like nature may be added, were they not obvious to the private reflection of every reader.

23. But the great point, and which ought to carry the chief weight with us in this case, is, that the alteration now proposed will give such a mighty power to the bulk of the English Commons, as can be never counterbalanced by the body of the nobility. Should we suppose two hundred and thirty-five Peers possest, one with another, of £5000 *per annum*, this would amount to no more than £1,175,000 *per annum*; and what is such a property, and the power arising out of it, compared with the power arising out of the property of those many millions possest by the Commons? Besides, that the great accessions of

wealth yearly made in the body of the Commons would give it continually an increase of property and power, which would accrue to the body of the nobles, in case their door was always open to men of overflowing fortunes, who might find no great difficulty in procuring an entrance.

24. I shall now offer two fair questions to any man who impartially weighs these matters.

First, If two schemes of government were proposed to him, in both of which the legislature should consist of three branches, whether he would prefer that scheme, in which one of the branches might be increased at pleasure by another of them; or that scheme in which every branch should be limited to a certain stated number. Nay, if the two schemes were placed in parallel with one another, and considered in their respective consequences, whether the first would not appear a most wild and indigested project?

In the second place, I would propose this question. If the Lords had been limited to a certain number by our constitution, whether it would not have been thought unpardonable in any one who should have proposed to have taken off that limitation, and left it to the pleasure of the Crown arbitrarily to add to them any number at any time.

Nobody can be at a loss to determine himself in these questions, who considers this subject by those plain lights which are already exhibited in this discourse, and which may be strengthened by many other considerations.

25. This subject naturally engages me in one talk more, which is, to examine the objections that have been started against this alteration proposed to be made in the constitution of the House of Peers. And here I cannot discover any inconvenience which can be said to follow from such an alteration, that does not now subsist, or is not answered by some much greater inconvenience in the present state of the Peerage. But, that I may not follow the example of those who have appeared in print on the other side of this debate, in putting weak arguments into the mouth of their antagonists, I shall answer such objections as have been the most approved by those who declare themselves against this bill, as they are laid together in a pamphlet, entitled, The Plebeian.

26. As for the introduction, the digression upon the Ephori, and the concluding paragraph, they are only arguments *ad conflandam invidiam* [for the incitement of anger], and such as are not to be an-

swered by reason, but by the same angry strain in which they are written, and which would discredit a cause that is able to support itself without such an assistance.

27. "At first sight," says the Plebeian, "this proposal must appear very shocking; it carries with it so great an alteration of the Constitution." This is the first general objection, and I wish it had been pursued regularly; but because it is dropped and resumed in the following part of the discourse, I must be forced to collect those scattered passages on this head, as I find them in different parts of the book. This great objection will be sufficiently answered, if this alteration of the Constitution is from worse to better; which I think has been fully proved. As everything is formed into perfection by degrees, the wisdom of all legislatures has embraced every opportunity of making such changes in their government, as have been advantageous to those who live under it. This author himself gives us an eminent instance of a great alteration of our Constitution in the Lower House, under the reign of Queen Elizabeth, "when the Crown erected several new corporations, and relieved several ancient and decayed ones from sending any members at all." I do not make use of this increase in the number of the Commons, as an argument for an increase in the number of Lords, which the author produces as the reasoning of some people who are for the bill. Such people, if any there are, must talk inconsistently with themselves, since it is the purport of the bill to prevent the House of Lords from growing too numerous. But it is an unanswerable argument to show that there has been as great an alteration in one branch of our legislature, as is now proposed to be made in another; and that such an alteration should be introduced into our form of government, when there are good reasons for it; on which account our author himself justifies the above-mentioned alteration in the House of Commons. Our author furnishes us with another very good argument in this particular against himself. "Whiggism," says he, "if I understand it aright, is a desire of liberty, and a spirit of opposition to all exorbitant power in any part of the Constitution. Formerly the danger on this account was from the Crown; but since the Habeas Corpus Act, and the many restraints laid upon the Crown in King William's time, and the great and numerous limitations of the Succession Acts, the prerogative of the Crown is reduced so low, that it is not at all dangerous to the Commons." As we have the author's confession in the afore-mentioned instance of an alteration in the Plebeian, he has here given us an account of as remarkable changes in the regal branch of our government. The prerogative was retrenched

in those several instances, because without such retrenchment the power of it appeared exorbitant and dangerous to the Commons. If therefore there still inheres in the Crown a power that is exorbitant and dangerous to the Commons, there is the same reason why the Commons should lay hold of the present opportunity to retrench it. This is the matter in debate betwixt us; but, be that as it will, the argument which the author here makes use of against the bill in question, "that it carries in it too great an alteration of the Constitution," would have been as good an argument against the Habeas Corpus Act, or any other of those above-mentioned. What is further said upon this subject . . . would make a handsome sentence in a popular speech, but will never stand the test of a strict examination in a discourse addressed to the reasons and not the passions of men. "In short, it has been for our ancient Constitution," says the author, "that we have struggled with so much vigour for many years together; it is for that we have poured out a river of English blood, and a treasure unheard of in any former age. This Constitution may have its imperfections; but, faulty as it is, our ancestors have conveyed down liberty to us through that channel: and we ought to continue it on, as well as we can, to our posterity, and not give way to the new-modelling schemes of every extraordinary genius." This is not arguing, but declaiming. Our ancestors remedied several imperfections from time to time, and we are obliged to them for having conveyed liberty down to us through the channel which they had so often altered and reformed. And will not our posterity be as thankful to us, if we transmit to them their liberty through the same channel, when it shall be only altered for the better conveyance of it?

28. Having taken off the force of this main objection, I shall follow others as the author leads me. He tells us that "the shutting up the door of the House of Lords, in the manner talked of, cannot but prove a great discouragement to virtuous actions, to learning and industry, and very detrimental to the House of Peers itself, by preventing such frequent supplies from going into it, as the nature of such a body requires: for want of which, it may in time become corrupt and offensive, like a stagnated pool, which hitherto has been preserved wholesome and pure by the fresh streams that pass continually into it." This consideration, if it has any force, cuts down all the other arguments drawn from the new accessions of figure and power, which he supposes would accrue to the House of Lords, by the passing of the bill so much talked of. Can it be detrimental to the House of Lords, and at the same time throw into their hands all the places and honours

that the Crown can confer upon them? Will that body of men, which would become mean and despicable, and offensive as a stagnated pool, by the means of this alteration, be raised by the same means to be the most formidable, and the most honoured part in our Constitution? Or could the same body degenerate into a public nuisance, as our author represents it, and at the same time be able to overawe both king and people? Can two such contrary effects be produced from one and the same cause? But could we suppose that this body of men might thus degenerate; would they be able, without numerous recruits of wealth, learning, and industry, to oppose anything for the good of the community, in contradiction to the king and people? But more of this hereafter.

29. Our author adds, "I am not unaware, it will be said, that the frequent extinctions of [noble] families will salve this inconvenience, and make room for the rewarding of merit. But," says he, "this expedient, I fear, is not much to be depended on; for the uncertainty of the time when the Crown will have any such power will make it much the same as if it were never to have it at all;" which is as much as to say, that unless the Crown has power of making what number of Lords it pleases, and at what time it pleases, and to serve what turn it pleases, it had as good have no power at all of making Peers, which the author supposes is the only adequate power it has of rewarding merit. Not to ask the author whether it be generally virtuous actions, learning, or industry, that recommend Commoners to the Peerage, or of what other kind the merit is which has been often thus rewarded; I shall only ask him, whether any man has so crying a merit as immediately requires a Peerage for its reward; or whether the extinction of two titles in a year will not leave room enough for the Crown to reward those extraordinary persons, whose merits give them such a demand upon it? As for another argument which the author puts into the mouth of those whom he calls patrons of the bill proposed, "that it will ease the Crown of importunities," as I think it has no great weight in it, I am not concerned to urge anything in its defence against the Plebeian's answer to it.

30. We come now to the most considerable paragraph of the whole book, which I shall therefore transcribe at length. "But another consequence, of a much higher nature, attending the limitation of the number of Peers, is the danger there will be of changing the Constitution by this means into an aristocracy. And this may at any time in such case be effected by the confederacy of two or three great families, which would form such a body in the House of Lords, as

the Crown would not be able to control. That this kind of government is one of the worst sorts of slavery, is too well known to be disputed. In a democracy, a great many different persons may come to have a share of power by several incidents, but in the other case it is birth only that entitles to superiority: and the milk such nobles are nursed up with, is hatred and contempt for every human creature but those of their own imaginary dignity." The question to be stated here is, Whether the House of Lords under their present constitution is not as likely to run into an aristocracy, as it would be in case their number should be limited. It appears very plain to me, that a body of Peers perpetually increasing, and capable of additions, has in it a natural tendency to an aristocracy. Supposing that the House of Lords from sixty members is now swelled to two hundred: these, if increased by the same proportion, would in the same number of years amount to six hundred and sixty-six, to which we may presume there would be still the like proportionable additions. By this means they would in time receive such vast accessions of property, as might encourage them, not only to entertain so ambitious a design, but in a great measure to render it effectual: especially when any men could be admitted into their own order, with their great abilities in parliament, or their great influence among the people, who might be most capable of opposing their encroachments upon the Commons. I do allow that such additions would be prejudicial to the Crown; but this is no reason why they would not be made, as it has not prevented the additions that have been made in our own memory. For though the Crown in general would be a sufferer by this method; yet it would naturally have re-course to it, as it has formerly, when it labours under any present exigency, that can only be removed by such an expedient. This danger of an aristocracy, every one must confess, would be very much abated, and, I think, utterly removed, by the limitation of the Lords to such a number as is now proposed. In such a case, their property would be so very inconsiderable, when compared with that of the Commons, (as I have before showed to a demonstration,) that it would render such a design in them the most chimerical, and the most impracticable. And since it is impossible that the whole body of Lords in their united strength could be able to establish themselves into an aristocracy, the author's imagination vanishes, that "this may at any time, in such a case, be effected by the confederacy of two or three great families, which would form such a body among the Lords as the Crown would not be able to control." If the author means in this place, by the Crown not being able to control the Lords, that it would be restrained from pouring in such a number as would sway them to its inclinations, it is what ought to be wished for. If he means that this want of power in the Crown would enable them to erect an aristocracy, it is certainly a wrong consequence, because not only the Crown, but the people, would have a superior power in them to the body of nobles, and are equally concerned to preserve their stations in the government. The author after this brings an argument to prove, that an aristocracy is a bad form of government, and that a democracy is preferable to it, in which I entirely agree with him; but must add, that a mixed government, made out of aristocracy, democracy, and monarchy, is better than either of them. The author subjoins, that "the milk which nobles are nursed up with is hatred and contempt of every human creature, but those of their own imaginary dignity." If so, the fewer of them the better. What Commoner would not desire to put a stop to the increase of them?

31. The next objection I meet with is from the great privileges the Lords are already possessed of, with relation to actions *de Scandalis Magnatum*, &c., which is likewise a very good reason why we should hinder the increase of persons invested with these privileges; and as for the judicial power, with that of imprisoning, they are such as subsist in their body as it is now constituted, and therefore cannot be objected to the proposed alteration, which would only leave them as they are.

32. "The increasing the number of Peers," says the author, "is always to be wished for by the Commons." We have seen sufficient reasons why it should not. "Because the greater their number, the less considerable they become;" the contrary of which has been evidently proved; "and the less within the influence of court favours." What! when by this very power of increasing them at will, it can secure any point among them that it pleases? "By which means alone ministers are kept in awe, and remain in a situation of being called to account for their actions. Were it otherwise, they would be out of the reach of any accusation. They would know exactly by whom they were to be tried, and their judges might be their accomplices. And should this once come to be the case, what might they not attempt with impunity?" Is this inconvenience better prevented in a House of Peers on the bottom it now stands? Can any one who has been a good minister be secure, if the Crown should add a sufficient number of his enemies to those who sit in judgment upon him? Or is a bad minister in any danger, when he may be sheltered by the addition of a sufficient number of his friends?

33. I must not pass over another remarkable paragraph of the

author upon the same argument for increasing the Lords at pleasure. "The great advantage," says he, "that the number of their body cannot be increased, is at present the most valuable privilege of the House of Commons, and the only thing that makes them considerable." This is indeed a very poor advantage, to found upon it the grandeur of the House of Commons. Is not the power of giving money and raising taxes confined to that body, and which can never fail to give them the greatest weight in the legislature? Will not this be always the most valuable privilege of the Commons? and what other privilege can make them more considerable? He goes on, "The Lords are possessed of many great privileges that they will not permit the Commons to share with them; and therefore the Commons would be highly wanting to themselves, if they should add this advantage likewise to the Lords, which is the only one that they can enjoy distinct from them." Our author, as it may turn to his account, sometimes considers the Lords in their personal privileges as they are individuals, and sometimes as they are a body of men in the legislature. If he here means their privileges in the former view, I do allow they are very great ones, and therefore certainly every Commoner cannot desire an increase of such individuals. But if he here means their privileges as a legislative body, it is certain that all their privileges together are not equal to that one of commanding the purse of the community. So that it is wonderful how he could advance, that the number of the House of Commons, not being subject to an increase, "is the only advantage that they enjoy distinct from the House of Lords."

34. Our author next proceeds to speak of the proportion of property between the two Houses of Lords and Commons, which is a point already so fully discussed, that I shall not trouble the reader with any repetitions; but cannot omit what the author asserts as an indisputable point, and which in itself is the greatest paradox I ever heard advanced. His words are, "Indeed, if a restraining bill should pass, I do not doubt but it would be soon followed with a bill to prevent Lords from alienating their estates, for which many plausible reasons are to be produced; and then, without all dispute, the balance of property will be soon turned on the side of their Lordships." Which is as much as to say, in plain English, that the Lords will have as much wealth amongst them as the whole body of the British Commons, or that one million will be a balance against a hundred millions. Indeed the House of Lords in their present constitution may be always approaching to a balance in property with the Commons, from whence they are continually receiving into their body such large supplies; but if their

number be once limited, you cut off their recruits, and lay them under an impossibility of ever rivaling the other branch of the legislature in this particular.

35. Our author's argument, that a new power would arise to the House of Lords from the alteration so much talked of, is founded upon a fact which every one denies at first sight. His words are these: "For as to what is commonly said, that the Lords would get nothing, no new power would be added to them by this means; I beg leave to state this matter in a proper light. Suppose the balance to be now even betwixt the Lords and the Crown, as it certainly is, or else the Constitution would not subsist in quiet; is it not plain to the most common capacity, that when two scales are upon an equal poise, if you take any weight out of one of them, you give the advantage to the other without putting anything into it?" The author here supposes that the balance between two parts of the legislature should be even; and so far I concur with him, that being the chief end which this alteration has in view. But I can by no means suppose with him that they are even, because it is contrary to matter of fact. For we plainly see that the Sovereign has it always in his power to make what division of party or opinion he pleases prevail in that House. As for the reason of their present supposed equality, "that otherwise they could not subsist in quiet," it has no force in it, because we see very ill-constituted governments will subsist in quiet for many ages, not that they are preserved by a rightly tempered Constitution, which would give them the greatest strength, but by other accidental causes. The ill consequences of such an inequality may be frequently felt and complained of, though they may not shake the tranquillity of the public.

36. I have now gone through everything that carries the face of an argument for the constitution of the House of Lords, as it now stands, or of an objection against the alteration proposed to be made; having only avoided saying anything in this case as it affects the Scottish nobility, because I have here considered it only as an English Commoner, and because I have thoughts of prosecuting the subject, as it relates to Scotland, in another pamphlet, being unwilling to swell this to a greater bulk.

37. Since the writing of the foregoing discourse, I have perused a pamphlet, entitled, "The Thoughts of a Member of the Lower House," &c., in which the author first approves our Constitution as divided into its three branches, and through the whole course of his book contends in effect that it should consist of no more than two; for he supposes the House of Lords instituted only as guardians and ornaments

to the throne, and to be augmented by the Crown in such a proportion, as may strengthen it in opposition, to the House of Commons. The reader may see his scheme in the following words: "There is not," says this writer, "a more certain maxim in politics, than that a monarchy must subsist by an army, or nobility. The first makes it despotic, and the latter a free government. I presume none of those nobler personages themselves, who have the honour to make up that illustrious body, do believe they are so distinguished and advanced above their fellow-subjects for their own sakes: they know they are intended the guardians, as well as ornaments of the monarchy, an essential prerogative of which it must be to add to and augment their number in such proportion, as to render them a proper balance against the democratical part of our Constitution, without being formidable to the monarchy itself, the support of which is the reason of their institution." This is a most extraordinary notion of government, that one branch of a legislature should be instituted, only to be subservient to the strength and support of another, but it is on this bottom that he founds his whole discourse; and as for his objections to the proposed alteration, I find they are such as I have already obviated in the course of this pamphlet. If anything remains in them unanswered, it will fall under the last objection against the matter in debate, which I should not take notice of, did not I find that it makes an impression upon some people's minds.

38. Suppose, says the objection, there should be an inflexible obstinacy in the House of Peers, what method would there be left to bring them to a concurrence with the two other branches of the legislature, when it will not be in the power of the King to bring them over to reason, by flinging in sufficient numbers among them? To this I answer, That if the Lords are obstinate in a point that is reasonable and beneficial to the community, it will be happy for their country that they should be invested with the proper power of a legislative branch, not to be overruled to wrong measures. This may sometimes be of great advantage to the public, if we can possibly suppose that the two other branches may concur in anything that is not consistent with justice, or the national interest. If the Peers are thus inflexibly obstinate in any methods that are *dishonourable, unjust,* or *pernicious* to their country; can we imagine they could not be influenced into a compliance by the authority of the two sharing branches in the legislature? Or can we think they would persist in measures which would draw upon them the displeasure of the Crown, and the resentments of the whole Commons of Great Britain? Every body of men takes as much

care as possible to preserve their credit, and to render themselves popular; and we cannot think that any branch of a legislature would be made up of madmen, or pursue such measures as must necessarily end in their infamy, or their destruction; especially when they are infinitely weaker than either of the other constituent parts of our legislature. Could any person apprehend such a behaviour from them, I am sure the same person cannot in his heart apprehend their growing up into an aristocracy. The Peers are so little a match for the Crown in power, or the Commons in property, much less able to cope with the united force of both; that it is wildness to suppose them guilty, of such an unjust and unreasonable obstinacy, as they know might endanger their very being in the British Constitution. And now I shall only propose it to every one's thoughts, whether an expedient, which will remedy the greatest inconvenience that may arise to us, from one of the branches of the legislature, and of which we have had experience, as has been already sufficiently explained, should prevail with us to lay it aside, out of a groundless fear, that it should expose us to an inconvenience from another branch of the legislature, which must suppose them destitute of common sense, void of honour and equity, and regardless of self-preservation, before it can possibly befall us. To this I shall only add, that whatever objections are made against this alteration in the Constitution, may be made against every form of government, in which the legislature consists of three distinct branches, and that is, against such a form as has been pronounced the most perfect by those who have been the most skilful politicians, and the most famous for their observations on the nature of government.

THE PLEBEIAN
No. 2. Monday, March 23, 1718–19
BY A MEMBER OF THE HOUSE OF COMMONS
CONSIDERATIONS UPON THE REPORTS RELATING TO THE PEERAGE CONTINUED;
AND REMARKS UPON THE PAMPHLETS THAT HAVE BEEN WRIT FOR THE
SUPPOSED BILL

Who sees not now through the Lords' thin disguise?
DRYDEN

Those who are not particularly acquainted with the vocation of Pamphlet-writing, have very much wondered that a matter of so great consequence as the affair of the Peerage, and espoused by such persons as are very well known to be its patrons, could have been so long a while upon the stage, and no champion appear for it; but others, who are more versed in this kind of business, know, there could not be wanting persons enough to make their court, by producing their lucubrations on this head. But as it is a subject that will not very well bear debating, their masters, without doubt, were of opinion, that the best way was, to let all manner of writing alone, and keep all that could be said on the subject for the time and place where it was absolutely necessary to say something.

The agitators for the bill assured themselves, that nobody would be so bold as to attack first; and consequently judged themselves out of all danger. But the Plebeian starting forth unexpectedly, they were forced, like people in a surprise, or on an invasion, to march immediately any troops they had; and indeed these are some of the most tattered I ever saw.

The first champion that appeared for this bill, was a person who exhibited himself in the St. James's Post, of Wednesday, March 18, in this advertisement: "Some Considerations relating to the Peerage of Great Britain. Wherein the arguments *for* the reasonableness and expediency of a bill, said to be depending, are stated *Pro* and *Con*."

This performance I have not been able to venture upon; for he that can state arguments *for* the bill, both *Pro* and *Con*, is too slippery a person for anybody to lay hold of.

The next that entered the lists, on the same side of the question, having been more fortunate than to *discover himself beforehand*, I have perused his labours. The account he gives of himself is, "That he is a member of the House of Commons, who has a friend with whom he uses to talk over in *private* all arguments and considerations which concern anything of moment, as far as they could collect and remember them: and they having both agreed that this was a matter of a very extraordinary nature, the one entreated the other to put his thoughts about it in writing, that he might be better able to judge of them all together. And in order to continue the privacy of this correspondence, those thoughts came out, printed for J. Roberts in Warwick-Lane."

This notable introduction was very near having the same effect upon me, as to this pamphlet, as the advertisement just mentioned had to the former; but with much ado I went through the performance. All I can learn from it is, that this gentleman was present at the debates of the House of Lords; where he does not seem to have been mightily enlightened as to the true state of the case, the debate having in all probability run pretty much one way.

The next that follows these two combatants for this bill, is somebody or other that is used to masquerading, as I suppose; and indeed he is so well disguised, that it is impossible to know him. When I first read the title, *The Old Whig*, I expected no less than the utmost wrath and indignation against the House of Lords. I could not help thinking but he would have been for *voting them useless* at least, as his ancestors did formerly: but I was extremely surprised to find just the contrary; that he is for giving them such a power, as would make the *House of Commons useless*; and therefore he might as well have taken any other title in the world, as *The Old Whig*. I am afraid he is *so old a Whig*, that he has quite *forgot his principles*.

But I shall show now more plainly, what is said in the former Plebeian, that this is neither a *Whig* nor a *Tory* point, but is a jumble, a hodge-podge, a confusion of all parties and all persons together; and must inevitably in its consequences destroy first *Whig* and *Tory*, and afterwards *Crown* and *people*. As all sorts of people unite for it, so ought all sorts, and of every denomination, that have any value for their Constitution, to unite against it.

This pamphlet, by the marks it appears with, being in all probability the best performance that is to come from that quarter, the Plebeian will consider it thoroughly; and in order to proceed more methodically, for this author's satisfaction—

First, I will answer the objections made to the last Plebeian.

Secondly, I will consider the argument, as the *Old Whig* states it himself.

The first objection the author of the Remarks makes to the Plebeian, is, "That the *Introduction*, the Digression upon the *Ephori*, and the *Conclusion*, are all arguments *ad conflandam invidiam*." He who says that arguments drawn from history, which can only show what has happened in former times, are arguments *ad conflandam invidiam*, gives up the matter in dispute, and lets the world know, by passing them so slightly over, that he feels their force: for it is a tacit admission, that in all probability the like disasters will happen from the alterations now projected in our Constitution, which, history informs us, were the real consequences of alterations of the like nature in other countries; otherwise those arguments could not now contribute to make persons invidious. Besides, I always thought that bringing examples from history was looked upon as the most impartial and unexceptionable method of arguing, as it is abstracted from the passions and interests of the present times; for what is learning and history, if it be not to draw inferences of what may happen, from what has happened?

.   .   .

The first argument of the Plebeian, which the *Old Whig* objects to, is, . . . "That though the Plebeian declares against the proposed bill, because it will make so great an alteration in our Constitution, yet he produces an eminent instance of a great alteration of our Constitution in the Lower House under the reign of Queen Elizabeth, when the Crown erected several new corporations, and relieved several ancient decayed ones from sending any members at all."

This, the Remarker says, was as great an alteration in one branch of our legislature, as is now proposed to be made in another. The Remarker quite mistakes this point; for, instead of being an alteration of so great consequence to the constitution of the Commons, as this new proposal is of that of the Lords, it was an alteration of no consequence at all. Suppose the towns of Watchet and Dunster, two seaports in Somersetshire, to have been destroyed in the wars with Ireland in Queen Elizabeth's time. The inhabitants, on account of poverty, apply to the Crown to be exempted from the charge of paying four members to represent them in parliament. The Crown some time after grants charters to two neighbouring towns in flourishing circumstances, and directs the writs at a following summons of a parliament to be sent to Tiverton and Honiton, instead of Watchet and Dunster. Let anybody judge if this alteration can be of any consequence to the House of Commons. Here is nothing else but the places changed; and four members from Tiverton and Honiton are the same thing as four from Watchet and Dunster. But to state this matter with nicety would require much more labour and time than I am able to allow it.

Another argument, which the Remarker says the Plebeian furnishes against himself, is, "That he owns the prerogative has been retrenched in several instances; because without such retrenchment the power of it appeared exorbitant and dangerous to the Commons." But these retrenchments being now made, the question at present is, Whether the Commons ought to go on stripping the Crown of every jewel, till it becomes less resplendent than a Doge of Venice's coronet, or less comfortable than the Sword-bearer's cap of maintenance; and, what is of the greatest moment to the Commons, less able to protect them against the power of a House of Lords, if ever their Lordships should be disposed to claim a larger share of authority than belongs to them?

As to the complaint the Remarker makes, That the Plebeian *applies to men's passions, and not their reasons; and declaims instead of arguing*; what must be said in answer to this is, That people must make use of what arm they have. On the one side, it is evident there can be nothing but arguing and reasoning, and declaiming and exemplifying; but on the other, the Plebeian is afraid there are more irresistible arts of applying to the *passions*, rather than to the *reasons* of men, or else he would not have one minute's pain for the issue of this question.

The manner in which the Remarker states the Plebeian's argument, relating to the *shutting up the door of the House of Lords*, shows he either wilfully or ignorantly mistakes that part of the controversy: "For, after having cited the words of the Plebeian, he asks, if it can be detrimental to the House of Lords, and at the same time throw into their hands all the places and honours that the Crown can confer upon them? Will that body of men, which would become mean and despicable, and offensive as a stagnated pool, by the means of this alteration, be raised by the same means to be the most formidable and most honoured part of the Constitution? Or would they be able, without numerous recruits of wealth, learning, and industry, to oppose anything for the good of the community?" To this I answer, It will not be detrimental to them in point of power, but will be detrimental on account of those talents that ought to accompany power; the want of which the Commons will feel in their *judicature*, and in many more particulars. They will be *offensive* to others, but not perceive it themselves; they will be *formidable*, but not *honoured*. These are natural *effects* that all *exorbitant power produces*. As to wealth, they will take it, it is to be feared, where they can find it; and learning and industry will be as useless baubles to their Lordships, as *dangling Peerages* (as my author describes them excellently well) are to men of sense amongst the Commons.

The next objection of the Old Whig to the Plebeian is, "That he avers the uncertainty of the extinction of families will leave so little opportunity for the Crown to reward merit by Patrician honours, that it will be much the same thing as if the Crown were never to have any such power at all." *Whereas* (says he) *there will be two titles extinct every year, according to the calculation generally received.*

By the *calculation generally received*, I suppose the Remarker means the list published by way of prelude to this project. Whether it be true or false, if some heralds know anything of this matter, would take more time to examine into, than, I dare say, the Constitution it is intended to introduce would subsist. But supposing, for argument' sake, that that calculation is right, and that in one hundred and sixteen years there have been one hundred and fifty-four extinctions, there will be found wanting seventy-eight to make up his number of two a year; so that the extinctions have not been during that time quite so many as after the rate of one *Lord and a half* per annum. But besides this error in arithmetic, there is another error of an *odd nature* in this *computa-*

tion; which, unless some method is proposed to ascertain it, will reduce the extinctions to fewer than even one a year. And if so, those who expect to have their services rewarded by reversions so uncertainly computed, may have time enough to try all their patience, and at last find that, instead of advancing themselves to dignity, they have been forging their own chains. In the *computations of the titles extinct*, all those are comprehended who have been extinguished by *the edge of the law, treason, rebellion, and other capital offences*; and who, without the spirit of prophecy, can foretell what *vacancies* may happen by such means for the future? But if, in favour of this *scheme*, it be admitted that in all probability there may be as many and as great *criminals* hereafter in that noble body as there have been for the time past, is it not to be feared that the *path to justice may be more difficult, after this narrowing the way up to the House of Peers, than it has been formerly*.

As to what the Remarker has objected to the arguments of the Plebeian, which prove, "That the limitation of the number of the Lords will run the Constitution into an aristocracy;" this matter shall be fully considered presently, when I come to examine the Old Whig's state of the case.

In a following paragraph, where the Remarker takes notice of what the Plebeian urges on the side of the King and Commons, viz. "That an ill minister might be screened against them both, if this law should take place, by reason that in such case he would know exactly his judges, (who might likewise be his accomplices,) and so act with impunity; the Remarker argues, That if this bill does not pass, an innocent minister cannot be secure, nor a guilty one punished, if the Crown should add to the House of Peers a sufficient number of the enemies of the one, or of the friends of the other." In either of which cases the utmost iniquity must be supposed in the Crown, which, I confess, I cannot bring myself to do, and therefore my argument remains entire. And it would grieve me to the heart, if I could think there were any *innocent ministers*, who ought to be emboldened by the consciousness of their integrity, and yet should have greater apprehensions from honest actions, than have been hitherto shown by men of the most guilty consciences, through the many ages that this Constitution has subsisted, without the alteration now desired.

The Remarker thinks it wonderful how the Plebeian could advance, "That the number of the House of Commons not being subject to an increase, is the only advantage that they enjoy distinct from the House of Lords;" and alleges, that *all their Lordships' privileges to-*

gether are not equal to that one of commanding the purse of the community. Were it true, that the Commoners enjoyed this privilege of *commanding the purse of the community,* distinct from the House of Lords, they would be very easy as to the increasing, or diminishing, or fixing their number, or as to anything else that might belong to that noble assembly. But, alas! this is not the case; for their Lordships' concurrence is as necessary to a money-bill, as to any other bill: nay, whether a money-bill may not originally take its rise in their House, is a point never yet clearly given up by their Lordships, if I am not very much misinformed; and whether they may not be more inclinable to dispute this matter, if ever their door comes to be shut in the manner now proposed, may deserve very serious reflection.

Thus having answered every objection made to the former Plebeian by the Old Whig, except such as will occur in considering this argument, as he states it himself; I shall now proceed to that point which I proposed at first setting out.

I agree with our author, "That the best kind of government is that which is composed of these three branches, the *regal,* the *noble,* and the *plebeian.*" This is at present our happy Constitution: "But then," says this author, "we have one imperfection or defect in it, which wants to be remedied; and that is, the Crown has too great a power over one branch of this Constitution, namely, the *noble;* in that the Crown can, whenever it pleases, add so many to their number as to influence their actions." And this author likewise assures us, . . . "That the Crown has power enough also to gain a House of Commons of what complexion it pleases." From whence I observe, first, That if it be a fault in the Constitution, that the Crown has so great power over one branch of the Constitution, the *noble,* as this author affirms, it is as great an imperfection that the Crown has so great a power, as he also affirms it has, over the Plebeian. And therefore this author should have proposed some method to have remedied this defect in the latter, as well as in the former branch; or else that perfection in the Constitution, he seems to be desirous of, cannot be arrived at. He contends, that it is absolutely necessary the *Lords should be entirely independent of the Crown.* An impartial friend to the *whole body of the people,* and to sound reason, would have said as much for the Commons. Then these two estates would have been upon a level. But even by such an alteration, which is the only equal one, our Constitution would not be mended, but made much worse; for if both Lords and Commons were as independent of the Crown as this author desires the

Lords may be, the unhappy consequence that must ensue would be, that if any discord should arise betwixt them, and each remain inflexibly resolved, here the Constitution would certainly want a casting power; and the only way of ending the dispute must be like a *Polish* Dyet, *by getting up on horseback.* And therefore this power now in the Crown, and which has been in it for so many ages, is necessary for the good of the whole community, to prevent the greatest confusion, which might otherwise arise from the passions of men.

The Crown once parted with this power out of its hands to the Commons; and that concession produced the ruin of the monarchy, and of the Peerage. If the Crown should part with the power now to the Lords, that it has over them, why may it not be very reasonably apprehended, that the same fatal consequence may ensue to the King and the Commons?

If it be necessary, as it has been plainly shown, that the power now in the Crown should remain there, for the good of the people in general; it is as necessary for the defence and advantage of the Crown itself. The Lords (by the power the Crown has of adding to their number) are a fluctuating, uncertain body. This is all that gives the Crown any influence over them, and prevents combinations, cabals, and factions against the Crown. But if the door comes once to be shut, so that the Crown cannot make any considerable addition to their number in any exigencies whatever, what a door is opened at the same time to form a power superior to that of the Crown, and superior to all human control! Then they will become a fixed certain body: and should three or four ambitious bold men combine together hereafter, of the greatest families and the greatest estates, where would the difficulty be of getting a majority of two hundred thirty-five? and, if once obtained, what remedy could be provided in so desperate a case? Whilst they act in the common methods of government, they would command all *favours*; and, should they ever act in an *arbitrary* manner, necessity and self-defence would make the union amongst them the stronger.

I will now examine what the author of the Old Whig calls the *great point*, and which ought to carry the chief weight with us in this case; which is, "That the alteration now proposed will give such a mighty power to the bulk of the *English* Commons, as can never be counterbalanced by the body of the nobility. Should we suppose two hundred thirty-five Peers possessed, one with another, of £5000 *per annum*, this would amount to no more than £1,175,000 *per annum*.

And what is such a property, and the power arising out of it, compared with the power arising out of the property of those many millions possessed by the Commons?"

By this state of the case, we are to suppose, on the one hand, a certain, limited, fixed, hereditary body, of two hundred thirty-five Peers, enjoying great privileges above the Commons, and possessed of an annual revenue amounting to £1,175,000, which they have entirely in their own power; and this estate not so equally divided as £5000 *per annum* to every individual, but to some the command of £50,000 a year apiece, others not £500 a year. On the other hand, you must suppose a body of above twice the number fluctuating, unfixed, in the power of their prince every moment, at furthest not able to subsist above a few years, and possessed of not near half the estate before-mentioned; is it not too evident which of these two bodies must destroy the other, if once this should come to be really the case? The Lords are principals, and act entirely for themselves: the Commoners are no further principals than as to the estates they possess themselves. As our author has stated this matter, in order to magnify the power of the wealth of the Commons, though he is all along speaking of the aggregate body, yet he would insinuate as if they had as great command over the universal body of the people, as the Lords have over themselves. This is as much as to say, that the four members of the city of London have as absolute command over the estates of all the inhabitants of that great *metropolis*, as any four Lords have over their tenants. Indeed, if the Commons had a power of laying taxes upon the estates of all those they represent, that would be the same thing in this case, provided they had it abstractedly from the Lords. But this fallacy, which is often insinuated in this pamphlet, has been already detected. The Commons have no more power over their fellow-subjects' estates than the Lords; they cannot lay any tax without their Lordships' concurrence. And all that is peculiar to the Commons in this matter is, that they have hitherto been allowed to choose what tax they judged easiest for the people: but every day's experience shows us, that, if the Lords differ in opinion from the Commons, their power is at an end. The better to illustrate this *great point*, as our author properly calls it; as he has computed the value of the wealth of the body of Peers, I will take the liberty to compute the value of the wealth of the body of the Commons. Supposing them to be worth, one with another, £800 *per annum*, including personal estates, which I am certain is not disparaging this, or any other House of Commons that has sat in a British parliament; the annual income of five hundred fifty-eight Commoners will amount to £446,400, which is so insignificant a sum, in proportion to the value of the property of the Lords, that I will beg leave to compute his Majesty's whole Civil List with the property of the Commons, both sums together making but one million forty-six thousand four hundred pounds; and there will still remain a balance on their Lordships' side, of one hundred twenty-eight thousand six hundred pounds *per annum*. *Therefore, if it is an uncontested maxim, That power follows property,* . . . here is power, here is property; and let the body that possesses both in such a degree be but once made so independent as is proposed, would not the Crown, would not the Commons, be absolutely under the dominion of the Lords, according to this author's own way of reasoning?

I am satisfied the controversy is ended here: but I will suppose my author not to have been mistaken so very grossly, and examine his argument upon an imagination that the property of the House of Commons was ten times superior to that of the Lords, whereas the property of the Lords is near three times as much as theirs; yet, even in this case, the Lords would have the advantage of them; because a united constant body of men, always acting for the same interest and grandeur, and pursuing a continued scheme, must be an over-match for so transitory a body, and made up of persons of such different views and interests, as the House of Commons is. To bring an example on this head. Let us imagine the stock of the Bank of England to be of the value of one million, and the stock or cash of all the bankers, scriveners, goldsmiths, and dealers in money throughout London, to be four times or eight times that sum; is there anybody who does not believe the bank, incorporated and well compacted in all respects for its own private interest, will not have a greater power, greater credit and authority, than all those particular proprietors of a much larger capital, who cannot possibly be ever put into any posture, so as to act with that weight for their interest, as the bank will do for itself in the circumstances above-mentioned? The great power of all such fixed bodies is chiefly owing to this circumstance, that two or three persons always govern the rest; and it is as well the common interest of the society that they should be so governed, as the particular interest of the governors. In this their strength chiefly consists; and for this reason five or six hundred Lords (if anybody can be so wild as to suppose the Crown will ever increase their number to such a degree) will not be so terrible to the Crown or the people, as two hundred thirty-five, or any such fixed number. For to suppose that the majority of two hundred thirty-five Lords, were they so fixed, would not be entirely directed and influenced by three or four amongst them of the greatest wealth, abilities, and resolution, is as absurd and improbable to common reason and constant experience, as anything that can be thought of.

If it be allowed then, as it certainly must be, that the weight of so great power, and of such disproportionable property, may by this means come into a very few hands; what havoc may it not make of the dignity of the Crown, and of the liberty of the people?

Thus I have shown the certain destructive consequences of this project, as stated by the Plebeian, and even as stated by the Old Whig himself. I must confess I do not believe that the authors of this scheme were apprehensive how far it would go; but since it is now so plain, that *he who runs may read*, I hope they themselves will desist from so desperate an undertaking.

I cannot help observing, that his Majesty is treated with great indignity by the author before me, in several passages of his pamphlet. In one place he says, "Whilst the door of the House of Lords is always open, people of overflowing fortunes may find no great difficulty in procuring an entrance." In another, he insinuates, that "there is another kind of merit besides what arises from virtuous actions, learning, and industry, that has been often rewarded with Peerage." I am satisfied his Majesty has used this prerogative, as he has done every other prerogative of the Crown, with the greatest discernment, and therefore I am willing to trust it still in his hands. The House of Lords is treated by this author still more *en cavalier* than his Majesty. His words are these: "If the English Commonalty should (by this bill) gain only this single advantage, I think it a very considerable one, that it will hinder the nation from being overrun with Lords. We know, that in the sale of an estate it is no small recommendation to the buyer, that there is no Lord within so many miles of it; and the distance of such a borderer is often looked upon as an equivalent to a year's purchase. But who can be secure from such a neighbour, whilst the species is so apt to increase and multiply? I shall not insist upon paying debts, which is looked upon as a moral duty amongst Commoners, who cannot but be sorry to see any additions to an order of men that are sheltered by privileges from the demands of their honest and industrious creditors. To which many considerations of the like nature might be added, were they not obvious to the private reflection of every reader."

I cannot very well account for it, how this author comes to take so great a liberty as he has done here; even so far, as to endeavour to make it believed, that the Lords are sheltered from their just debts; whereas every one knows, a Lord's goods and effects are liable to the pursuit of his creditors, though his person is always protected. This author and I differ on every account, as to what relates to this branch of the legislature. They seem to me to have been for many years, and to be at present, a just and honourable body. This, I think, is owing to the frame of that body, and the situation it is in. I am against altering either, lest they should become tyrannical and odious. The Old Whig represents them to be at present a species of such a nature as I dare not venture to repeat, but must refer to his own words; and yet contends to vest them with much greater powers than they now have.

I have but one remark more to make upon this author, which is indeed in a matter of the last consequence, and which cannot be thoroughly considered till the next paper. The author of the Old Whig has very truly stated the power of the Crown, as it relates to the legislature, in these words:

"The Crown, as a branch of the legislature, cannot desire a greater prerogative, than that of a negative in the passing of a law: and as it ought not to influence either House in their debates, what can a good king desire more, than the power of approving or rejecting any such bill as cannot pass into a law without the royal assent?"

As I readily admit of all that is here advanced, That the regal part of the legislature is to wait for the advice of its great council, both Houses of parliament, and to give its negative to what it does not approve; that doing otherwise would be influencing the debates of one or both Houses, and turning the Constitution quite upside down: as I sincerely allow, a good king cannot desire any more than the approving or rejecting any bill offered him; and as I believe, from the bottom of my heart, that we never had so good a king as we have now: what credit can I give to what this author asserts, that *his Majesty has already signified his consent on this point*, of so great consequence to himself, and to the very being of his faithful Commons, before he has so much as once heard their opinion? Our author calls this an *act of unparalleled goodness*. But what I have to say upon this subject, I shall reserve to another opportunity, if what this author seems to be assured of should prove true.

THE OLD WHIG

No. 2. Thursday, April 2, 1719

WITH REMARKS UPON THE PLEBEIAN

> Why stand you thus? whence springs this strange delay?
> None will be blessed, yet every mortal may,
> Since Heaven, incensed, no more will condescend
> To their next suit a gracious ear to lend.
>
> SHARD

The author of the Plebeian, to show himself a perfect master in the vocation of pamphlet-writing, begins like a son of Grub Street, with declaring the great esteem he has for himself, and the contempt he entertains for the scribblers of the age. One would think, by his way of presenting it, that the unexpected appearance of his pamphlet was as great a surprise upon the world as that of the late meteor, or indeed something more terrible, if you will believe the author's magnificent description of his own performance. . . .

Our author, in his triumphant progress, first animadverts on a writer, whom he says he never read, which being my own case, I shall leave that writer to defend himself. The second he mentions, considering the strength of his arguments, and the closeness of his reasoning, deserved a little more regard from the Plebeian, who, it seems, with much ado went through the performance. This would certainly have been true, had he gone through it with a design to answer it.

Having routed Baronius, and confounded Bellarmine, pass we on to the next, said the country curate to his admiring audience. Our author pursues his conquests with the same satisfaction and intrepidity. In the first place, ⋅he is angry with a writer for assuming the name of the Old Whig, who may more justly recriminate upon this author for taking that of the Plebeian, a title which he is by no means fond of retaining, if we may give credit to many shrewd guessers. But he tells the Old Whig, that he expected from that title no less than the utmost wrath and indignation against the House of Lords. How does this agree with the censure he passes upon him afterwards, for treating that species in such a manner as he dares not venture to repeat? I must however remind this author of the milk with which he nurses our nobles, not to omit his stagnated pool. . . .

The author, in the next paragraph, gives us a definition of the point in debate, viz. that it is a jumble and a hodgepodge; a most clear, comprehensive, and elegant account of the matter!

.   .   .

The Plebeian proceeds to detect the imaginary mistake in the Old Whig, for having asserted that there has been as great an alteration in one branch of the legislature, as is now proposed to be made in another. A fact immediately puts an end to a dispute, and, in the case before us, stands thus:

King Henry VIII added to the House of Commons	38 members
King Edward VI	44
Queen Mary	25
Queen Elizabeth	62
King James I	27

The question now is, whether the restraining the number of the House of Commons to what it is at present, was not as great an alteration in that branch of the legislature, as the restriction now proposed would be to the other branch of the legislature, should it take place in it. To which I shall add the following question: Whether the inconveniences, arising from that continual increase in the House of Commons, did not make the restraint upon it prudent and necessary; and, Whether, if the like inconveniences arise from this perpetually increasing House of Lords, it is not as necessary and as prudent to put a stop to it? As for the little towns of Watchet and Dunster, our author can draw nothing from them to the advantage of his cause, if he can bestow labour and time enough, of which he finds it necessary to be very sparing in this argument, to peruse the printed list of counties and boroughs, to whom the privilege of sending representatives to parliament was granted or restored by the several princes above-mentioned; and to answer the short query proposed to him at the end of it, with relation to Queen Elizabeth:

After having proposed these questions in plain terms, I come, in the next place, to one of the Plebeian's, which is carried on in metaphor, till it ends in something that is past my understanding. But these retrenchments being now made, the question, says he, at present is, whether the Commons ought to go on stripping the Crown of every jewel, till it becomes less resplendent than the Doge of Venice's coronet, or less comfortable than the Sword-bearer's cap of Maintenance? I shall only confront this metaphorical query with one that is adapted to men of ordinary capacities. "These retrenchments being made, whether the Commons ought to accept the offer of the Crown, to part with a prerogative that is still exorbitant and dangerous to the community?"

But our author's chief concern is for the poor House of Commons, whom he represents as naked and defenceless, when the Crown, by losing this prerogative, would be less able to protect them against the power of a House of Lords. Who forbears laughing, when the Spanish friar represents *Little Dickey*, under the person of Gomez, insulting the colonel that was able to fright him out of his wits with a single frown? This Gomez, says he, flew upon him like a dragon, got him down, the devil being strong in him, and gave him bastinado on bastinado, and buffet upon buffet, which the poor meek colonel, being prostrate, suffered with a most Christian patience. The improbability of the fact never fails to raise mirth in the audience; and one may venture to answer for a British House of Commons, if we may guess from its conduct hitherto, that it will scarce be either so tame or so weak, as our author supposes.

The Plebeian, to turn off the force of the remark upon another paragraph, has recourse to a shift that is of great use to controversial writers, by affirming that his antagonist mistakes his meaning. Let the impartial reader judge whether an answer, that proves this alteration would not be detrimental to the House of Peers, is not suited to an objection which says in so many words, that it would be detrimental to the House itself. But, says the Plebeian in this his reply to the Old Whig, it will not be detrimental to them in point of power, but it will be detrimental on account of those talents which ought to accompany power, the want of which the Commons will feel in their judicature. Which is, in other words, "I do not mean when I say that it will be detrimental to the House of Peers itself, that it will be detrimental to the Peers, but that it will be detrimental to the Commons." I appeal to any man, whether the Old Whig ignorantly mistook the natural sense of those words, or whether the Plebeian ignorantly expressed that which he now says was his meaning in those words. The Plebeian having in his former paper represented, that this old standing body of Peers, without receiving numerous additions from time to time, would become corrupt and offensive like a stagnated pool, tells us here in excuse for them, that they will be offensive to others, but not perceive it themselves. If I could suppose, with the author, that they would ever be in this lamentable pickle, I should be of his opinion, that they ought to be sweetened by such wholesome, pure, and fresh streams as are continually passing into them.

The Plebeian next objects to the Old Whig's calculation of the probable extinction of two titles, taking one year with another. By the calculation generally received, says this author, I suppose he means the list published by way of prelude to this project. Whereas,

the Old Whig could not take that list for his calculation, but formed
his calculation from that list, and from the nature of the alteration
which is proposed. This objection will immediately vanish upon dis-
covering the fallacy of the Plebeian's argument. He supposes no greater
number of extinctions would happen among the English Lords, were
their numbers settled at 184, than happened in that body when they
were only 59, 104, 142, 153, 162, or 168. At this rate of calculating,
the Plebeian will be sure of gaining his point, and affirms very truly
that the extinctions by a just medium amount to no more than a Peer
and a half for every year. But I appeal to honest Mr. Wingate, who
was never looked upon as a party-writer, whether my calculation will
not appear very just, if examined by his golden rule, and other curious
operations of arithmetic, which are to be met with in his works; especially when the bill, as it evidently tends to multiply extinctions, by
preventing the Peerage from running into collateral lines, or descend-
ing to females, will more than answer my computation, if I should
have the misfortune to disagree with the Plebeian about some very
minute fraction of a Lord, that might happen in the space of 116 years.
As for those contingent vacancies which may be made by the edge of
the law, our author regards the uncertainty of them as a very un-
comfortable prospect to the candidates for Patrician honours, since
they may have time enough to try all their patience, if they live in
hopes of such an expedient for their promotion. The ascertaining of
this point is indeed what I am not equal to, and must therefore leave
it to the masters of political calculation. But our author is afraid, that
if such lucky opportunities of extinction should happen, Lords may
still sit with their heads on, unless a seasonable increase may be made
to them in such critical junctures. This, I must confess, is to me one
very great reason for the alteration proposed; being fully of opinion
with the Old Whig, as expressed in the following words, "Is this inconvenience better prevented in a House of Peers on the bottom it
now stands? Can any who has been a good minister be secure, if the
Crown should add a sufficient number of his enemies to those who sit
in judgment upon him? Or is a bad minister in any danger, when he
may be sheltered by the addition of a sufficient number of his friends?"
The Plebeian's answer to this passage is highly satisfactory: In either
of these cases, says he, the utmost iniquity must be supposed in the
Crown, which I must confess I cannot bring myself to do, and therefore my argument remains entire. I very much approve of the author's
dutiful and submissive behaviour to the Crown, which puts one in mind
of the worthy alderman, who, upon hearing a member of the common

council call the emperor Nero a monster of cruelty, told him, he ought not to speak disrespectfully of a crowned head. But if the author will only go such lengths with me, as to allow there ever has been a bad sovereign, or, not to shock him with such a supposition, that there ever has been a wicked ministry, and that it is not utterly impossible but there may be such in times to come, my argument stands entire. God be thanked, we are now blessed with a good king, and with the prospect of such for our days, but cannot answer for those who are yet unborn, since they will still be men, and therefore liable to imperfection.

The Plebeian was hard-set by the answer of the Old Whig to his arguments, That the limitation of the number of the Lords would run the Constitution into an aristocracy, and has therefore very prudently shuffled the consideration of that point under another head, where he forgets the Old Whig's reply to what was urged against his opinion in that case, so that he has visibly given up the point which was most material in his first Plebeian. The Old Whig's remark therefore still stands out against him unanswered, and plainly turns his own ill consequence upon him, by showing there is a visible tendency to an aristocracy as the Constitution now stands, which would be taken away by the alteration proposed. But it is ungenerous to insult a baffled adversary; I shall therefore proceed to the next particular in dispute.

The Old Whig affirms, that the power of giving money and raising taxes is confined to the body of the Commons, and that all the privileges together of the Lords are not equal to that one of commanding the purse of the community. The Plebeian allows the consequence, but cavils at the position, which is a received maxim among the Commons of England, the doctrine of the House of Commons in particular, and established by the practice of every parliament in the memory of man. Let us now see what the Plebeian affirms in contradiction to it, and by the way observe whether he personates his part well, and speaks the language of one who writes himself a member of the House of Commons. The author asserts, That whether a money-bill may not originally take its rise in the House of Lords, is a point never yet clearly given up by their Lordships, if he is not very much misinformed. This point, if I am not very much misinformed, was never claimed by the House of Lords, and has not a single precedent in the practice of that body in the legislature. He afterwards asserts that the Commons have no more power over their fellow-subjects' estates than the Lords. Is not the power of granting a supply, fixing the quantum of that supply, appropriating every part of it to particular uses, and settling the ways

and means for raising it; is not this power over their fellow-subjects'
estates much greater than that of the Lords, who can neither add to,
diminish, nor alter any one of these particulars? And if the power of
the Commons extends itself to all these points, how can the author
further affirm, that all which is peculiar to the Commons in this matter
is, that they have hitherto been allowed to choose what tax they judged
easiest for the people! But what shadow of reason is there for him to
proceed in asserting, that every day's experience shows us, that if the
Lords differ in opinion from the Commons, their power is at an end;
since, on the contrary, experience shows us, that whenever the Lords
have pretended to such a power, they have always been over-ruled by
the Commons! Our author tells us, the concurrence of the Lords is as
necessary to a money-bill as to any other bill. That is not denied; but
he must allow that the Lords' concurrence to a money-bill is not of
the same nature with their concurrence to any other bill, which they
may undoubtedly change, amend, and return, upon the hands of the
House of Commons, for their concurrence in such amendments as the
Lords shall think proper. Besides, to show the Plebeian how much the
purse of the community is at the command of the Commons, let him
consider the case of a vote of credit, which is transacted wholly between the sovereign and the Lower House. To this we may add, that
the sovereign himself, in his speeches to parliament, applies that part
which relates to money to the House of Commons, distinct from that
of the Lords; by which method it is plain the Crown supposes those
privileges are vested in the House of Commons, to which every member of that House has always pretended, except the present author.

The Plebeian in the next paragraph makes use of a very sure and
wise method of confounding his antagonist, by putting his own sense
upon a passage in that author's pamphlet. The Old Whig represents
how dangerous it would be to our Constitution, if the Crown, which
is already possessed of a certain means to over-rule one branch of the
legislature, should ever be able to influence the elections of a House of
Commons, so as to gain one to its measures; in which case, if liberty
was endangered in the Lower House, it could not make a stand in the
other. The Plebeian perverts this meaning after the following manner:
This author, says he, assures us, that the Crown has power enough to
gain a House of Commons of what complexion it pleases; and, after
puzzling himself in his own voluntary blunder, is displeased with the
Old Whig for not proposing to cure an inconvenience which he never
affirmed to be in the House of Commons, as well as that which he
proves to be in the House of Lords; so that he would have had him

quit the subject which he had undertaken, to speak of one which he had nothing to do with. But, supposing the Plebeian had rightly stated the sense of the author, the inconvenience in the House of Lords is that which is woven into its very Constitution, and therefore at all times exposes us to its ill consequences; whereas what the Plebeian suggests with regard to the House of Commons is only extrinsic, and accidental to that body, if it ever happens in it.

It is not probable that this dispute between the Plebeian and the Old Whig will last many weeks; but, if there was time to discuss the whole point, I think it may be shown to a demonstration, that the check of the Crown upon the House of Commons, which is the power of dissolution, is, by infinite degrees a weaker check than that it has in the present Constitution upon the House of Lords, which is the power of adding to it what number, at what time, and for what purpose it pleases: nay, that the power of dissolution is also in its nature a check upon the House of Lords, as it dissolves them in a legislative capacity, and may break the most dangerous cabals against the Crown, which are such as may be formed between the leaders of the two Houses. These two points, if drawn out into such considerations as naturally rise from them, would fully establish the necessity of three branches in a perfect legislature, and demonstrate that they should be so far separate and distinct from each other, as is essential to legislative bodies: or, as the Old Whig has before explained it, "If one part of the legislature may any ways be invested with a power to force either of the other two to concur with it, the legislative power is in reality, whatever it may pretend to, divided into no more than two branches."

I have hitherto followed the Plebeian in his own method, by examining, first, his replies to the objections made by the Old Whig; and come now to his second general head, wherein he formally proposes to consider the argument as the Old Whig states it himself. And here I was not a little surprised to find, that, instead of answering the several distinct arguments urged by that author in defence of the bill as drawn from the nature of government in general, from the British Constitution, from its effects on the Crown, on the House of Commons, on the whole body of the English commonalty, and from the ill consequences it would remedy in the present Constitution; the Plebeian contents himself with attacking but one single argument of his antagonist. Till the Plebeian shall have answered those other points, I shall take it for granted that he gives them up. Not to multiply words, I believe every reader will allow me that an author is not to be much regarded, who writes professedly in answer to a discourse which proceeds on many arguments, when he singles out that argument only which he thinks is the weakest; especially when he fails in his answer even to that single argument. A famous French author compares the imaginary triumphs of such a kind of disputant, whom he was then dealing with, to those of Claudius, which, instead of being represented by the strong towns he had taken, and the armies he had defeated, were testified to the people of Rome, by a present of cockle-shells that he had gathered up on the sea-shore.

But to come to the matter before us. The Old Whig, after having considered it in several views, examines it with regard to the whole bulk of the British Commons. Under this head he has the following words: "But the great point, and which ought to carry the chief weight with us in this case, is, that the alterations now proposed will give such a mighty power to the bulk of the English Commons, as can be never counterbalanced by the body of the nobility." Now, what the Old Whig here calls the great point with regard to the commonalty of England, the Plebeian insinuates he calls the great point with regard to the whole controversy, and descants upon it accordingly. Whereas it is evident the author insists upon many points as great as this in other views of the question. The Old Whig affirms, that the commonalty has infinitely more wealth than the nobility, which was the proper consideration of this place. The Plebeian returns for answer, that the commonalty is indeed much richer than the nobility, but that the House of Commons is not so rich; which was not the proper consideration of this place. It is impossible for a disputant to lose the cause, who is a master of such distinctions. I remember I was once present at an university disputation, which was managed on the one side by a notable Peripatetic. The question which he defended in the negative was, Whether comets are above the moon? The sophister, being pressed very hard by the force of demonstration, very gravely extricated himself out of it by the following distinction. Comets, said he, are two-fold, supra-lunar and sub-lunar. That supra-lunar comets are above the moon I do allow; but that sub-lunar comets are above the moon I utterly deny. And it is of this latter kind of comets that the question is to be understood.

The fallacy of the Plebeian's answer being thus far discovered, all that he further adds in his own way of arguing will be easily confuted by unravelling the matter which he has very artificially perplexed. The Old Whig supposes that every Lord in the legislature, taken one with another, may be worth £500 a year, in which, for argument's sake, every one knows his concession has been vastly too liberal. The Plebeian values every member of the House of Commons at £800 per annum one with another, in which it is plain he has been exceeding scanty. Nay, many are of opinion, that upon casting up the whole sum of property that now resides in the House of Lords, it would not exceed that which is in the House of Commons. If this particular approaches to the truth, all arguments of a superior power arising from its greater property fall to the ground of themselves, as being raised on a false foundation. To which I must further add, that if this increasing power still continues in the Crown, the property of the House of Peers will indisputably surmount that of the House of Commons; and that, on the contrary, if the bill passes, it visibly tends to prevent the impoverishment of the House of Commons in point of property, and to fill it with men of such estates as in a few years will be more than a counter-balance to the House of Lords, even under this view.

But further, to show the weakness of the Plebeian's reasonings upon this head, I will allow that the House of Lords enjoy at present, and may still continue to enjoy, a greater share of property than the House of Commons. But not withstanding this concession, to which the nature of the thing does not oblige me, it is still evident that the immense property which subsists in the bulk of the English Commons will render their representatives more powerful than the body of the Lords. This will plainly appear from considering the very nature of representatives; from those junctures which can possibly give them an occasion of exerting their power; and from matter of fact.

It is implied in the very nature of representatives, that they are backed with the power of those whom they represent; as the demands of a plenipotentiary, let his personal wealth or power be as little as you please, have the same weight with them as if they were made by the person of his principal. I will beg leave to borrow from the Plebeian an example of the bank of England, which, as he makes use of it, has no manner of analogy with the subject of the dispute. Is not the whole flock of that numerous community under the guidance of a few directors? And will any one say, that these directors have no other influence on the public, than what arises to them from the share which they personally enjoy in that stock? The author urges that the Peers are principals, which in reality is the reason why their power is not to be apprehended in opposition to that of the Commons: whereas, were they only representatives of a body immensely rich and numerous, they would, beside their own personal property, have such a support as would make them truly formidable. The whole Commons of England are the principals on one side, as the Lords are the principals on the other; and which of these principals are armed with most power and property?

To consider, in the next place, those junctures that can possibly give them an occasion of exerting their power. It is on both sides supposed to be in such cases as will affect the rights of the English commonalty, in which case every commoner of England is as much concerned as any of their representatives. Thus, if four London citizens, to make the case exactly parallel, were deputed to maintain the rights of their principals, as citizens, who can imagine that they would not be supported by the whole power and property of the city, and not be too hard for any two or three great men, who had ten times their personal estates? Now as the Plebeian's supposition reduces things to the last extremity, it can only take place in a rupture, which is never likely to happen. And in that case, as these two great bodies must act separately, there is no room for considering how far the concurrence of the House of Lords is necessary in a money-bill, which entirely takes away the author's reasoning. . . .

But matters of fact are the best arguments. We both agree that power arises out of property; and the author himself has given an instance of the power of the House of Commons, in having been able to effect the ruin of the Monarchy and Peerage. Whence had the Commons this power, but from being supported by their principals?

The Plebeian thinks he strengthens his point, by adding that the Lords are a fixed body. To this I might reply, that the principals of the House of Commons are as fixed a body as the Lords; and therefore, however their representatives may vary, they will continue intent, from age to age, to assert and vindicate their peculiar rights and privileges, unless we can believe that any body of men will act against those two strong motives of self-interest and self-preservation. I might further venture to say, that men of the greatest wealth and weight in the House of Commons are almost as sure of a seat there, as if it came to them by inheritance. But supposing the House of Lords never so much fixed, and so manageable by two or three great men, (for which very reason, additions are very often made to them, which the alteration would prevent,) we have seen that their united power, if their number is limited, can never be a match for that of the House of Commons, supposing still such a rupture as the Plebeian all along imagines, in which each body is to act separately for itself.

The author, in the remaining part of his pamphlet, appears like every writer that is driven out of all his holds. He endeavours to set the Crown, and the whole body of Peers, upon his adversary; accuses him in effect of *Scandalum Magnatum*; nay, and gives very broad intimations that he ought to be indicted for high-treason.

I should not have given myself, or the public, all this trouble, had I not been so peremptorily called to it by the last Plebeian. I do assure him, my silence hitherto was not the effect of old age, as it has made me slow, but to tell him the truth, as it has made me a little testy, and consequently impatient of contradiction, when I find myself in the right. I must own, however, that the writer of the Plebeian has made the most of a weak cause, and do believe that a good one would shine in his hands; for which reason, I shall advise him, as a friend, if he goes on in his new vocation, to take care that he be as happy in the choice of his subject, as he is in the talents of a pamphleteer.

Some Reflections upon a Pamphlet, called The Old Whig

> The ills that I have done cannot be safe,
> But by attempting greater; and I find
> A spirit within me chides my sluggish hands,
> And says, Go on.
> CATALINE, *Conspiracy*

Since the publishing of *The Thoughts*, the town has been informed by two pamphlets on the other side: one entitled, *Considerations*, etc., and the other, *The Old Whig*. The last gentleman seems to be sensible of his defect in point of length, and so promises another, which puts me in mind of a country girl who offered her services to a gentlewoman. This lady being over-nice, observed to the wench that she made her curtsies very awkwardly; to which the other replied, "Indeed, Madam, I make them very ill, but you shall have the more of them, the more of them, the more of them." And so she ducked for half an hour together.

However, to do justice to this author, I acknowledge he has unanswerably shown the great inconvenience which will happen to the crown and people if the Lords are multiplied too fast: I was in great hopes he had convinced those who set him to work of the unreasonableness of creating thirty-one, or, if he will have it so, but fifteen at once, when he gives us such shrewd hints that we have too many already. But upon perusal of his performance the second time, I find that this is not the thing aimed at. We have a very good ministry at present, which God bless. The author seems to be of my opinion that

London, 1719.

we shall never have such another; therefore it is wise to secure them during their own time, and let those who come next look to themselves.

I find this gentleman is of the opinion of the law books, that the crown is always in its infancy, and therefore it is proper to take away from it all knives, scissors, etc. by which it might cut its fingers. He thinks it is no safer to trust it with any prerogative for its own good, than for that of the people; whereas I was weak enough to believe that the weapons for its own preservation could not be placed in better hands than its own.

It's evidently the interest of the crown to make enough lords to keep the balance of the government even, and yet not so many, as to make them terrible to itself. It's as plain, in the opinions of the projectors themselves, that the crown has never yet committed an excess in the latter; since there were never so many lords as there are now, and yet by their intending to make more, they confess they have not enough already. But why they should prophesy that for the future the crown and all other subsequent ministers shall conspire against themselves as well as their country, if such a law does not pass, I can't imagine. As for my part, I should think a man stark mad, if he called out in the streets, "Help! Help!" that the neighbors might come in and hinder him from killing himself.

These considerations, I am persuaded, would have some weight with our author, if he did not think we were blessed with so foreseeing and virtuous a ministry, as could minutely hit the just proportion and balance of power which will exactly suit the several parts of our constitution at present, and in all generations to come, and that they will make no ill use of any power they are trusted with. To this I confess myself unable to give any answer.

I agree also with our author in several other useful discoveries dispersed throughout his pamphlet: that men of great estates had rather be lords than commoners, and that the more of them which are taken out of the House of Commons, the fewer will remain behind; that commoners for the most part have more wit than————; that lords have not always been made for merit; that the more of them there are, the more privileges there will be (I don't say, with the author, the more mischief); that any prerogative in the crown against the public interest will do more harm than good; that ministers will do their own business, whatever becomes of the king or people; that the negative power is useful to the crown; that an ill king, if he has no more wit, may throw his troop of horse into the House of Lords (I pray God keep them out of the House of Commons!). And with several other seasonable and important maxims in politics, very necessary to be well understood in this controversy.

And so having done him all the justice due from a fair adversary, in owning everything which is material in his pamphlet, I shall just hint at one or two things that I think are not so, and in which I cannot agree with him.

He says that though I admit with him that our present government consists of three estates, yet by the reasoning of my pamphlet I make them but two; this seems to be his own opinion. The reason is, according to his own emphatic way of expression, that the king may add a troop of horse to the Lords, and then in all likelihood he may get a majority. But this pregnant objection notwithstanding, I can't help thinking the Lords are one estate with a witness. They have an equal power in making all laws, and the execution of all them in the last instance, when they are made, without being accountable. They have the sole possession of all honors; their persons are like holy ground, sacred, and not to be profaned or touched with lay hands: whatever they think fit to do, we must say nothing of it at the peril of *Scan' Mag'*. If they should commit high treason or felony, they can't be punished unless they have a mind to it. As for any judgment that can be given against them in other courts for crimes which are not capital, they can appeal to themselves and so cannot fail of equal justice. There was once upon a time a general council of ecclesiastics (who surely must be more holy than any laymen) who made a canon, that the evidence of a layman should not be valid against a clergyman.

There is another thing in which this author has expressed himself so cautiously, that I cannot tell whether we are agreed or not. He says, "The three estates should be entirely separate and distinct from each other, so that no one of them may lie too much under the influence and control of either of the collateral branches." If he means by these significant words *too much*, not at all, then I beg leave to differ from him; I appeal to the reader, whether he has not formed a state of war instead of a civil state. But if he means they ought to have such an influence and control upon each other, as to prevent extremes coming to pass, I don't see but we are well agreed, and I beg of him to read over my pamphlet once more.

However, there is one point in which I must beg leave to differ altogether from him, and which indeed is the only thing he has offered against my pamphlet: viz., if you trust a wise body of men with such power, they will never play paw-paw tricks with it. But since we authors for the most part have more wit than money, which may happen to be the case of my present brother, I doubt he will not be able to give good city-security for it. And therefore I recommend to his consideration, that in the paper he has promised he will propose a remedy, how we shall help ourselves if it happens otherwise.

So I conclude, with due deference to his performance, which I confess has said not only all the subject will admit of, but a great deal more.

POLITICAL CORRESPONDENCE AND DEBATE, JUNE 1719–FEBRUARY 1721

Secretary Craggs to Mr. Schaub

Whitehall, June 30, 1719, O.S.

I cannot sufficiently thank you for the useful intelligence you gave me in your letters of the 24th and 30th N.S., nor can I sufficiently lament with you the bad situation of affairs in the North. I should not, however, regard it in that light, were we permitted to employ such means as may be found to extricate ourselves with honour. But as long as that mischievous old man [Bernstorff] retains his influence, it will hardly be possible. So contracted are his views with regard to the public, and so confined his ideas to his own Mecklenburg and his three villages, that the credit and security of all Europe are not able to rouse him. Besides, as he minds nothing but his own interest and prerogatives in particular districts, and the gratifying of his resentment against Monsieur Ilgen, &c., such principles will never advance our affairs. Wherefore, happen what may, I am entirely of opinion, that we should adopt the method proposed by the Duchess [of Kendal], of making everyone speak who possesses the least degree of influence.

You see that, at the rate we are now going on, Lord Stanhope is on the point of resigning every day. It is possible that his friends may continue in, out of pure respect to the King; but without hoping to do the least good, and thus becoming certain victims to an useless point of honour. Besides, you would see a new faction. Those who serve the King would have just credit enough to be sacrificed to the rage of one party, or to the interested views and adulations of another. Believe me, my friend, consult with the Duchess and Lord Stanhope,

Philip Henry Stanhope (Viscount Mahon), *History of England from the peace of Utrecht to the peace of Versailles, 1713–1783* (London, 1836–1854), vol. II.

and exert your utmost efforts; for nothing worse can happen than what I foresee. My most humble and sincere compliments to the Duchess. Show her this letter, which will save her the trouble of one from me. I have but one objection to Gortz's coming, which is, the filling of a new purse. It is incredible what prejudice all these sales of offices and other underhand dealings occasion to the King's service; for, to complete our misfortunes, I have remarked that there is no distinction of persons or circumstances: Jacobites, Tories, Papists, at the Exchange or in the Church, by land or by sea, during the Session or in the Recess,—nothing is objected to, provided there is money. You see that I, too, write pretty freely to you. I have burnt your letters. Should you show mine, there is not a thought of which I am ashamed, nor any consequences that I dread. But, to conclude, as long as we are in the boat we must pull with all our might, and meet difficulties only to surmount them. I desire you will continue your informations with the same punctuality. Among the very few reasons which induce me to support the burthen of business as well as I am able, the hope of being one day of some use to you is not the least.

Earl Stanhope to Secretary Craggs

Hanover, July 10, 1719, N.S.

We have been in very great agitation here for some time, but have, at last, got a complete victory over the old man [Bernstorff]. The King has twice, in council, before all his German Ministers, overruled him with an air of authority in relation to our negotiation with Prussia. One of these rebukes ought to be the more sensible to him, as it concerned the three villages you have so often heard of. The old gentleman affects to appear very supple to me since, and the new instructions for M. Hensch are preparing as I would have them.

Mr. Secretary Craggs to the Earl of Stair

Cockpit, Oct. 1, 1719

. . . You may have perceived from several of my private letters and heard from other means that we were not likely to be well with that old woman Bernstorff. 'Twas he who last year underhand gave

out the king was against the peerage bill; 'twas on his credit and
support that so many of the Whigs were running riot; 'twas on the
hopes of his powerful interest that Lord Cadogan was endeavouring to
do mischief, and that the party, uncertain who had credit at court and
what changes were going to be made, were divided, hawling and pull-
ing twenty different ways. Every man was let into a secret, and when
they were told the truth or pressed with ill consequences, you could
see every jackanapes as wise and mysterious as the old man himself,
shrinking up his shoulders or shaking an empty head, as if each of
them knew much better things than what you told them. Now you
must know this stupid old creature, with the profoundest ignorance
that ever I knew, enjoys also the greatest share of pride, resentment,
and avarice that you can imagine. He had puzzled and muddled in
those northern affairs with the adroitness of a cow, till at last nobody
knew what to make of them, but everybody saw ruin and destruction
advancing with great strides from that quarter. Upon this we began to
resolve not to murder ourselves for fear of dying, and all of us one
after another attacked our master on the subject. The old woman had
an ascendant of habit and custom, but we had argument and reason,
which I must say I never but saw the king yield to when he had
digested it. And thus we so far got the better that Carteret was sent
to Stockholm and afterwards Whitworth to Berlin. You cannot imagine
by what little artifices and knavery Bernstorff has endeavoured to
traverse their negotiations; but, to be short, in spite of them all, your
lordship sees that those matters are pretty happily concluded. This
success has very much opened his Majesty's eyes, and he has seen
with wonder all that he has been engaged in for the sake of three
villages which Bernstorff claims as his own, for the sake of his estate
in Mecklenburg, and of his personal hatred to Ilgen, &c., of the same
nature. And I believe you will no longer find that heavy clog to every
wheel that was set agoing. . . .

Lord Polwarth to J. Robethon

1719, September [19] 30, Copenhagen. I begin to lose hopes of
seeing you at Göhre, or indeed before you return to Britain. I am
extremely sorry for it, beside what I had to say concerning my master's
service here, which for many good reasons is the most difficult I know.
I had also some concerns of my own, and that of the greatest con-

Historical Manuscripts Commission, *The Polwarth Papers*, vol. II (London, 1916).

sequence to me was to know, if possible, what is resolved upon the subject of the peerage, if that is to be tried this winter, and if I may flatter myself not to be forgot, if it is. If it is not, there is in any case at present what I cannot think will continue very long. My father is alive, and if it should please His Majesty to call me up to the House of Peers, there is my Lord Duplin, now Lord of Kinnoul, a precedent for it, and what possibly there may be no opposition to. I beg you'll be so kind as to try the Earl of Sutherland upon that head. I'll make no step without his approbation, and as he thinks advisable. I write this only to myself. Though I have written to his Lordship today, I would not say a word of it till I know how he would relish it. I know he has a regard for my father, and I hope for me, and he with good reason may reckon upon us for every true humble servants to him; therefore I rely entirely upon his advice and assistance.

J. Robethon to Lord Polwarth

1719, [September 26] October 7, Göhre . . . We leave this in three weeks and will be only eight days at Hanover, as His Majesty wishes to be in London by 20th November and has fixed the opening of the session for 4th December (23rd November, o.s.). Parliament will meet on that day for business. . . . Lord Sunderland is to have the Peerage Bill on next session and bids me to tell you that in the list of the twenty-five Lord Marchmont will not be forgotten; but as for calling your Lordship to the House of Peers during your father's lifetime that is an impossibility. . . .

Polwarth Papers, vol. II.

J. Robethon to Lord Polwarth

1719, October [6] 17, Göhre . . . You will see that your visit here at the present moment was impossible and that you have done better service to the King and his ministers in remaining at Copenhagen. I assure you that they are very sensible of these and thoroughly satisfied with you. Those great services will put my Lord Sunderland under a necessity of putting your good father upon the list of the twenty-five additional peers, if the Peerage Bill be carried, as I hope it will. My Lord Sunderland assured me positively yesterday again that your

Polwarth Papers, vol. II.

father should not be forgotten in that case. I think it will not be amiss that you should write to my Lord Sunderland two words about it in this juncture.

Newcastle to Stanhope

My dear Lord,   October 14, 1719

The good news you have sent us of the King's resolution to return soon to us, has put new life into us all here, and the great success you have had in everything you have undertaken abroad will I hope make everything easy the next session, for I believe the most sanguine man among us could hardly have imagined that so many great and substantial advantages could have been procured for us in so short time. You will give me leave to have a double pleasure in that everyone must see to whose integrity and ability all our success is owing. I am very glad to find by my friend Craggs that Lord Sunderland and yourself are entirely of opinion for pushing the Peerage Bill: I must own I can never think our constitution settled or the king entirely safe till it be passed. The miscarriage of it last year I chiefly attribute to the under hand insinuations of some, and the open opposition of others, whom some people would fancy had, if not the first, at least a very great share of credit. This I think will now certainly be removed for I think it appears very plain that our master places his confidence where all honest men must wish it, which in my opinion will go a long way towards making everything easy, and when once people come to see, somebody [i.e., George I] at present will think himself as ill-used if the Bill does not pass, as anybody hereafter can do if it be. I should think they would be afraid of acting as they did last year. I entirely agree that everything ought to be proposed that may be an inducement to bring about so solid a good as this Bill would be, and therefore I cannot but think that the University Bill is proper to that end, as being agreeable to the party and a solid advantage to the public. I must own, my dear Stanhope, I am not of the same opinion as to the repeal of the Septennial Bill, for I think we shall evidently lose much more by it than we can possibly get. In the first place, I am far from thinking that it will make the Peerage Bill go down better: some I am sure who are very good friends to the latter will strenuously oppose the former. Though I own we have but a small chance for any Tories, yet that undoubtedly would make them more

Williams, *Stanhope*, Appendix E. Punctuation, etc., revised by the editor.

determined. I took the liberty to tell Lord Sunderland, when he dropped something of the kind at the Comptroller's, that I found that it had displeased some of our friends. Besides I must own I cannot apprehend that we have any reason to fear coming to a new election provided this Parliament sets out its time, for then the party can by no means pretend to be disobliged. Should this Parliament be continued it would show a great distrust of the King's interest in England, and look as if our past conduct would not be approved of, when on the contrary we have all the reason to think that before this Parliament ends, the King's affairs will be on so glorious a foot it will [be] almost impossible to oppose him. The merit of having settled a universal peace in Europe, which by the assistance of his servants he will in all probability have done, will make him so popular that I cannot but think he may have with Parliament as he pleases, and his steady adherence to the Whig interest must and will make that unanimous on our side. Towards the close of the last session there was a great many ill humors stirring; should this Parliament be continued beyond its time nobody knows in what shape they may appear. Upon the whole, my dear Lord, I am of opinion and have long been so that we shall not fail of a better Parliament than this is at present, provided we do not disoblige the party, by parting with this sooner than its time. I think when I have the happiness and pleasure of seeing you, I can convince you on the many alterations which must be made for the better: almost all the P——— family [supporters of the Prince of Wales] will be turned out. Most of those that had the chief hand in choosing the Parliament brought in their own creatures, most of whom I believe we shall be able to deal with; I will take the liberty to say that I myself will make the difference of sixteen votes, many others can and will do the same, and if the court would upon such an occasion, and sure 'tis worth while, use one proper method, and yet but very sparingly, I should think we cannot fail. Many private persons will be at expenses for the government, and few I fancy will have the heart to do against it. I am sure I speak against my own interest, but I could not forbear giving you my thought upon a point I thought so essential. Give me leave only to suggest one thing, yet this point may be undetermined till we have the happiness of seeing you on our side of the water: then we may take our lists and see when we shall mend and where otherwise, and then I dare say the advantage will appear so great on our side, that you will be of my opinion. The great point I think we ought to aim at is that there should be but two parties, the one for and the other against the goverment, and I cannot but think that by a new election, Mr. Walpole and those few friends his party will be able to bring in, will be so incorporated with the Jacobites, that we shall have but little difficulty in dealing with them.

My dear Stanhope, forgive my long impertinence; I could not forbear troubling you with my opinion because I was sure you would excuse it, and be assured that nothing upon earth can ever alter my perfect love and esteem with which I am. Pray my compliments to Lord Sunderland. We all here wish Dr. Boulter may be Bishop of Bristol and Dean of Christ Church as being the best able to stem the torrent of the minority.

Stanhope to Newcastle

My dear Lord,   Hanover, October the 27th O.S. 1719
The King of Prussia will dine here tomorrow and stay only two days; this visit will I hope in reality as well as appearance amply make amends for our staying here three days longer than was intended. The King will certainly set out this day a week hence. You will by this messenger receive our convention with Denmark; we have a project on foot for satisfying even the Duke of Holstein by engaging him to join his interest with the Prince of Hesse in order to get the Crown settled on the Prince of Hesse for life, and the Duke of Holstein by the same act of the states to be recognized as heir presumptive after the Queen and the Prince, if Her Majesty should leave no issue. We shall I believe make some use of Count Fleming, though not so much as it would seem reasonable to expect from the apparent interest of Poland to curb the Czar. Lord Cadogan is ordered to get ready to make a trip to Vienna; by his last letters we are made to hope that his negotiation at The Hague is concluded in a better way than has been expected of late. Lord Stair, contrary to custom, writes in a most sanguine manner from Paris and prepares us to expect speedily the submission of Spain to our terms; even the Czar by letters received this day from Berlin is said to put water in his wine. Thus we have a very reasonable prospect of seeing a peace in the south and the north before next spring; this good situation of affairs will probably put our friends in good humor at our opening the Parliament and it seems to us here very advisable to make the best use and advantage possible of this good humor by getting the Peerage Bill, which if dropped or

Williams, *Stanhope.*

delayed must in my poor opinion be looked upon as lost forever. It remains only to be considered by those who think this Bill necessary, whether the most certain way to secure a majority for it in the House of Commons, be not to secure at the same time in favor of all those who think the continuance of this Parliament advantageous either to the public or to themselves, the power of continuing it. I beg your Grace to think of what has been suggested from hence touching the Septennial Bill in this view, if you think we can carry the Peerage Bill through the House of Commons without the existence of so strong an argument *ad hominem* of the continuing of this House of Commons will be to great numbers there. It will be pretty indifferent to me whether we meddle with the Septennial or not (though I confess to your Grace that I think it for the interest of our country to repeal it if it stood singly upon its own merits) but whatever my opinion may be of that matter I should very readily submit my opinion touching it to my friends because I think there is no danger in delaying it; on the contrary I am persuaded that it will at some time or other force its own way through, but the Peerage Bill is of a very different nature. I think we must carry it now or never, since it will probably never happen again that a king and ministry will be for it. Your Grace will easily imagine that nobody can be so mad as to think of proposing any fixed resolution to the King upon matters of this consequence without knowing previously the sense of our friends in England: they must govern us and especially our friends of the House of Commons; if what is decided as a service to this House of Commons and to the Whig party be taken otherwise by them, it must undoubtedly be dropped, but at the same time give me leave, my dear Lord, to tell you very freely my thought that if they are against repealing the Septennial I shall have very little hope of succeeding in the Peerage. When your Grace shall see our good master you will learn from himself how much he has heart not to be baffled a second time in this matter, and you will therefore be so good as to turn in your thoughts until we do meet, which is the most likely method to succeed. I am very glad to find your Grace, who can judge as well as anybody, so sanguine upon the choice of a new Parliament, but the best new parliament will come too late if the Peerage Bill be not passed in this. This is my point of view which if I lay too great a stress I shall be forgiven by your Grace, whom I know to be equally zealous for it; if there be any difference of opinion between us it seems only to be which is the best and most certain way to come at it, which as I said before, all private opinions must be submitted to what shall appear to be the sense of the bulk of our friends in the House of Commons. It would indeed for this and many other reasons have been happy if we could have been a fortnight sooner in England, but we must now make the best use we can of the time we have. I cannot promise that the old man [Bernstorff] will be left behind but I may safely assure your Grace that though he should come, the King will do whatever shall be proposed to him to make everybody sensible that he is not to meddle in English business; he is very piqued and mortified at his declining credit and has taken a very slight occasion to vent his spleen and resentment against poor Robethon, where he cruely affronted without rhyme or reason. Robethon, being his immediate subordinate in the German chancery, may be insulted with impunity; whilst we are excluding the Germans avowedly from meddling in English business, we cannot openly support him. However, we shall I hope disengage him by the assistance of our good Duchess [of Munster].

October the 28th O.S. at ten in the evening
The King of Prussia is not yet come but is hourly expected and you may depend upon it that the King's journey will hold for Tuesday next; I am ever with the most sincere respect, my very good Lord.

Lord Sunderland to Lord Carlisle

1719, November 18, London. I was in hopes upon our arrival in England we should have had the honor of seeing your Lordship here, but I am sorry to hear you are going a further northern journey; however I hope it will not be a long one, and that after it we may have the satisfaction of seeing you in town. I beg leave to congratulate with you the good situation of the King's affairs in all parts, which gives a reasonable and near propsect of peace, both in north and south; I must also congratulate you upon another thing, which I know you have long had at heart, and which will contribute more to the King's and the public service more than any other thing, that is, the resolution the King has taken, not to suffer his Germans to meddle in English affairs, he having forbidden them to presume so much as to speak to him about them. This he has ordered all his servants to declare to everybody to be his resolution, and tells it himself to as many as come to him. He is determined to recommend the Peerage Bill in his speech,

Historical Manuscripts Commission, *The Carlisle Papers* (London, 1897).

and to have it brought in the first week of the sessions; and if the Whigs will be reasonable in that, he intends his servants shall push the bill for the effectual reforming [of] the universities, and every other Whig point.

This is the situation we are in, and since we can't yet have your presence here, I hope you will be so good as [to] excuse my sending enclosed a blank proxy, which if you please to sign, and seal, and let me know with whose name you would have it filled, I will obey your commands.

Peerage Bill Revived

The King's Speech on Opening the Session. November 23. The King went to the House of Peers with the usual state, when the Lord Chancellor, by his majesty's command, read the following Speech to both Houses:

My Lords and Gentlemen;

The satisfaction, with which I always meet you, is very much increased at this time, when it has pleased Almighty God so to strengthen the arms of Great Britain and our confederates, and so to prosper our several negotiations, that, by his blessing on our endeavours, we may promise ourselves to reap very soon the fruits of our successes. I am persuaded it will be accounted, by all my good subjects, a sufficient reward for some extraordinary expence, that all Europe, as well as these kingdoms, is upon the point of being delivered from the calamities of war by the influence of British arms and counsels. One Protestant kingdom has already been relieved by our seasonable interposition; and such a foundation is laid by our late Treaties for an union amongst other great Protestant powers, as will very much tend to the security of our holy religion.

I believe you cannot but be surprized at the continuation of a war, where our enemies have nothing to hope, and so much to fear. It is indeed difficult to frame any judgment of those counsels, which have broken out of late in so many rash and ill-concerted measures: If they depend upon our divisions at home, I doubt not but in a very short time, their hopes, founded upon this expectation, will prove as vain and ill-grounded as any of their former projects.

In congratulating with you on this happy posture of affairs, I must tell you, that as I have been very just and faithful to my engagements,

Parliamentary History, 6 George I, 1719.

so I have met such frank and powerful returns of assistance from my allies, as will, I doubt not, establish a lasting friendship among us.

Gentlemen of the House of Commons;

You will see, by the accounts I have ordered to be delivered to you, how moderate a use I have made of the power entrusted with me to augment my forces by sea and land. I depend upon the eminent duty and affection you have always shewn to my person and government, that you will be vigorous in dispatching the necessary Supplies for the year: to which purpose I have ordered the Estimates to be laid before you. And, at the same time, I must desire you to turn your thoughts to all proper means for lessening the Debts of the Nation.

My Lords and Gentlemen;

You all must be sensible of the many undeserved and unnatural troubles I have met with during the course of my reign. Our divisions at home have gone magnified abroad, and by inspiring into some foreign powers a false opinion of our force, have encouraged them to treat us in a manner which the crown of Great Britain shall never endure while I wear it. The trouble and expence which this hath brought upon us have been the most loudly complained of by those, who were the occasion of them. But with your assistance I have hitherto got through all those difficulties, and by the continuance of your help, I hope very soon to overcome them, since the hand of God hath so visibly been with us in all our undertakings.

If the necessities of my government have sometimes engaged your duty and affection to trust me with powers, of which you have always with good reason been jealous, the whole world must acknowledge they have been so used, as to justify the confidence you have reposed in me. And as I can truly affirm, that no prince was ever more zealous to increase his own áuthority, than I am to perpetuate the liberty of my people, I hope you will think of all proper methods to establish and transmit to your posterity the freedom of our happy constitution, and particularly to secure that part which is most liable to abuse. I value myself upon being the first who hath given you an opportunity of doing it; and I must recommend it to you to complete those measures which remained imperfect the last session.

So far as human prudence can foretell, the unanimity of this session of parliament must establish, with the peace of all Europe, the glory and trade of these kingdoms on a lasting foundation. I think every man may set the end of our labours. All I have to ask of you, is, that you would agree to be a great and flourishing people, since it is the only means by which I desire to become a happy king.

The Lords' Address of Thanks and Congratulation. As soon as the King was withdrawn and the Commons were returned to their House, the duke of Manchester made a motion for an Address of Thanks and Congratulation to his majesty; and being seconded by the earl of Holderness, the same was unanimously agreed to, the archbishop of Canterbury only desiring that a clause might be added to the said Address, to acknowledge his majesty's seasonable interposition in favour of the Protestants abroad, which was readily complied with. The Address was as follows:

Most Gracious Sovereign:
We, your majesty's most dutiful and loyal subjects, the Lords Spiritual and Temporal in parliament assembled, beg leave to congratulate your majesty, on your safe and happy return to this kingdom, and upon the great success with which it has pleased God to bless the wise measures taken by your majesty, to procure and establish peace in Europe.

It is with the utmost pleasure and satisfaction, that we see the present happy union between your majesty and the other great Protestant powers, which does so visibly tend to the security of our holy religion: and we desire to express the deep sense which we have of your majesty's seasonable interposition, for the poor persecuted Protestant's abroad; and we humbly beseech your majesty, that you would be pleased to continue your powerful protection and offices in favour of them.

We also beg leave to assure your majesty, that we will, to the utmost of our power, stand by and support your majesty, in the prosecution of such measures as you shall think farther necessary to take, for the completing the great ends your majesty has in view, for the security of trade and glory of these kingdoms, and the general tranquillity of all Europe: and we promise ourselves, that the whole world will soon be convinced with how little foundation the enemies of your majesty and your kingdoms have flattered themselves to reap any benefit from our intestine divisions.

We should be wanting in our duty to your majesty and our country, if we did not return your majesty our most hearty Thanks, for that tender and unprecedented care and concern your majesty has been pleased to express, in your most gracious Speech from the throne, for the liberties of your people, and the freedom of our happy constitution; which must necessarily draw all suitable returns of the utmost gratitude from all your majesty's faithful subjects, who have a true value for such inestimable blessings.

The King's Answer. To this Address the King gave the following Answer:

My Lords;
The sense you express, in this dutiful Address, of my endeavours for the common good, is most acceptable to me. The assurances of your support will very much contribute towards bringing about the great and good ends we have in view: and you may depend upon the continuance of my best offices every where, in behalf of the Protestant cause and interest.

Debate in the Commons on the King's Speech. The Commons being returned to their House, the earl of Hertford moved for an Address of Thanks, Though this motion was carried without dividing, yet it did not pass without opposition.

Mr Shippen in particular said, That no man was more ready than himself to concur in giving his majesty unfeigned assurances of the zeal and affection of that House to his person and government, in returning him Thanks for his care and endeavours to procure the tranquillity of Europe, and in congratulating his safe return amongst us; but he could not forbear observing that his majesty's Speech contained many heads, of different nature, and of great importance; and as he remembered that this House had formerly been reflected on, for approving the measures of the ministry by the lump, and without knowing what those measures were, he therefore was of opinion, they ought to proceed with caution in this juncture, the rather, because mention was made in his majesty's Speech, of a thing of the highest consequence, viz. the altering some part of our constitution; that it was plain enough that thereby was meant the Bill of Peerage; but it was surprising, that this affair should be brought again upon the stage, after it had miscarried the last session in the other House, and that the major part of this House had expressed such an aversion to it; concluding with a motion to congratulate his majesty upon his safe return, and to give him Thanks for part of his Speech, and appoint a day to take the rest into consideration.

Mr. Herne hereupon seconded Mr. Shippen; but

Mr. Hungerford foreseeing, that if the House should divide, a negative was like to be put upon Mr. Shippen's motion, said, That Addresses of this nature were but customary compliments; but he hoped that in the course of this session they should have opportunities enough to inquire into the grievances of the nation, and the conduct of the ministry; that as to the Bill of Peerage in particular, since the court seemed to have it at heart, he doubted not but it would soon pass the other House, and be sent down to them, and then, and no sooner, he hoped to see a great division in that House. Hereupon Mr. Shippen waived his motion.

The Commons' Address of Thanks and Congratulation. November 24. The Commons presented their Address to his majesty, as follows:

May it please your Majesty:

We your majesty's most dutiful and loyal subjects, the Commons of Great Britain in parliament assembled, do return our most unfeigned thanks to your majesty for your most gracious Speech from the throne, and assure your majesty, that our hearts are filled with unspeakable joy, upon your safe and happy return to these your kingdoms, and with the most just and grateful sense of your unwearied labours for our welfare, and the security of the Protestant religion.

We heartily congratulate with your majesty on the success of your British arms, and return the thanks of this House in the most dutiful manner, for such measures taken by the influence of British counsels, as afford the nearest prospect of a general peace abroad, and of enjoying with glory the benefit of trade and tranquillity.

And we crave leave to assure your majesty, that we will, on our parts, by the vigour of our resolutions for the support of your government, and by the dispatch which we will give to the necessary Supplies, convince the world, that if our enemies have conceived any hopes from our divisions at home, this hath been the vainest of all their projects. And we will enable your majesty, in concert with your allies, effectually to support and perfect those just and equitable measures which have been taken to establish a general peace.

And we further assure your majesty, That we will apply ourselves to find out the best means for lessening the Debts of the nation, and supporting the public Credit; and will concur in all proper methods to establish and preserve the freedom of our happy constitution, for which your sacred majesty has given so many tender proofs of your care and affection.

The King's Answer. To which Address the King returned the following Answer:

Gentlemen:
This loyal Address deserves my best thanks. It contains the most dutiful and affectionate expressions to my person and government; and you shall perceive my sense of them, by the endeavours I will always use to procure your welfare and prosperity.

Debate in the Lords on the Peerage Bill. November 25. The duke of Buckingham brought into the House of Lords the Bill of Peerage, which was read the first time; and being read a second time the next day, upon a motion that the same be committed,

Earl Cowper said, That besides the reasons that induced him last session to be against this bill, he had now another that weighed no less with him than the rest, viz. The earnestness with which it was recommended, and the eagerness with which it was brought before them, at the beginning of a session; that he had observed, both from history, and his own experience, that in affairs of moment, precipitation was ever dangerous, and, in many cases, to be suspected; and, for his own part, he could not help being of opinion, that if there were no secret meaning in this bill, some men would not be so pressing for it. To this

The Earl of Sunderland answered, That it could not with any justice be said, that any precipitation had been used in this affair, since the bill in question had been brought in the last session, and then thoroughly examined; so that he doubted not but every member of that House was fully apprized of it, and ready to give his vote for or against it: that the reason why it was brought in so soon at this time, he conceived to be, that it might give no interruption to the other important affairs, which the king had recommended to his parliament: and as for any secret meaning in this bill, his lordship solemnly declared, that he knew of no other, but what his majesty had been pleased graciously to intimate in his speech, viz. the securing the freedom of our constitution, by preventing, for the future, the abuse of one branch of the royal prerogative, of which they had a fatal instance in the last reign, and which had given just offence, and terrible apprehensions to all sober men.

To this it was replied, That if it was foreseen that bill might interrupt the other important affairs, it had been adviseable to keep it until the middle, or towards the end of the session, and to begin with the king's business. But

The Duke of Buckingham compromised the matter, by saying, That, for his own part, he apprehended no danger from this bill, and if it was attended with any inconveniences, as all human affairs are apt to be, time would discover it; and then, as in all other cases, they might apply a remedy to it. As to the time of bringing of it in, his grace thought it no material objection, since this House had no other business to go upon: but that he foresaw, that whatsoever dispatch they made in that bill, it would not get so quick a passage in the other House.

The Peerage Bill passes the House of Lords. Hereupon the Bill was committed to a committee of the whole House, who went through it the next day; and on the 28th, the earl of Clarendon, chairman of that committee, having made his report, the same was agreed to, and the Bill ordered to be ingrossed. On the 30th of this month, the Lords read the said Bill the third time; passed the same, and ordered it to be sent down to the Commons.

Debate in the Commons on the Peerage Bill. December 1. Upon a message from the Lords, by the lord chief justice King, and the lord chief baron Bury, that the Lords had passed a Bill, intitled, 'An Act for the Settling the Peerage of Great Britain:' to which they desired the concurrence of the Commons, the said Bill was read the first time, and a motion being made, That the said bill be read a second time the Friday next ensuing, the same was opposed by a great many members, who moved, That this important affair might be put off to the 18th of this month; which last motion, after a long and warm debate, was carried by a majority of 203 against 158.

Sir John Norris to Lord Polwarth

1719, December 1, London. After passing through nothing but storms I arrived yesterday at our court and kissed our master's hands and found a great desire your court [Denmark] would come to a good understanding with us. Today the Peerage Bill was brought to the Parliament and though I could have kissed our shore upon landing I wished myself back in a sea storm; you know my unfortunate sentiments. Being desirous to preserve the favor of our great men gave me the ultimate concern. I have not yet had time to eat. I am tired to death. My compliments to our friends. . . .

Polwarth Papers, vol. II.

George Baillie of Jerviswood to Lord Polwarth

1719, December 1. This day the Peerage Bill came down to the Commons, was read a first time and ordered a second reading, but upon a debate of several hours as to the day of the second reading it was by a majority of forty-five put off for a week, when those for the Bill would have had it done on Friday next. I look upon this to be equivalent to the rejection of the Bill, which likely will be the fate of it, Tuesday next, unless some great change happen in the disposition of the members, which for my part I do not expect. The consequence of this may make it a very uneasy session and I do not know how much further it may go. But God guides the world. . . .

Polwarth Papers, vol. II.

J. Robethon to Lord Polwarth

1719, December [8] 19, St. James . . . The Peerage Bill has already been read twice in the House of Lords and committed. They go this day through it in the committee and are likely to sit late. There will be no manner of difficulty in that house, and it is hoped we shall carry it in the other. I did recommend yesterday again the business of the peerage to my Lord Sunderland, which promises very fair and has a great esteem for your Lordship. Mr. Darcy, brother to my Lord Olderness, comes again to the King's party and is to have the late Mr. Dunch's place as Master of the Household. They talk of Sir William Strickland to be general-muster-master. In a word, our ministers are very busy to get friends for their Bill. . . .

Polwarth Papers, vol. II.

Debate and Decision

December 18. The engrossed Bill from the Lords, intitled, 'An Act for the Settling the Peerage of Great Britain,' was read a second time, and a motion being made by the lord William Paulet, teller of the Exchequer and member for Winchester, for committing the Bill, which was seconded by sir Charles Hotham, the same occasioned a warm debate, which lasted from one o'clock in the afternoon till near nine at night. The members who spoke for committing the Bill, were lord

Parliamentary History, 6 George I, 1719.

William Paulet, sir Charles Hotham, col. Moreton, Mr. Hampden, Mr. Craggs, Mr. Plummer, Mr. Lechmere, Mr. Aislabie, serjeant Pengelly, and Mr. Hungerford; against committing it, Sir Richard Steele, Mr. Pitt, sir Wilfrid Lawson, Mr. Horatio Walpole, Mr. Wykes, sir John Packington, Mr. Methuen, Mr. Herne, Mr. Tuffnell, Mr. R. Walpole, and Mr. John Smith.

Sir Richard Steele spoke first against committing the Bill as follows:

Mr. Speaker; I am against the Bill, because I fear it may change this free state into the worst of tyrannies, that of an aristocracy, which is the most likely consequence to attend such a law as this would be: the whole tenor of the Bill is very unfortunately put together, if anything, but an addition of power to the peers, is intended by it. All mankind must allow, that the only plausible reason for this law, was what happened in the last reign, when twelve peers were made in one day; but the Preamble assigns no such reasons, but says, That sixteen peers of Scotland, by reason of many new creations since the Union, are not a sufficient and proportionable representative of that nobility. And therefore they shall hereafter not be represented at all: but, A thing much more suitable to the peerage of Scotland ought to be done for them, to wit, That twenty-five of them should, at all times hereafter, have hereditary seats in parliament.

I always imagined that no man could judge what was suitable to him but himself; and that it could be no manner of comfort to one who has anything taken from him, that the possession of it is more suitably placed in another. How it is suitable to the peerage of Scotland, that instead of having a representative of sixteen sitting by their election, they are hereafter to be favoured with having 25 there instead of them, and not one there in their behalf? It must be confessed, that the peers of Scotland cannot complain of anything like being tricked; but their potential seats in parliament are barred and taken from them, not by collusion and double dealing, but by the most unreserved and candid usurpation imaginable: but though this is done with so much ease, and no reason given but that they who do it, are pleased to say it is most suitable; it is to be presumed, that those, whose consent is necessary for the divesting innocent men of their liberty and honour, will desire some better account of the matter, before they deprive their fellow-subjects of their undoubted rights. I cannot but, from a natural detestation of injustice, say, that is the highest wrong done to the indulgence mentioned in the preamble, to expect it will be granted in favour of any men in wrong of any other;

and I doubt not but this House will alarm that benignity from being employed to the destruction of itself, or oppression of others.

I hope the best man and best prince in the world, will be gracious, so as to have it always in his power to be gracious: I am sure he will never give his people any reason to complain, but of his too great goodness: happy the sovereign and happy the people, when excessive grace is all that can be feared of him.

The Peers of Scotland have an indefeasible right, by the Act of Union, to be elected and serve in parliament as peers of Great Britain, in the manner therein stipulated, and it would be but more cruel, not more unjust, to take from them their lives and fortunes, than this honour and privilege, which their ancestors purchased by the frequent hazard of theirs: the terms of the Union are plain and absolute; nor can any privilege, liberty, or property secured by it to the meanest subject of either nation, by violated or altered against his will, and no satisfactory reparation done him, without infringement of the whole act, and leaving the persons so injured, at liberty to avenge by force what was done by it: for protection and obedience are reciprocal, and withdrawing the one, discharges the other. What then it the condition of these unhappy men, who are to be divested of their rights and privileges of subjects, and yet, no doubt, to be deemed traitors, should they fly to any foreign power, or invader of that nation, which has in the dearest and greatest considerations, those of honour and distinction, made them foreigners? The terms of the Union cannot be revoked without disuniting the kingdoms; for when that is done they are no longer held together by the law, but by force; and the power which then keeps us together must be arbitrary, not legal; or if legal, not righteous; for a law, not supported by justice, is in itself null and void; nor are the makers of it legislators, but oppressors. It appears, without any possible contradiction, that the parliament of Great Britain cannot exclude the peers of Scotland from the benefit of the 23d Article in the Act of Union,* without becoming an arbitrary power, acting with an indifference to good and evil, on the foundation of might only.

We are safer under the prerogative in the king, than we can be under an aristocracy. The prerogative is a power in the sovereign, not ex-

[*Article XXIII stipulates that the sixteen elected peers ". . . shall have all privileges of Parliament which the peers of England now have, and which they or any peers of Great Britain shall have after the union." As for the others, ". . . all peers of Scotland and their successors to their honours and dignities shall from and after the union be peers of Great Britain . . . and shall enjoy all privileges of peers as fully as the peers of England do now, or as they or any other peers of Great Britain may hereafter enjoy the same, except the right and privilege of sitting in the House of Lords and the privileges depending thereon. . . ."—Ed.]

pressed or described in the laws, but to be exercised in the preservation of them by the rule of the general good: and if it could be proved, that the business of the twelve gentlemen, (meaning the twelve lords created by queen Anne in the time of the earl of Oxford's ministry) was purely done to save the nation, and that it was done for the good of the whole, the statesman, who advised it, would deserve the thanks of all mankind, for exposing himself to the misrepresentation and resentment of future parliaments, for the good of his fellow-subjects.

I will not pretend to doubt but those noble personages have, under the hands and seals of all and every of their electors, the peers of Scotland, full power and authority for this alteration, without which their proceeding could not be reconciled to common honour: and if the thirty odd, who are to be ennobled by this Bill, are to be made up by present members of the House of Commons, such members are to climb to honour through infamy.

The Bill seems to me to be calculated for nothing but an aristocracy, and indeed, has not so much as the appearance of anything else; for though a man of honour and conscious integrity knows, that he is a peer for the sake of his fellow-subjects, and that this right is vested in him and his family for the sake of society, not for himself and successors only, yet is there no part of society considered in this bill, but merely the peers and nobles. The Lords exercise a power in the last resource: and an appeal lies to them from all the courts of Westmister-hall, for determining all the property of Great Britain, and yet they are willing to have a law, which, must necessarily disable them from being a capable court of justice for the future; for the Bill even provides for their insufficiency as to this purpose; and there is a clause, which, instead of looking out for great and knowing men, is very careful to leave the power in the king to give titles, in case of extinctions, to minors: much of the same stamp is the partiality of the Bill, that females are excluded from their future right; as if a lady of good sense were not as capable of bringing into the world a man of sense, as a boy, under age, is of becoming a man of justice and honour from the mere recommendation of his fortune; for it is not to be doubted but that would be his best pretensions; but lords have thought it more eligible to have in view the providing rich husbands for their daughters from among the Commons, than the leaving it to their female heirs, to make Lords of the descendents of meritorious commoners.

Thus the aristocracy is set out by this bill; for all the provisions and limitations of it regard only the titles and honours of the peers, and prodigious care is taken, that no one should suffer from possible contingencies and distant incidents among themselves, but no regard had to the known immediate present rights of those who do not sit in their House, but have title of election into it: there is no difficulty of destroying those whom they know to have titles, but they are prodigious tender of hurting those who may have titles, of which they do not know: the lords will be judges, and give and admit to whom they please incident claims; but extinctions are to be supplied only by the king, and he might possibly give them to persons they should not like. The restraint of the peers to a certain number will make the most powerful of them have the rest under their direction; and all the property disposed before them will be bestowed, not by judgment, but by vote and humour, or worse. Judges so make by the blind order of birth will be capable of no other way of decision.

It is said that power attends property; but it is as true, that power will command property; and according to the degeneracy of human nature, the Lords may as well grow corrupt as other men; and if they should do so, how will this be amended, but by the consent of those, who shall become so corrupt? What shall we say then? Shall we expose ourselves to probable evils, with the foresight of impossible remedies against them?

It is hardly to be read seriously, when the Bill in a grave style and sober contradiction has these words, viz. The twenty five peers on the part of the peerage of Scotland, as if they who were made instead of the peers of Scotland, could, without a banter, be called peers on the part of the peerage of Scotland; the true description of them is, peers made when the peers of Scotland were no more to be peers; for the titles resting in their families, without hopes of succession in the peerage and legislature, is only a bar against any participation of power and interest in their country; is it putting them into the condition of papists convict, as to what ought to be most dear to them, their honour and reputation. It is held by true politicians a most dangerous thing to give the meanest of the people just cause of provocation; much more to enrage men of spirit and distinction, and that too with downright injuries.

We may flatter ourselves, that property is always the source of power; but property, like all other possessions, has its effects according to the talents and abilities of the owner; and as it is allowed, that courage and learning are very common qualities in that nation, it seems not very advisable to provoke the greatest, and, for ought we can tell, the best men among them. Thus we are barred from making this law by prudential reasons, as well as from the inviolable rule of justice and common right, with relation to the Scots Peers.

If we consider the matter with regard to the king's prerogative, this law will diminish it to an irreparable degree; and it is a strange time to take away power, when it is in the possession of a prince, who uses it with so much moderation, that he is willing to resign it; but we are to consider the prerogative as part of the estate of the crown, and not consent to the taking it out of the crown, till we see just occasion for it. His majesty's indulgence makes it safe in his royal breast; and we know of nothing, any other of the family has done, to alter it for fear of him.

The Prerogative can do no hurt, when ministers do their duty; but a settled number of Peers may abuse their power, when no man is answerable for them, or can call them to an account for their encroachments. It is said, and truly too, that the manner of their power will be the same as now; but then the application of it may be altered, when they are an unchangeable body: schemes of grandeur and oppression can be formed to invade the property, as well as liberty, of their fellow-subjects; which would, according to the present establishment, be vain to undertake, when they are subject to an alteration, before their project could be ripened into practice and usurpation.

As for any sudden and surprizing way of creation, That lies before the legislature for censure; and the great diminution which all creations bring upon the king's authority, is a sufficient defence against the abusive employment of that authority this way: For when the king makes peers, he makes perpetual opponents of his will and power, if they shall think fit; which one consideration cannot but render frequent creations terrible to the crown. This Constitution has subsisted in spite of convulsions and factions, without restraining or repressing the extent of the legislative powers; nor is it possible for any man, or assembly of men, to circumscribe their distinct authorities: No, they are to be left eternally at large; and the safety of each part, and the good of the whole, are to be the rules of their conduct: And as it is impossible to foresee all the circumstances which must arise before them, there is no safe way but leaving them at large, as vigilant checks upon each other, unconfined, but by reason and justice.

If there was an outrage committed in the case of the twelve gentlemen, the peers should have then withstood the receiving of them, or done what they thought fit at another season for their satisfaction; and not, when it is too late, instead of asserting their liberties, mediate their future security in unreasonable concessions from the crown, and discouragements upon the merits of the Commons: and can the gentlemen in present power reasonably think, that the consummation of the English glory and merit, is to close and rest in their persons?

After the Bill has sufficiently provided for the aristocracy over these dominions, it goes into a kind of economy and order among themselves, which relates to their nobility and not to their Peerage. We plain men and Commoners will not dispute about any thing which we know to be merely trifling and ornamental; and if they will be satisfied with a power in them as peers, they shall be dukes, marquises, earls, or whatever other words they please, without our envy or opposition: But when we come seriously to consider what we are going to do, we must take the liberty to be very jealous, at the last time, that it may be in our power to make a stand for ourselves and posterity; and noblemen cannot blame commoners, who are as shy in bestowing, as they are importunate in urging, the grant of such a power in themselves, which can be of no use or advantage but to themselves: at the same time one cannot resist observing to them, that, with respect to the prerogative, the peerage of Scotland, and the rights of the whole body of the people of Great Britain, they cannot be more exorbitant in the use of this Bill, should it become a law, than in the circumstances under which they send it to us for our concurrence; and it is not thirst of power, but moderation in the demands made of it, which can recommend men to farther trust; and I cannot but apprehend that what is founded on usurpation, will be exerted in tyranny.

It is to be hoped, that this unreasonable Bill will be entirely rejected, since none can pretend to amend what is in its very nature incorrigible; for it would be in vain to attempt a good superstructure, upon a foundation which deserves nothing but indignation and contempt.

It is a melancholy consideration, that under the pressure of debts, the necessities of a war, the perplexities of trade, and the calamities of the poor, the legislature should thus be taken up and employed in schemes for the advancement of the power, pride, and luxury, of the rich and noble. It is true, this affair ought to be treated in a most solemn manner, by reason of the awful authority from whence it comes; but we must not, on such occasions, be oppressed by outward things, but look to the bottom of the matter before us, divested of everything that can divert us from seeing the true reason of what passes, and the pretensions to what is asked.

If this Bill is required for preventing the creation of occasional peers, why, at the same time, are twenty-five Scots, and eight English, to be now made? Is not this the same thing, as to say, if you will let us make so many this one time, under the sanction of a law, we will make no more, for we shall have no occasion for any more? The latter end of this Bill seems to have some compassion towards the prerogative, and enacts something gracious towards the descendents of the sovereign, before the commencement of the Aristocracy, viz. 'Provided always nevertheless, That nothing in this act contained, shall be taken or construed to lay any restraint upon the king's majesty, his heirs or successors, from advancing or promoting any peer having vote and seat in parliament, to any higher rank or degree of dignity or nobility; nor from creating or making any of the princes of the blood peers of Great Britain, or Lords of Parliament; and such princes of the blood, so created, shall not be esteemed to be any part of the number to which the peers of Great Britain are by this act restrained.' This is the grace and favour, which, as soon as all their own posterity and accidents that could befall them, are provided for, is most bounteously bestowed on the children of the royal family; As this goodness is conferred on those of it, who are not yet intitled to that honour, it is to be presumed, that nothing vested in others of them will be assaulted; but that whatever becomes of this Bill, their present estates, their then remaining estates, will be still inviolable.

Since there is so full a House at this debate, I doubt not but it will infallibly end according to justice; for I can never think the liberty of Great Britain in danger at such a meeting; but for my part, I am against committing of this bill, because I think it would be committing of sin.

Mr. Pitt, member for Old Sarum, spoke next against the projectors of this Bill, whom he taxed with mean obsequiousness to foreigners, and with designs against the liberties of their countrymen.

Sir Wilfred Lawson, and Mr. Horatio Walpole, who spoke on the same side, were answered by colonel Moreton.

Sir John Packington spoke as follows:

Mr. Speaker: We have all the reason in the world to acknowledge the good intentions his majesty has been pleased to express in his speech for the good of his subjects and the liberty of our constitution; but, in my opinion, his majesty is not rightly informed of the manner of making his subjects feel the effects of those gracious intentions; and in particular, the Bill now before us is a very improper return to all the demonstrations of duty, zeal, and affection, which his faithful Commons have given since his majesty's happy accession to the throne. When the king and his ministers thought fit to enter into a strict alliance with France, and thereby give that ancient and almost irreconcilable enemy of England, an opportunity to retrieve the extreme low and desperate condition of their affairs, the Commons did not oppose those measures. When his majesty judged it necessary, either for the good of his subjects, or to secure some acquisitions in Germany, to declare war against Sweden, and to send strong squadrons into the Baltic, his faithful Commons readily provided for those great expences. When afterwards it was thought proper to deprive his majesty's subjects of the beneficial trade to Spain, by declaring war against that crown, and sending a fleet into the Mediterranean to serve as ferry boats for the emperor's troops, the good natured Commons approved those wise counsels: After all these and several other instances of obsequiousness and complaisance, which this House has shewn for the ministers, it is matter of wonder we should, at last, be no better rewarded, than by a Bill, visibly calculated to exclude the Commons from titles of honour, and to raise the dignity and power of the peers. It seems to have been the principal design of the ministry, since the beginning of this reign in particular, to give one family the absolute disposal of all honours and favours. For my own part, I never desire to be a lord, but I have a son, who may one day have that ambition; and I hope to leave him a better claim to it, than a certain great man (meaning general Stanhope) had, when he was made a peer. It is, indeed, an extraordinary and unexampled condescension in his majesty, to part with so valuable a branch of his royal prerogative, as is the bestowing marks of honour and distinction on such as have deserved them, by their eminent virtues and services to their king and country; however, considering what equivalent is given by this bill to his majesty, nobody will wonder at this concession, if it reached no farther than his majesty: but I hope this House will never concur in depriving of so bright a jewel of the crown, the prince, who, in his proper turn, is to wear it; and who is so worthy of it by all the royal virtues that shine in his person; and which, during his regency, have gained him the hearts and affections of all true Englishmen. And if some persons have, through their indiscretion, occasioned an unhappy difference, I am apprehensive, that if this Bill, so prejudicial to the rights of the presumptive heir, should pass into a law, it may render that division irreconcileable; and therefore I am against the committing this Bill.

Mr. Hampden answered one of the most material objections against the Bill, viz. That it would give the peerage an aristocratical authority; and endeavoured to shew on the contrary, That the limiting the number of the peers would rather diminish than increase their power and interest, since these were mainly owing to the constant addition of riches which the peerage receives by the ennobling of weathly commoners.

Mr. Craggs spoke on the same side, and urged, That his majesty, since his accession to the throne, had had no other view than to procure the good and happiness of his subjects and to secure their rights, and liberties. That having, in his royal wisdom considered the abuse that was made, in the last reign, of that branch of the prerogative, relating to the creating of peers, which abuse had brought the liberties of Great Britain, and of all Europe, into imminent danger; his majesty through a condescension worthy of a prince truly magnanimous, had graciously been pleased to consent, that such bounds be set to that part of the prerogative, as may prevent any exorbitant and dangerous exercise of it for the time to come: That it was only in the reigns of good princes, that legislators had opportunities to remedy and amend the defects to which all human institutions are subject; and, that, if the present occasion of rectifying that apparent flaw in our constitution were lost, it might perhaps never be retrieved.

Mr. Methuen answered Mr. Craggs, and shewed the danger of making alterations in the fundamental laws and ancient constitution; urging the comparison of a building, in which the removing one single stone from the foundation may endanger the whole edifice.

Mr. Herne spoke on the same side.

Mr. Lechmere owned, That he did not like this bill, as it was sent down to them, yet he did not doubt but it might be made a good one, provided the Lords would give the Commons an equivalent, and suffer them to share several privileges and advantages, which their lordships enjoy. Therefore he insisted on the committing of the bill, that they might make amendments to it; and as to the objection, that it was dangerous to make any innovations in the constitution, he alleged several instances, particularly, the act for limiting the Succession and the Act of Union, which, indeed had altered, but, on the other hand, had rather improved and strengthened, than prejudiced the original constitution.

Mr. Robert Walpole next rose, and spoke as follows:

Among the Romans, the wisest people upon earth, the Temple of Fame was placed behind the Temple of Virtue, to denote that there was no coming to the Temple of Fame, but through that of Virtue. But if this Bill is passed into a law, one of the most powerful incentives to virtue would be taken away, since there would be no arriving at honour, but through the winding-sheet of an old decrepit lord, or the grave of an extinct noble family; a policy very different from that glorious and enlightened nation, who made it their pride to hold out to the world illustrious examples of merited elevation,

> Patere honoris scirent ut cuncti viam. [It is evident that all men know the way of honor.]

It is very far from my thoughts to depreciate the advantages, or detract from the respect due to illustrious birth; for though the philosopher may say with the poet,

> Et genus et proavos, et quae non facimus ipsi, Vix ea nostra voco; [Both race and ancestor and those things which we do not do ourselves, these things I hardly call our own.]

yet the claim derived from that advantage, though fortuitous, is so generally and so justly conceded; that every endeavour to subvert the principle, would merit contempt and abhorrence. But though illustrious birth forms one undisputed title to pre-eminence, and superior consideration, yet surely it ought not to be the only one. The origin of high titles was derived from the will of the sovereign to reward signal services, or conspicuous merit, by a recompence which, surviving to posterity, should display in all ages the virtues of the receiver, and the gratitude of the donor. Is merit then so rarely discernible, or is gratitude so small a virtue in our days, that the one must be supposed to be its own reward, and the other limited to a barren display of impotent good-will? Had this bill originated with some noble peer of distinguished ancestry, it would have excited less surprize; a desire to exclude others from a participation of honours, is no novelty in persons of that class:

> Quod ex aliorum meritis sibi arrogant, id mihi ex meis ascribi nolunt. [Since they have taken the credit themselves for what others have done, they will not credit me for my merits.]

But it is matter of just surprise, that a bill of this nature should either have been projected, or at least promoted by a gentleman, who was, not long ago, seated amongst us, and who, having got into the Houses of Peers, is now desirous to shut the door after him.

When great alterations in the constitution are to be made, the experiment should be tried for a short time before the proposed chance is finally carried into execution, lest it should produce evil instead of good; but in this case, when the bill is once sanctioned by parliament, there can be no future hopes of redress, because the upper House will always oppose the repeal of an act, which has so considerably increased their power. The great unanimity with which this Bill has passed the Lords, ought to inspire some jealousy in the Commons; for it must be obvious, that whatever the Lords gain, must be acquired at the loss of the Commons, and the diminution of the regal prerogative; and that in all disputes between the Lords and Commons, when the House of Lords is immutable, the Commons must sooner or later, be obliged to recede.

The view of the ministry in framing this bill, is plainly nothing but to secure their power in the House of Lords. The principal argument on which the necessity of it is founded, is drawn from the mischief occasioned by the creation of twelve peers, during the reign of queen Anne, for the purpose of carrying an infamous Peace through the House of Lords; that was only a temporary measure, whereas, the mischief to be occasioned by this bill, will be perpetual. It creates thirty-one peers by authority of parliament; so extraordinary a step cannot be supposed to be taken without some sinister design in future. The ministry want no additional strength in the House of Lords, for conducting the common affairs of government, as is sufficiently proved by the unanimity with which they have carried through this bill. If, therefore, they think it necessary to acquire additional strength, it must be done with views and intentions more extravagant and hostile to the constitution, than any which have yet been attempted. The bill itself is of a most insidious and artful nature. The immediate creation of nine Scotch peers, and the reservation of six English peers for a necessary occasion, is of double use; to be ready for the House of Lords if wanted, and to engage three times the number in the House of Commons by hopes and promises.

To sanction this attempt, the king is induced to affect to wave some part of his prerogative; but this is merely an ostensible renunication, unfounded in fact, or reason. I am desirous to treat of all points relating to the private affairs of his majesty, with the utmost tenderness and caution, but I should wish to ask the House, and I think I can anticipate the answer; has any such question been upon the tapis, as no man would forgive the authors, that should put them under the necessity of voting against either side?* Are there any misfortunes, which every honest man secretly laments, and bewails, and would think the last of mischiefs, should they ever become the subject of public and parliamentary conversations? Cannot numbers that hear me testify, from the solicitations and whispers they have met with, that there are men ready and determined to attempt these things if they had a prospect of success? If they have thought, but I hope they are mistaken in their opinion of the House, that the chief obstacle would arise in the House of Lords, where they have always been tender upon personal points, especially to any of their own body, does not this

[*He here probably alluded to the misunderstanding between the king and prince of Wales. Cobbett]

project enable them to carry any question through the House of Lords? Must not the twenty-five Scots Peers accept, upon any terms, or be for ever excluded? Or will not twenty-five be found in all Scotland that will? How great will the temptation be likewise to six English, to fill the present vacancies? And shall we then, with our eyes open, take this step, which I cannot but look upon as the beginning of woe and confusion; and shall we, under these apprehensions, break through the Union, and shut up the door of honour? It certainly will have that effect; nay, the very argument advanced in its support, that it will add weight to the Commons, by keeping the rich men there, admits that it will be an exclusion.

But we are told, that his majesty has voluntarily consented to this limitation of his prerogative. It may be true; but may not the king have been deceived? Which if it is ever to be supposed, must be admitted in this case. It is incontrovertible, that kings have been over-ruled by the importunity of their ministers to remove, or to take into administration, persons who are disagreeable to them. The character of the king furnishes us also a strong proof that he has been deceived; for although it is a fact, that in Hanover, where he possesses absolute power, he never tyrannised over his subjects, or despotically exercised his authority, yet, can one instance be produced when he ever gave up a prerogative?

If the constitution is to be amended in the House of Lords, the greatest abuses ought to be first corrected. But what is the abuse, against which this bill so vehemently inveighs, and which it is intended to correct? The abuse of the prerogative in creating an occasional number of peers, is a prejudice only to the Lords, it can rarely be a prejudice to the Commons, but must generally be exercised in their favour; and should it be argued, that in case of a difference between the two Houses, the king may exercise that branch of his prerogative, with a view to force the Commons to recede, we may reply, that upon a difference with the Commons, the king possesses his negative, and the exercise of that negative would be less culpable than making peers to screen himself.

But the strongest argument against the bill is, that it will not only be a discouragement to virtue and merit, but would endanger our ex-cellent constitution; for as there is a due balance between the three branches of the legislature, it will destroy that balance, and con-sequently subvert the whole constitution, by causing one of the three powers, which are now dependent on each other, to preponderate in the scale. The Crown is dependent upon the Commons by the power of granting money; the Commons are dependent on the Crown by the power of dissolution: the Lords will now be made independent of both.

The sixteen elective Scotch peers already admit themselves to be a dead court weight, yet the same sixteen are now to be made hereditary, and nine added to their number. These twenty-five, under the influence of corrupt ministers, may find their account in betraying their trust; the majority of the Lords may also find their account in supporting such ministers; but the Commons, and the Commons only, must suffer for all, and be deprived of every advantage. If the proposed measure destroys two negatives in the crown, it gives a negative to these twenty-five united, and confers a power, superior to that of the king himself, on the head of a clan, who will have the power of recommending many. The Scotch commoners can have no other view in supporting this measure, but the expected aggrandizement of their own chiefs. It will dissolve the allegiance of the Scotch peers who are not amongst the twenty-five, and who can never hope for the benefit of an election to be peers of parliament, and almost enact obedience from the sovereign to the betrayers of the constitution.

The present view of the Bill is dangerous; the view to posterity, personal and unpardonable; it will make the Lords masters of the king, according to their own confession, when they admit, that a change of administration renders a new creation of peers necessary; for by precluding the king from making peers in future, it at the same time precludes him from changing the present administration, who will naturally fill the vacancies with their own creatures; and the new peers will adhere to the first minister, with the same zeal and unanimity as those created by Oxford adhered to him.

If when the parliament was made septennial, the power of dissolving it before the end of seven years had been wrested from the crown, would not such an alteration have added immense authority to the Commons? And yet, the prerogative of the crown in dissolving parliaments, may be, and has been oftener abused, than the power of creating peers.

But it may be observed, that the king, for his own sake, will rarely make a great number of peers, for they, being usually created by the influence of the first minister, soon become, upon a change of administration, a weight against the crown; and had queen Anne lived, the truth of this observation would have been verified in the case of most of the twelve peers made by Oxford. Let me ask, however, is the abuse of any prerogative a sufficient reason for totally annihilating that prerogative? Under that consideration, the power of dissolving parliaments ought to be taken away, because that power has been more exercised, and more abused than any of the other prerogatives; yet in 1641, when the king had assented to a law that disabled him from proroguing or dissolving parliament, without the consent of both Houses, he was from that time under subjection to the parliament, and from thence followed all the subsequent mischiefs, and his own destruction. It may also be asked, Whether the prerogative of making peace and war has never been abused? I might here call to your recollection the Peace of Utrecht, and the present war with Spain. Yet who will presume to advise that the power of making war and peace, should be taken from the crown?

How can the Lords expect the Commons to give their concurrence to a bill by which they and their posterity are to be for ever excluded from the peerage? How would they themselves receive a bill which should prevent a baron from being made a viscount, a viscount an earl, an earl a marquis, and a marquis a duke? Would they consent to limit the number of any rank of peerage? Certainly none; unless, perhaps, the dukes. If the pretence for this measure is, that it will tend to secure the freedom of parliament, I say that there are many other steps more important and less equivocal, such as the discontinuance of bribes and pensions.

That this bill will secure the liberty of parliament, I totally deny; it will secure a great preponderance to the peers; it will form them into a compact impenetrable phalanx, by giving them the power to exclude, in all cases of extinction and creation, all such persons from their body, who may be obnoxious to them. In the instances we have seen of their judgment in some late cases, sufficient marks of partiality may be found to put us on our guard against the committing to them the power they would derive from this bill, of judging the right of latent or dormant titles, when their verdict would be of such immense importance. If gentlemen will not be convinced by argument, at least, let them not shut their ears to the dreadful example of former times; let them recollect that the overweening disposition of the great barons, to aggrandize their own dignity, occasioned them to exclude the lesser barons, and to that circumstance may be fairly attributed the sanguinary wars which so long desolated the country.

Mr. Aislabie, Chancellor of the Exchequer, stood up next, and answered a material objection that had been raised against the bill, viz. 'That it was dangerous to make any innovations in the constitution;' and made it appear, that several alterations had been made in the original constitution by Magna Charta, the Habeas Corpus Act, and several other laws made for the benefit of the subject; and upon the whole was for committing the bill. He was backed by serjeant Pengelly, but they were opposed by

Mr. Smith, who urged, that the foundation of this bill being wrong and faulty, there was no room for amendments, and therefore he was against committing it.

Mr. Hungerford, who brought up the rear, was for committing the bill.

The Peerage Bill rejected by the Commons. At about a quarter past eight in the evening, the question being put upon lord William Paulet's motion, the same was carried in the negative, by a majority of 269 voices against 177, so that including the two tellers on each side, there were 450 members in the House. After this the prevailing party, to signalize their victory, moved, and it was resolved without a division, "That the Bill be rejected."

Charles de la Faye to Lord Polwarth

1719, December 8, Whitehall.— . . . Your lordship will find we have suffered a defeat in the House of Commons in losing the Peerage Bill by 269 against 177. But that is not conclusive for the remainder of the session. I mean that many who voted against the Bill will upon every other occasion agree to whatever will be proposed for the King's service, and I have every reason to believe that others will affect more complaisance in any thing else than they would have shewn at another juncture.

Lord Chancellor Middleton to Thomas Brodrick

(Endorsed in his own hand-writing, "The grounds and steps of the duke of Bolton's coolness to me.")

Dear Brother,   Dublin, Dec. 14, 1719

I am obliged to you for the account you give me of the fate of the peerage bill on Tuesday last, it was what I expected as well as wished; though I confess, I was and am a good deal confounded how to account for their prudence; who after a former unsuccessful attempt,

resolved on renewing it so very soon after, without having taken a
more exact muster of the troops they should be able to bring into the
field on the day of battle. You know last spring, what my sentiments
were on this subject, and I remember to have told you in what a
manner my giving into the bill, was pressed upon me, and by whom.
For fear of mistakes, I wrote down my resolution, and read it to a
certain great man, which was in the words following. I cannot with
honour or conscience vote for the peerage bill, it being perfectly
against my judgement. I desire I may without displeasing his majesty,
be absent from the house, while that bill is under consideration; not
thinking it becoming me to give opposition, by voting or debating
against a bill introduced and carried on as this has been. If this be too
great a favour to be allowed me, I am ready, with the most dutiful
submission, and without the least reluctancy, to suffer anything which
I may be thought to deserve, for not being able to perceive the reasonableness or expediency of the bill. This I read on 17th March, 1718,
and desired the person I read it to, that he would acquaint the king
with it. He seemed much out of humour; said he was sorry, nay surprised to find me to have taken this resolution; having formerly thought
I had been for the bill, but promised to acquaint lord Sunderland
with it. On the 19th, I went to his house, and asked him if he had seen
his Majesty; he told me he had not, but should see him that day. About
an hour after, he called at my lodging, expressed great kindness for
me, recommended the Old Whig to me, and hoped I would be convinced: I gave him no reason to expect it, and so we parted. From
that time, I suppose it was resolved, he should leave town without so
much as letting me know it, much less giving me an opportunity of
going at the time he did: and though I knew that he was preparing
for Ireland, yet he never mentioned it to me, till after his footmen had
talked with mine, of the day they meant to be ready.

I knew the meaning was, to try whether I would not stand it; and
resolved not only to have stayed in town, but to have been at the
debate, and to have voted as my judgement led me: soon after his
going out of town, I had a visit from lord Sunderland, by whom I was
pressed on the same subject, but I continued firm; and after some expressions of concern (with a good deal of warmth) we parted: and
soon after, I was told, I might prepare for Ireland, without loss of
time, &c. At this time, it was not determined to drop the bill in the
lords house, without sending it down to the commons. Hence arose
the coolness of a certain person towards me, insomuch, that when I
landed in Ireland, I found he had taken other people entirely into his

bosom; and I also found, that some measures which they had resolved upon, about pushing the matter in favour of the dissenters, were so unpalatable, that they would prevent doing as much for them, as might have been attained, if no wrong steps had been taken at his first landing: but it had obtained (I suppose, from the great favour and intimacy a certain person was taken into) that an entire repeal of the test was intended; and this had taken so deep a root before I came over, that it was impossible to get people free from engagements they had mutually entered into, to go thus far and no farther; and to convince the world they were not under the direction of one man. Notwithstanding the countenance I saw given to one person, and the court paid by all the attendants of a great man to him, I went on in my constant course of carrying on the public affairs in the easiest and best manner; and by doing everything that could be done, and assuring him, that the imaginary fears with which he had been possessed, would come to nothing; and showing him from time to time, that what I had said, had come to pass; as on the contrary, what they had suggested, never did; I brought him to see, that I sincerely wished him well, and served him effectually; so that I think he had entirely good wishes toward me, till toward the end of the session; I mean, till after he returned from a certain place, during the recess; when I received your letter from Newmarket, which I communicated to him, and told him I was sorry to find, that everybody as well as I, observed in him a coolness toward me, in comparison of the favourite. He said, I was ill used by him who wrote the letter, who he believed must be Mr. Conolly's friends; professed great kindness, &c. but when so senseless an objection as my being against the popery bill, is made the foundation of resentment, I must think otherwise. In short, I was again urged (by order) whether I should have leave given me to attend the session of parliament, and told the bill would again come in: I said, I had rather remain here, than go over and disoblige (as I certainly should) in that particular. From that time, I take it, the fixed and grounded distaste is taken. This is written for your own satisfaction.

Secretary Craggs to Earl Stanhope

Cockpit, December 27, 1719

. . . the town is very empty. That fool, Tom Vernon, moved for a call of the House, which I was forced to second for the appearance, the day we adjourned. I believe our project to pay the debts, or rather to lessen them, will succeed: and I do not despair of the Civil List, but I am not so sanguine as our good friend the Earl of Sunderland. When that is done, we shall have, in my mind, made no bad Session. We may begin next year, at least by the Scotch part of the Peerage Bill; and I will tell you that the report of a new Parliament seems to me to frighten several of our mutinous friends into better manners.

The alternative of having a more consistent tractable majority does not suit with these petulant and interested humours, always ready to take advantage of the King's necessities.

Earl Stanhope to Lord Polwarth

1720, January 22, Whitehall

I shall now likewise acknowledge the receipt of your lordship's to me relating to a peerage of Great Britain for yourself. Your lordship may be well assured that no one is more convinced of both your's and your father's merits and would more cordially embrace any opportunity of serving your lordship than myself, but I find the King lies under so many difficulties to do what you desired in your letter to his Majesty that I hope your lordship will excuse me if I don't press the point. But as we must necessarily endeavour again next session to get the Peerage Bill, at least what relates to Scotland, past if possible, I shall upon that occasion be very mindful to do your lordship all the service that lies in my power. . . .

Lord Chancellor Middleton to Thomas Brodrick

Dear Brother,   Dublin, June 12, 1720

Yesterday I had a letter from the duke of Bolton, of the seventh, by which I find he is to be out, though he will not understand so entirely; but I take it for granted, our next packets will bring authentic accounts of the duke of Grafton being declared. In the postscript, he tells me, that he believes I shall partake of his fate; and indeed, I little doubted being removed, as soon as it was found to be convenient to their affairs. He [Lord Sunderland] whose nose burst out bleeding, on my utterly refusing to be for the peerage bill, has resentment enough mixed with his passion for that bill to seek the ruin of all who opposed it; and there is no withstanding the current of his present power. I believe too, your riding resty this session, has increased the weight of my sins. I am preparing for quitting all thoughts of Dublin or public affairs, during my life; and believe, I shall find more happiness and peace in a private retirement at Peperhara, [his country seat in Surrey] than I should ever have met with, if my zeal for his majesty's service had met better returns from some who serve him, than they have done: but you and I have not learned to be servile enough, or to bring everybody else into a necessity of dancing after the pipe of one set of men. Farewell. Though my fortune be not great, I shall be able to live independent, and yet handsomely. My services to all where you are.

Lord Chancellor Middleton to Thomas Brodrick

Dear Brother,   June 26, 1720

I thank you for your letter of the one and twentieth, but cannot be of your opinion, in relation to what you fancy will not happen: I have all along taken it for granted, I should be removed, from the time I could not promise to go into the darling bill; and you may remember, I told you, I had it more than hinted to me by lord Sunderland and the duke of Bolton what the consequences of persisting in my own sentiments, and not going implicitly into that scheme, would prove to me. It is impossible for a proud man to forgive being denied the most unreasonable request; and you may be sure, it caused no little ferment in his blood, when it burst out so plentifully at his nose, as it did on his finding me immovable after all the soft and rough arguments had been made use of. But, in my opinion, the late order from the lords of the admiralty, for the yacht to attend immediately at Chester, to bring over the lord chief baron Gilbert, with his servants, and *equipage*, shows he is to return a greater man than he went over: the usual method has been to apply here for an order for the yacht, which would have been granted immediately; but this being new, makes the thing more taken notice of, and creates the same opinion in the rest of the town, that it did in me, when captain Lawson first showed me the order. It is pretty odd, if it be determined, that I am to be removed, that it is kept so much a secret; after its being none that some people have for a good while been preparing the way for doing it. We are not strangers to the offer made sergeant Pengelly, and the terms of the treaty; nor to the sending for sir R. L. to return to London: but there is something not yet adjusted finally to the satisfaction of the schemers. If my good friends fancy I will throw up, they shall find themselves mistaken; for though I know when I am ill used, I resolve not to give them a handle, for doing what they have only wanted a pretence for doing some time past. If I consulted my own interest, I know not that man alive whom I would rather have to succeed me, than the person who I think will do so.

My honest endeavours to prevent our lords from doing some things in the last parliament (for which I cannot but think most of them are a good deal concerned, though they cannot bring their stomachs to own it) rendered me for some time the butt of the rancour and malice of all who were infatuated with a notion, that the lords were doing the kingdom service; and that those who opposed their proceedings, did it to make their court in England; they and their abettors were patriots, those who differed from them were betrayers of their country; thus I suffered for some time in the opinion of weak men, and you may be sure my personal enemies took care to blow the coals. Nay, I was so injuriously treated, that when the chief baron had refused to take any notice of an order of the lords here, on an appeal from a decree in the exchequer, though there was no appeal brought before the lords of Britain, I was said to have been privy to it, and to have advised the chief baron to do so: though between you and me, I never heard of the thing till after it was done, and Mr. Gibbon told the story at the chief baron's table, when the duke of Bolton dined there, and I happened to be of the company. I think people begin now to think, that they were not so much to blame, who told them what the consequence of their hot proceedings would be, as they were once thought to be; and perhaps, it may be now thought they meant better to the kingdom, or saw farther into consequences, than some of the furious drivers of that extraordinary proceeding. This is a thing one would wish should come to pass, as I plainly foresaw it would in a little time: but when that man is made chancellor, and sits among the lords, who formerly used him very cavalierly, I cannot but think it will be looked on as the last indication in how heinous a manner his treatment and some people's behaviour to him is relished in England; and their characters must fall very low, who assured people, that they were weary of the thing in England, that it was an hot iron, which they resolved to let fall, &c. An archbishop and a certain viscount of your acquaintance, though not your friend or mine, were ever harping on this string. This step, therefore cannot, I think, fail of having this effect, that people will see I advised against doing those things which would never be born in England, but on the contrary, would irritate them to the last degree, and acted honestly in giving that advice; and had the prudence to judge better of the event, than the managers of that hot headed project. I cannot, at the same time, but think this step will lay my lord lieutenant under a good many unforeseen difficulties: whether an unacceptable man will be able to do much service among the lords, I leave you to judge, as well as whether he will be so; but as to the matter of doing the business of a speaker in the house, or of a chancellor, in preparing the bills at the council board, I cannot but think he will, by application, make himself a master of both. We have it here, that our parliament is to be dissolved, and a new one called: if this be so, I cannot dive into the secret, unless it be this, that a certain person desires to get out of a post, in which he may foresee more rubs than he has yet met with, or can well remove. But I fancy the thing is only conjecture; though Mr. Horace Walpole, I know, has sent over for a list of the lords and commons. I will not conclude without telling you, that it is given out among the people confided in, that I was at the bottom in promoting the proceedings against the barons: is this so? if it be, no man on earth was ever more injuriously treated on both sides than I have been.

Lord Townshend to Colonel William Stanhope

Sir,   Whitehall, February 9, 1720/1

The King having been pleased to honor me with the Seals [as Secretary of State for the Northern Department, though Townshend had joined Stanhope's administration in 1720 as Lord President of the Council— Ed.] I can with great truth assure you that it is a very great mortification for me to find myself under a necessity of beginning our correspondence by condoling with you on the death of Lord Stanhope. You have lost in him a very kind and sincere friend and relation, and the King an able and faithful servant at a juncture when he had great occasion for his help and assistance. I heartily wish I could say anything to you upon this melancholy occasion that might give you ease and relief under your present affliction, for though I have not the happiness of being personally acquainted with you, yet your character and the services you have done the King in the stations you are in are so well known to me, that I can without flattery assure you that you may

Historical Manuscripts Commission, *The Townshend Papers* (London, 1887).

upon all occasions command my best services. It is a great addition to our present misfortune that Mr. Craggs is fallen ill of the smallpox and I fear is in some danger. I have not seen your last letters; I am told they are before the King from whom I have nothing particular at present in command for you, but believe I shall dispatch a messenger to you in a few days. I have therefore now nothing further to add but only to let you know that His Majesty is resolved to pursue the same measures and to support steadily all the engagements he is entered into. . . .

RETROSPECTIVE ACCOUNTS

Memorandum by Lord Chancellor Middleton

Showing, that the chief cause of his disgrace, was derived from his refusal to vote in favour of the peerage bill. Without date, but evidently written between his dismissal in 1725 and his death in 1729.

Archbishop Abbott, having received some usage, which he thought severe, held it fit, that the reason of it, might be truly understood, least it might some way turn to the scandal of his person and calling, and therefore drew up a declaration or narrative, of the manner of his treatment; but not with an intent to communicate it to any, but to let it lie by him privately, that things being set down impartially, whilst they were fresh in his memory, he might have recourse to it, if question should be made of anything contained in that relation.

I hope I may be excused for doing something in imitation of that great man, in circumstances, which seem to me to have some likeness to his, without the imputation, of having the vanity to believe, my services to the public to be anyway equal to those of that pious and good archbishop. My years are very near the same [Archbishop Abbot was sixty-five in 1627] as his were, when he fell into disgrace. I had spent many of them in places of great service; and (as he said of himself) I may truly say of myself, for ought I know, untainted in any of my actions. I have been made, as he was, *fabula vulgi*, tossed upon the tongues of friends and foes, of protestants and papists, of court and country; but in nothing does my case more nearly resemble his, than in his falling under the displeasure of the then duke of Buckingham, who could not endure any man that would not depend upon him, and so stoop to him, as to become his vassal. The great power which that minister and favorite had with his unfortunate and ill advised master, inclined him to expect more submission to his pleasure, than the archbishop thought was due to him, having learned a lesson, to be no man's servant but the king's. And it was my misfortune to fall into the disfavor of a certain minister, who was believed to have as great credit and power with his master, as the duke of Buckingham had with his, whose name, I decline to mention, since it hath pleased God to call him out of the world. But it will be necessary to show, for what reasons, and by what steps, that great man was induced to treat me in the manner he did, for some time before his death.

Upon his present majesty's accession to the throne, he was pleased to entertain a very good opinion of me, as having in an eminent manner, espoused and served the interests of king George, in the life of the late queen, particularly in the parliament held in 1713, under the duke of Shrewsbury, by standing to be speaker, in opposition to the court, ministry, tories, jacobites, and all people in employment. What effect that session of parliament had on the English councils, was visible in the succeeding session of the British parliament; at which time, it was generally believed, the court intended to have brought in a bill to empower the queen to have appointed her successor by will; but the vigorous proceedings of the Irish parliament in favor of the protestant succession, cast such a damp on their project, that the session *opened* with declarations, upon every occasion, in the house of commons, of firmly adhering to the succession, as settled in the protestant line; and I am persuaded, that if his majesty had been fully apprised with what zeal and affection I served him at that time, it would not have been in the power of any minister to have procured my disgrace, which afterwards happened. It is now time to show what were the inducements which made lord Sunderland, from being my friend (for I think it was to his recommendation, I owed being made chancellor of Ireland) to become so bitter an enemy to me as he afterwards proved. In the session of the British parliament in the year 1718, a scheme was formed, to bring in a bill to restrain the number of peers in Great Britain, which bill had two views; one was to gratify some great lords of North Britain, by turning their elective seats in parliament into hereditary ones; the other was to restrain the prince, when he should come to the crown, from creating lords.

The duke of Bolton was at that time lord lieutenant of Ireland, and spoke to me in the end of February 1718, that such a thing was in agitation, and endeavoured to explain it to me, and to convince me of the reasonableness of it; but either had not at that time the resolutions which the lords intended to come to in that affair, or else did not think fit to communicate them to me. He was very warm for my going into it, as a thing much for the good of the public, and seemed to admire a whig's being of another mind, after the queen had created those twelve lords at one time. At that time, I did not in any sort relish the scheme, but refrained expressing myself, with any warmth or bitterness against it.

I waited on his grace again, after the lords had come to the resolutions in that matter, which the house did come to, and was then again attacked by him with an air of confidence, of his making me a friend to the bill, which, I suppose, proceeded from my not having declared myself with zeal against it, on the first mentioning it. He then began to use arguments to incline my judgement, which not making any impression on me, I told him my mind in plain terms, that I thought the bill was a very dangerous and pernicious one to the constitution, and that it would not pass, at least that it would not have my concurrence; at which he seemed a little startled, and by his manner, I conceived, that he had so good an opinion of his interest in me, or so ill an one of my resolution as to my voting in parliament, that he concluded, I should not be against what he so warmly recommended, especially when he told me that the king had been acquainted with it, and that the ministry thought it to be much for the good of the kingdom; and that if the bill should not succeed, the consequence would be of necessity, the alteration of a whiggish into a tory ministry. I could not see any such consequence of the throwing the bill out, and declared myself determined not to vote for it; but that I should not be under any obligation to give any vote at all in it, if his grace went soon into Ireland, and I attended him over. I expressed myself not fond of speaking or voting against a bill, which I was told the king and ministry had so much at heart, as probably I should do, if I should happen to be in the house, when the bill came before the commons. The surprise and concern the duke expressed on this occasion, induce me to believe, that he had the weakness to have engaged to the ministry, that I would be for the bill, on no better grounds, than my silence, when he first moved the thing, or the interest he thought he had in me, to influence my vote in parliament.

A Manuscript Belonging to the Earl of Onslow

Anecdotes and other Miscellaneous Pieces left by the Right Honorable Arthur Onslow, late Speaker of the House of Commons, &c. and now copied into this Book, for the sake of their being the better preserved in his family, whose greatest Honor will be in future ages, as it is in this, the being descended from him. Copied, for their instruction and entertainment, as well as my own, by me his only son, who admired his character when living, and shall to the last Hour of my Life feel and lament his Loss.

GEORGE ONSLOW, 1769

On Opposition

We have often heard of men who have left one party to join another, without any change of principle or inclination, avowedly, and only to force the Crown, by distressing the Administration in Parliament, to bring themselves back to, or to obtain, those seats of power they had lost or quitted, or sought after, and without designing to continue any longer with their new friends than should be sufficient for that purpose. A practice that has tended more to corrupt and debase the minds of men that use it and to distress and confound the affairs of the public than any other public evil this age has produced. And however strange and offensive such tergiversations must appear to men of strict minds, and of little acquaintance with the world (for to such only they can appear strange) yet there is nothing more certain than that by some fatal darkness of understanding or imbecility of heart many persons otherwise of great probity and honour have suffered themselves to be made instruments and supports of these factions, and have been brought to believe, what is in truth the common band of all party unions, and only justifiable where the Constitution is really in danger, from the settled plan of an Administration for that purpose that they might very honestly act against their conscience in particulars, in order in general to pull down one man they did not like, and to set up another they did, nay to make it a point of honour and fidelity to their friends so to do.

Upon this foundation, I mean of distressing the Administration, I have reason to think it was that Mr. Walpole (afterwards Sir Robert) exerted himself so eminently and effectually against the Bill to restrain the making of Peers. I have told you, before, the nature of this Bill, and that it was much approved of by very many of the Whigs. What

Historical Manuscripts Commission, *Buckinghamshire . . . and Onslow Papers* (London, 1895).

occasioned them to like it so well was the recent memory of the extraordinary creation of twelve Peers at once and of a sudden under the Administration of Mr. Harley, Earl of Oxford and Lord Treasurer, done as it was supposed to save him from some disagreeable attack he expected in the House of Lords. It was I remember universally disapproved of, and by the Whigs so much detested, that it was one of the principal subjects of their clamour against him and afterwards one of the articles of his impeachment.

When this Bill therefore which had the plausibleness of preventing such an abuse for the future was first brought in, the opposing of it so looked so like a contradiction in the Whigs to what they had said and done on the former occasion, that it was thought by the malcontents to be too strong a point and would be of too much reproach for them to set themselves against (the Lords among them perhaps somewhat biased by the advantage the Bill brought to their body), and at a meeting of the most considerable of them, it was the opinion of all except Mr. Walpole to give in to it; but he dissented so vehemently and passionately to the so doing, that, after much altercation and heat, they yielded to his opposing it in the House of Commons, or rather because they found that he resolved to do it, whatever they had said or should do upon it. He told them it was the most maintainable point they could make a stand upon in the House of Commons against the Ministry. He was sure he could put it in such a light as to fire with indignation at it every independent commoner in England; and that he saw a spirit rising against it among some of the warmest of the Whigs that were country gentlemen, and not in other things averse to the Administration. That the first discovery of this to him was from what he overheard one Mr. ————— member for ————— say upon it, a plain country gentleman of about eight hundred pounds a year of a rank equal only to that and with no expectations or views to himself beyond what his condition at that time gave him. But this person talking with another member about this Bill, he said with heat and some oaths (which was what Mr. Walpole overheard and catched at)— "What, shall I consent to the shutting the door upon my family ever coming into the House of Lords!" This Mr. Walpole told the company struck him with conviction, that the same sentiment might easily be made to run through the whole body of country gentlemen, be their estates then what they would. And so it proved, to a very thorough defeat of the Ministers in this instance. His performance in this debate, I have heard, for I was not then come into Parliament, was very great, and had as much of natural eloquence and of genius in it as had been heard by any of the audience within those walls. His topics were popular and made for those he hoped to bring over, from the story I have just now told you. He talked of the honours of peerage as the constitutional reward of great qualities and actions only in the service of the Commonwealth, and to be kept open for that purpose. That the usual path to the Temple of Honour had been through the Temple of Virtue; but by this Bill it was now to be *only* through the sepulchre of a dead ancestor, without merit or fame. In this strain he bore down everything before them, even against very able performances by many very considerable persons who spoke on the other side of the question.

The debate for the Bill was managed and principally supported by Mr. Craggs the younger, then one of the Secretaries of State, with parts and every other ability proper for the subject and his own station; and this I have been told to the wonder of everybody, who heard him that day and who did not imagine his talents to have been at all equal to such an undertaking, and to me it is still more amazing, who have very undoubted authority for saying, that no man in England was more against, in his own judgment, this measure than he was, or opposed it more any where than he did in the private consultations of the Ministers upon it. I have spoken of him before and therefore shall say no more of him in this place, but that I have often wondered at and been sorry for the contempt Sir Robert Walpole used always to express of him. It was plainly affected and therefore unworthy of him, and did arise as I have been told from some private personal insults he had received from him, to which indeed the other was too much given, and which I know was among the few things Sir Robert Walpole never forgave in anybody; as scarcely any man does, it perpetually bringing to his own breast a disgusting proof of his want of natural courage, which every man hates to think of himself, and therefore very naturally hates those who occasion that reflection in him. And I must also here say a few things to you on another particular I have mentioned of Mr. Craggs—the defending and supporting in public what he was really against and opposed in private—I know it is the common practice among Ministers.

I know it is said that Ministers cannot otherwise be kept together or the business of a Government be otherwise carried on, and that one man's scruples ought to yield to the judgment of the many, and he to suppose himself in the wrong. I know also that this practice has been sanctified by very good men conforming to it, and particularly by the example of that great and excellent Minister my Lord Chancellor Clarendon . . . than whom a wiser or more virtuous man never was in power. I know likewise that the not doing this, brings upon a man the disagreeable imputation of intractableness and obstinacy and of being impracticable in business, and draws often not only odium but contempt on those who do it not. Yet what shall a man say where conscience is concerned, or what will he be able to say when he is to answer for every action of his, not by the conscience of others but by his own, and how miserable is all worldly business, take it for a course of time, that is not carried on by men who make a conscience of what they do in it? And is there anything so likely to make men lose all conscience at last as to be deluded out of it in some perhaps very few particulars at first by the speciousness of worldly wisdom, convenience and complaisance? I don't say nor would I be thought to contend for this strictness in trifles, they are not subjects of conscience, nor where the matter is doubtful, though where I doubt I would rather not do. But I mean it in points of great importance, where conviction is clear and where the error may be dangerous. In such cases, advised as I am, I think he cannot be an honest man that does not use all the talents and means he is master of everywhere to oppose and prevent the thing he even singly disapproves of, be his station and bindings with others what they will. How much evil to the public may not one just man properly situated be able to stop by his resolution and perseverance? If he cannot do it in private consultations, he may in public councils and thither he ought to follow it.

The Cabinet, the Privy Council, and the Parliament are all of them the King's Councils, and I can see no reason why a man's conscience is to govern him in one or two and not in all; why he may be allowed to differ with his fellow ministers in the Cabinet and not in Parliament; why difference of opinion there should break Ministerial union more than in the other, provided decency and proper deference be observed in the one place as well as the other. But Ministers seldom love Parliaments; never bring business there for counsel, but to carry points that must have the authority of the Legislature; and in order to carry such points must previously strengthen themselves there by collecting all the force they can for it. This polity I own requires the firmest connection among the Ministers; but then it is a polity that I have ever found to produce far more evil to the State than good, and to the Crown too.

The Crown and Ministers also have been always most safe and strong when they have had the free and fair determinations of Parliament for their direction, and I know nothing is so likely to procure this and all that a Court almost can wish to have done there, as to let the Parliament see the Ministers are not in a combination to force things upon them, and nothing can demonstrate that more than Ministers allowing one another the leave to differ in their actings there according to the real difference of their opinions. If the difference of opinion be not real, it is faction, and the Crown ought, in a proper way, to check that among the Ministers; but that is not what I am speaking of. I mean the conscientious difference of sentiment that may happen among honest men, and when it is among such only, it will not be so frequent as to confound or disturb business. The general difference among Ministers is not from this, but from envy, emulation, jealousy and lust of superiority, and from thence arises disorder and confusion in counsels often fatal to the Government. Good men bear with one another, it is the bad only who ruin because they differ. But it may be said, what shall an honest man do in company with those who are not so? Few Ministries are constituted only of honest men, and the good yield sometimes to the others to prevent greater mischief; but nothing is more false, specious as it is, or more dangerous. The best men have been corrupted by this, and seldom have answered the good design they had in it, and by it have often ruined their characters and their ability to do any future good. Daguesseau, the Chancellor of France, one of the most upright men of his time and by that a very troublesome check on the Councils to the Regent, was as it is said undone in his reputation by one false compliance the Regent drew him into. As soon as the Regent found that, he ventured to lay him aside, which before that he was afraid to do. How miserable was the case of this great man? He was disgraced because of his virtue, but lost the benefit of that in his own mind and in the opinion of the world too, by this one false step he had made, and the advantage the Regent took of it. By which the one got the character of a weak man and the other the credit of over-reaching him.

And now the answer will be very easy to the question—what shall an honest Minister do who is in office with those who are not so? Pursue his conscience. If it removes him from power, his disgrace will be his honour and if he be wise man his comfort too. If he still remains in his public employment, it will be generally a mark of virtue in the Government, will do honour to his Prince and may reform a bad age by bringing disinterestedness and integrity into fashion. As to the case of my Lord Clarendon, I have only to say, where he did it, he did wrong, and that the best men are often ensnared into errors by the false appearances of right, which I am satisfied governed him whenever he was wrong; but I have the best authority for saying that in a very trying and difficult instance he did not do it, but strenuously and

effectually withstood in Parliament a very favourite Court measure
much pressed by the King himself but which the Chancellor thought
destructive of his and the nation's interest. And the Lord Treasurer
Southampton at that time did it often, and when he even differed in
judgment from his great friend the Chancellor, it was indeed much
disliked by the King who bore it only in him because he feared the
scandal of removing such a man, and to whom he had been so much
obliged, and was besides in constant expectation of his resigning of
himself, or of his dying through the violence of a distemper he had
some years laboured with. To the Chancellor there was not so much
complaisance, for the design of his ruin seemed to be fixed by that
opposition. And who does not now revere the memory of both the
one and the other of these truly great men, in the particulars I have last
mentioned? And who does not now wish my Lord Clarendon had ever
done in this what he once did at least, and what his colleague in power
my Lord Southampton always did. Men should not act for the sake
of fame alone; but it is a very justifiable and useful ambition to desire
it, not only whilst men are alive but after their deaths and fame after
a man's death is never but for real virtue. Be therefore of the first
Duke of Ormonde's opinion, who used to say "However ill I may
stand at Court, I am resolved to lie well in the Chronicle."

The British Peerage

Even in very early stages of society, the evils of pure despotism and
of pure democracy were severely felt, and found to be nearly akin.
The same violent bursts of passion, the same sudden changes of purpose, and the same blind fondness for favourites, which are the vices
of a single tyrant, were seen no less to prevail in the assemblies of
the sovereign people. "When once democracy," says Thucydides, "became unrestrained at Athens, rival statesmen applied themselves only
to please the multitude, and let go the care of the commonwealth." In
absolute monarchies, likewise, men looked rather to the favour of the
sovereign than to the service of the state. In both cases, therefore, was
felt the necessity of some check, and in both cases was soon established
an assembly of chief men to take some part of the sovereign power,
and to give moderation and steadiness to the government.

It is remarkable, however, that this institution has in different states
proceeded on quite opposite principles. In free cities the original

Stanhope, *History of England* . . . , vol. I.

intention has been to give increased authority to old age. This idea will be found to run throughout, and the titles Gerontes, Senators, Patricians, Presbyters, Signori, Aldermen, have all the same primitive meaning. In early stages of society, when all men are equally un-educated, age and experience would of course possess much more value than when mental cultivation may sometimes raise a schoolboy of sixteen above a ploughman of sixty.

In conquered countries, on the other hand, the principal followers of the conqueror, dividing the lands amongst themselves or holding military fiefs for life, have commonly formed an assembly as a check upon absolute power. This assembly was composed, not on the princi-ple of seniority or superior wisdom, but on the principle either of military courage or of a large stake in the commonwealth. Such was the case with most of the kingdoms that arose from the ruins of the Roman Empire; such was the case also with the Norman rulers of England.

But though these institutions have sprung from such opposite origins, it is very remarkable that they all have tended to the same result. Though neither the wisdom of age nor courage in the field have ever been thought hereditary qualities, yet the hereditary principle has nearly every where prevailed over the elective. The modes have indeed been very various. In many cases where the hereditary principle was not established by law, it has been adopted in practice. In many others it was favoured by the law of allowing the Senators to fill up their vacancies by officers (and such were the Roman Censors) of their own body. Sometimes a right of primogeniture has been acknowl-edged, sometimes there has been an equal enjoyment but a perpetual inalienability of the family estates. In England the elder son is usually expected to marry, in Venice it was the younger. These, however, are only different means to a common end—the hereditary transmission of power.

The reason why this should be is apparent even from so slight a sketch as I have given. If a Senate be intended as a check on Kings or on multitudes, it follows that to have all its members appointed either by the prerogative of the King or by the election of the multi-tude, is to recur to that very power which it was wished to control. It is to change the operation but not to diminish the force of a single or a many-headed tyranny. Thus therefore he who desires to see an Upper House chosen by the people or appointed by the Crown for life, seems to me utterly to mistake the true origin and object of the institution itself.

Of the practical value of this hereditary principle there was never, perhaps, a higher testimony nor a more striking illustration than that which was given, in his later days, by one of the great masters over mankind. "I have heard Napoleon," says M. de Sismondi, "observe during the Hundred Days, that government might be compared to sailing. It is necessary to have two elements before your ship can sail. You must, in like manner, have two elements before you can direct the vessel of the State, so that you may have a stay in the one against the other. You can never direct a balloon, because floating as it does in a single element you have no *point d'appui* to withstand the storms which agitate that element. Thus also there can be no *point d'appui*, no possibility of direction, in pure democracy; but when combined with aristocracy, you may work the one element against the other, and steer the vessel by their different powers."

Inheritance is therefore a fundamental and necessary principle of the Peerage. But it has, I conceive, another principle not less fundamental,—that this assembly should always be recruited by the most eminent warriors, statesmen, and lawyers of every age. It is this constant influx that keeps the current clear, and prevents it from degenerating into a torpid and stagnant pool. Without such accessions, I do not hesitate to say that the House of Lords neither could nor should exist. The limitations proposed by Stanhope and Sunderland would, indeed, have increased the power and importance of the Lords for a season; but would, most surely, by impairing their utility, have undermined their foundation and produced their downfall. The Peers, shut up in inaccessible dignity, would have learnt to look down on him whom even the highest services could not raise to an equality with themselves, unless by the previous extinction of one of their own number. The aspiring soldier or statesman would have lost one great motive for exertion. Even a Nelson could no longer have expected the same honours which had formerly rewarded an Anson or a Hawke. In many minds a sense of emulation would be altogether deadened. Many others (for such will always be the case with men of genius), finding that they could not rise to dignity by the institutions of the State, would attempt to rise over those institutions, and become noisy agitators instead of useful citizens. What has been the cause of the continued usefulness and authority of the British Peerage? —What has kept it firm and unshaken while so many neighbouring aristocracies have tottered to decay, or fallen before political convulsions? It is because their families are constantly coming from the people and returning to the people—they have been an institution, not a caste—not a separate and jealous oligarchy, like that of Venice, asserting for themselves and for all their descendants an inborn superiority over their brother men. With us, how many sons of ploughmen or of weavers, ennobled for their services, sit side by side with the loftiest of the Somersets and Howards! With us the younger children of the Peer return to the rank of Commoners, and his grand-children merge again completely in the great body of the people. Such is the true principle of usefulness and vitality in the British Peerage; and he who would limit its number, is as much its enemy and the country's, as he who endeavours to sap its hereditary honours.

It is true that the King's power of increasing the Peerage might be stretched to an unlimited extent, and for a factious purpose, so as utterly to overthrow the Constitution. But many other branches of the Royal prerogative are, in like manner, liable to abuse and encroach-ment. Yet, we look upon the responsibility of Ministers as in almost every case a sufficient barrier; and in the opinion of one of our greatest Judges, "such public oppressions as tend to dissolve the Con-stitution are cases which the law will not, out of decency, suppose, being incapable of distrusting those whom it has invested with any part of the supreme power, since such distrust would render the exercise of that power precarious and impracticable." I may add, that while the advantages of the King's prerogative to create Peers are constant and unceasing, the danger of its abuse is extremely rare. During the peaceful reigns of the four Georges such an idea was never at any moment entertained by any statesman. It was reserved for the tumultu-ous times which preceded and which followed them. And on the whole, I would no more forego the benefits of the Royal prerogative from the possibility of its misuse than I would prohibit navigation to prevent the danger of shipwrecks!

BIBLIOGRAPHICAL NOTE

This bibliography is intended to supplement the reader's own reconstruction, from primary sources, of the Peerage Bill. It lists and evaluates secondary sources: consideration of these materials will sharpen the reader's understanding of the events and personalities involved in the controversy. These books will also broaden his knowledge of the political world of early Georgian England.

Most readers will have previous acquaintance with several general studies dealing with events of which the Peerage Bill is but a small part. Basil Williams's *The Whig Supremacy, 1714–1760* (Oxford, 1939; 2nd revised edition, edited by C. H. Stuart, 1962) is detailed and authoritative, though consistently Whiggish in interpretation; Dorothy Marshall's *Eighteenth Century England* (London, 1962) is broader in scope, but although easier to read is ultimately less rewarding. Sir Charles Grant Robertson's *England under the Hanoverians* (London, 1911; 18th edition, 1962), though in certain regards dated, has on the whole stood the test of time. William Edward Hartpole Lecky's classic *A History of England in the Eighteenth Century*, vol. I (New York, 1878), ch. 2, yields useful material about the nature and utility of the aristocracy, culminating in a treatment of the Peerage Bill. For the period immediately preceding the Hanoverian accession, George Macaulay Trevelyan's magisterial *England under Queen Anne* (3 vols., London, 1930–34), though squarely in the Whig tradition, is enlightening and entertaining; his treatment of the Union in vol. II, *Ramillies and the Union with Scotland*, is difficult to better. A useful corrective to Trevelyan's simplified treatment of party is found in Robert Walcott's *English Politics in the Early Eighteenth Century* (Cambridge, Mass., 1956); his conclusions have not, however, received unanimous acceptance among historians of the period. For the early Hanoverian period, the relevant volumes of Wolfgang Michael's *Englische Geschichte im achtzehnten Jahrhundert* (5 vols., Leipzig, 1896–1945), fortunately, have been translated and adapted under the supervision of Sir Lewis Namier: Vol. I, *The Beginnings of the Hanoverian Dynasty* (London, 1936), and vol. II, *The Quadruple Alliance* (London, 1939), draw extensively upon Hanoverian and other continental archive collections and include material not available elsewhere, which Michael used effectively. Another older account utilizing private collections, Lewis Melville's (a pseudonym for Lewis Saul Benjamin) *The First George in Hanover and England* (2 vols., New York, 1909) assesses the character of George I in a more favorable light than had been the fashion and opens the way toward a more charitable view of the monarch as a person. W. T. Laprade's *Public Opinion and Politics in Eighteenth Century England to the Fall of Walpole* (New York, 1936) explores that relationship by the use of pamphlet materials and other political writings. Recently Archibald S. Foord, concentrating particularly upon early Hanoverian times, in *His Majesty's Opposition, 1714–1830* (Oxford, 1964), analyzed in a clear and convincing fashion the development of successive opposition groups, along with the idea and techniques of opposition; the activities of the Walpole-Townshend faction and of the Jacobite opposition are of particular relevance. Though the editor has not had the opportunity to use John H. Plumb's *The Origins of Political Stability: England, 1675–1725* (Boston, 1967), reviews of the book indicate it is a valuable interpretative contribution to the literature of the period.

Both houses of Parliament have received serious attention: Arthur Stanley Turberville has examined *The House of Lords in the Eighteenth Century* (Oxford, 1927) and Edward Porritt *The Unreformed House of Commons* (2 vols., Cambridge, 1903). One will better understand the century's own view of the functions of the House of Commons by reference to the first two chapters of Sir Lewis Namier's seminal *The Structure of Politics at the Accession of George III* (London, 1929; 2nd edition, 1957). Constitutional matters are discussed by Sir David Lindsay Keir, *The Constitutional History of Modern Britain since 1485* (London, 1938; 8th edition, 1966), chs. 5 and 6; and in a less formal but scholarly fashion by Betty Kemp, *King and Commons, 1660–1832* (London, 1957). E. Neville Williams, *The Eighteenth-Century Constitution* (Cambridge, 1960), has assembled a collection of materials wide in scope and introduced in a perceptive fashion.

Biographies traditionally supplement such politically oriented accounts as those cited above, but the yield for the early eighteenth century is not a particularly rich one. To be sure Walpole is spoken for, first by Archdeacon William Coxe, *Memoirs of the Life and Administration of Sir Robert Walpole* (3 vols., London, 1798), a venerable and accurate biography built upon source materials lavishly included, and in recent times by J. H. Plumb, who like Coxe will devote a trilogy to his subject. The first volume, *Sir Robert Walpole: The Making of a Statesman* (London, 1956), treats his rise to power, which was not so foreordained as previous accounts have had it. Plumb, able disciple of Trevelyan that he is, adds chapters dealing with the political and social milieu, which were lacking in Coxe. Basil Williams's biography, *Stanhope: A Study in Eighteenth Century War and Diplomacy* (Oxford, 1932), is a convincing assessment of Stanhope's career, but the man does not emerge in a compelling fashion. Plumb contributes an incisive, though necessarily brief, biographical sketch of George I in his *The First Four Georges* (London, 1956); his few pages compare favorably with Melville's two volumes or Thackeray's more humorous treatment. No serious biography has yet been written about Walpole's ally Townshend or his rival Sunderland, which is the more surprising in view of the relative abundance of materials. Consequently a serious gap persists in our knowledge of the period. The sometimes surprising results of closing such a gap have lately been demonstrated through the efforts of two men. Maurice Cranston's *John Locke: A Biography* (New York, 1957) is a detailed account of Locke's life; further, he anticipated proof subsequently supplied by Peter Laslett in his introduction to *Two Treatises of Government* (Cambridge, 1960) that these were both Exclusionist tracts, but in other regards his account of Locke's relationship to political events must be modified in accordance with Laslett's essay; the latter offers better comments on Locke's thought.

English foreign policy is analyzed especially well in Michael's volumes, but three other studies deserve note: Adolphus William Ward, *Electress Sophia and the Hanoverian Succession* (London, 1903; 2nd edition, 1909) and *Great Britain and Hanover: Some Aspects of the Personal Union* (Oxford, 1899) show the peculiar nature of the relationship between the two unequal portions of George's domains; James Frederick Chance, *George I and the Northern War* (London, 1909), studies Anglo-Hanoverian policy in the north of Europe from 1709 to 1721. G. C. Gibbs, "Parliament and Foreign Policy in the

Age of Stanhope and Walpole," *English Historical Review*, 77:18–37 (January 1962) sheds new light upon the influence of Parliament in the formulation of foreign policy.

To their regret, ministers in the eighteenth century had occasionally to conduct what amounted to a foreign policy in response to events in Scotland, the Union notwithstanding. For an excellent brief essay commenting upon the origins and evolution of that Union, including the text of the treaty, consult George S. Pryde, *The Treaty of Union of England and Scotland, 1707* (London, 1950). The standard detailed account is Peter Hume Brown, *The Legislative Union of England and Scotland* (Oxford, 1914). A particularly trying event is recounted by Alistair and Henrietta Tayler, *1715: Story of the Rising* (London, 1936). Studies of the Jacobites more often than not reflect a romantic sympathy for the Pretenders; clearly, this is the case with Sir Charles Petrie's *The Jacobite Movement* (London, 1932; 3rd edition, 1958), which may account for the liveliness of the work, at the expense of objectivity. More controlled sympathies are shown by George Hilton Jones, *The Main Stream of Jacobitism* (Cambridge, Mass., 1954), a fully documented account of the negotiations carried on between the court of "James III" and various governments, by a succession of agents.

Religious issues only touched upon in this book are surveyed in a comprehensive fashion by Norman Sykes, *Church and State in England in the Eighteenth Century* (Cambridge, 1934), establishing the existence of able and dedicated prelates as well as their more wordly brethren in the Church of England. George Every's *The High Church Party, 1688–1715* (London, 1956) concentrates on that party, with emphasis upon religious rather than political issues.

The only major secondary account of the Peerage Bill is Edward Raymond Turner, "The Peerage Bill of 1719," *English Historical Review*, 28:243–59 (April 1913), which is not consistently convincing despite a full consideration of the relevant documents. Turner's documentation supplements a list of contemporary pamphlets relating to the Bill, compiled, with an introduction, in "The Peerage Bill in 1719," *Retrospective Review*, series 2, 2:118–34 (1828). The Houghton Library at Harvard University possesses a number of these pamphlets. Finally, the published materials of the Historical Manuscripts Commission provide a valuable collection for the early eighteenth century, though no comprehensive index exists and the various volumes can be difficult to assess quickly.